Praise for Over the Top & Back

"This is my favorite kind of adventure tale: Against all odds, in the face of health, weather, interpersonal, navigational and culinary issues, Brandon Wilson and his somewhat reluctant wife hike it because it's there – or, it's supposed to be. I laughed, I winced, and then I started checking to see when I was next scheduled to be anywhere near the Via Alpina." ~ Kyle Wagner, travel editor, *The Denver Post*

"In upping the venerable French saying, "*jamais deux sans trois*," Wilson explores not just three, but pushes the alpine experience to extremes by traversing eight countries, and they have been fortunate for this laureate. He brings his considerable intellect and wry sense of humor to this epic adventure, and the result is brilliantly accessible and wonderfully subversive." ~ Richard Bangs, author of *Quest for the Sublime, PEAKS* and books that celebrate travel and adventure (richardbangs.com)

"Informative, entertaining, and original. Award-winning author Brandon Wilson is a pioneer in a groundbreaking genre of travel writing."
~ Richard R. Blake, *Midwest Book Review*

"Wilson's the king of 'tell it like it is' travel writing! Few writers admit their missteps and appreciate that readers really do want to know what happens on a long, arduous trek, be it scary, life changing or just downright painful. You'll feel the chill from the sleet, steam from the shower and the aroma wafting from a well-earned meal as you trek along from chapter to chapter!" ~ Donna Coomer, *Between the Lines Reviews*

"Loved Brandon's humor, gutsiness and *joie de vivre*." ~ Ron Strickland, founder of the Pacific Northwest National Scenic Trail and author of *Leave A Trail*

"Wilson is my favorite travel writer. ...A completely captivating read. Throughout there is a sense of suspense in this wild adventure. This is perfect for armchair travelers as well as those who aspire to hike the same trail."
~ *Rebecca Review,* Amazon Top 10 Reviewer

"He walks the way Forrest Gump runs. Brandon's driven to it. As for the connection between the outer journey and the inner journey, he never pushes it. You get it in small bits, as he does, because that's the way it comes. ...Wilson's books point the way toward this happy state of mind: just be bold and endure a few vicissitudes."
~ Stephen Hartshorne, GoNOMAD.com

"It's great fun trekking through the Alps with the Wilsons. They do all the hard work – and we get all the pleasures – all rendered with warmth, insight and humor in Brandon's inimitable style."
~ Rick Chatenever, Entertainment & Features Editor, *The Maui News*

"Wilson has reached his pinnacle of achievement, both in his wonderfully written story and the adventure. ...A tale both grand and simple, both exciting and humorous, both real and spectacular."   ~ Jim Damico, WanderingtheWorld.com

"A gift to hikers. ...Bravo to this adventurous pair for putting 'normal' life on hold so that they could trek the backbone of the Alps and bring this insightful tale to us."
        ~ Susan Alcorn, author of *Camino Chronicle: Walking to Santiago*

"Wilson's ultimate test, full of discovery, fear, laughter and, of course, a few tears too. ...Fans of his other books will take much delight. It will please young and old alike..."   ~ Jessica Roberts, Bookpleasures.com

"A fascinating and harrowing tale. ...A MUST READ for hikers, travelers, outdoors people and adventurers."   ~ Bonnie Neely, RealTravelAdventures.com

"Wilson always transcends the mundane and the ordinary. At the same time, he makes his grassroots travel experiences fully accessible to the mind and imagination of the reader... A dramatic but also very humorous story which proves once again how physical landscapes shape the human psyche." ~ Bob Fisher, Travelosophy.com

"Walking jazz – improvisation at its best, with stunning high notes (it's the Alps!) and a trill of rain and wet, slick rhythms. Played by ear, backed by deep experience, a persistent off beat, (and a lot of humor)...it rocks!"
        ~ Kathy Gower, American Pilgrims

"Not only do we discover idyllic, yet vanishing Alpine villages and people who have made the mountains their home for generations, but we're inspired and encouraged to summit our own personal Alps."   ~ Simone diSanti, ARoadReTraveled.com

"The thrill of victory, the agony of de feet! ...The book is sprinkled with humor and cartoons to make the journey special. Hikers and non-hikers will enjoy this travelogue of conquering the mountains and valleys of *mittel Europa*."
        ~ Barbara Hudgins, author of *Crafting the Travel Guidebook*

"Their spirit of teamwork, love of nature and people, and great courage facing and overcoming many difficult unknowns along the Alpine trails makes this Brandon's very best book and adventure to date."   ~ Linda D. Delgado, Author and Publisher

"Many dream. Some try. Brandon and Cheryl do. Well told."
        ~ Marcus Wilder, author of the *Naïve and Abroad* travel series

"Another unique adventure for the world nomad or armchair traveler alike to read and enjoy without getting your feet wet and cold. Part travelogue, part travel guide and all humor and adventure."   ~ Tammy Wetzel, Yileen Press

Over
the Top
&
Back Again

Hiking X the Alps

also in the true travel adventure series by Brandon Wilson:

Along the Templar Trail

Dead Men Don't Leave Tips: Adventures X Africa

Yak Butter Blues

Over the Top & Back Again

Hiking X the Alps

by
Brandon Wilson
Lowell Thomas Gold Award-Winning
Author of *Along the Templar Trail*

with illustrations by
Ken Plumb

PILGRIM'S TALES

Over the Top & Back Again

Photos: Brandon Wilson
Illustrations: Ken Plumb
Editor: Dr. Bob Rich
Cover design: Teri Kahan Design, Costa Mesa, CA
Cover marmot photo: © iStockphoto Images
Printed and bound in the United States of America

Although this story is true, some people's names and descriptions have been changed to protect their privacy.

All activities include a certain amount of risk. The publisher and author disclaim any responsibility and any liability for any injury, harm or illness that may occur through or by use of any information in this book.

For more information about this book and others in the series, visit: www.pilgrimstales.com.

Pilgrim's Tales books are available from Ingram and Baker & Taylor in the U.S., Agapea in Spain, and from Gardners and Bertrams in the U.K. and abroad.

Publisher's Cataloging-in-Publication Data
> Wilson, Brandon.
> Over the Top & Back Again / Brandon Wilson
> Library of Congress Control Number: 2010904328
> ISBN-13: 978-0-9770536-3-6 (hardcover)
> ISBN-13: 978-0-9770536-2-9 (perfect paperback)
>
> 1. Travel   2. Alps—Description and travel
> 3. Adventure and adventurers–United States Biography
> 4. Europe—Description and travel   5. Wilson, Brandon—Travel

To Cheryl, my first editor and researcher, my biggest fan and harshest critic, for her courage, humor, and eagerness to say, "Sure, why not?"

ugspitze
Birkkarspitze
Innsbruck
Hochgall / Collalto
▲ Weiße Spitze
Austria
Brixen / Bressanone
▲ Triglav
Italy
Slovenia
Trieste
Venezia
Adriatic
Sea

Trans-Alpina
— Route on Via Alpina
-- Valley Options
···· National Borders (approx.)

1

Leaps Into Madness

STRANGE THINGS FLY THROUGH YOUR MIND WHEN YOU'RE DANGLING by a thin blue rope in the pelting rain, hanging on in a white-knuckled grip as a freezing wind pushes you back and forth like a pendulum over a 1000-meter chasm.

Take my word for it. Unlike a Hollywood movie, my life didn't flash before me. Oddly enough, only one thing came to mind: Ötzi. Who? Ötzi the Iceman, the Alpine hunter who disappeared high in the Alps some 5300 years ago. Only recently did some hapless hikers discover his mummified body, freeze-dried with a grimace on his face.

Though it's nice to be ageless, I sure didn't want to end up like him.

Did he know that fateful day of marmot hunting would be his last? Of course not. Likewise, we had no clear-cut idea what we were getting ourselves into. We took a leap of faith. It's like a leap into the abyss; only with one the outcome's more certain. And just like the thin blue rope that now kept us connected to life, an equally fine line separates "adventure" from sheer madness.

This time, something told me we'd stepped over the line.

Let me explain.

As with past adventures, once again, it all started innocently enough. My ever-trusting wife, Cheryl, and I had heard about new hiking paths named the Via Alpina, which cross eight countries and cover 200,000 square kilometers. Its five trails run some 5000 kilometers or 3100 miles across the backbone of the Alps connecting existing long distance trails, many dating back to the days of the Romans and early traders.

I hoped some improvements had been made since then.

Five variations on the route come in a variety of colors: red, green, blue, purple and yellow. The longest, the red route, consists of 161 stages and runs from Trieste, Italy on the Adriatic Sea through Slovenia, Austria, Germany, Liechtenstein, Switzerland, and France to finish in Monaco on the Mediterranean Sea. Although geographically separated by mountains, these trails occasionally intersect, allowing a hiker to hop from one to the other to explore whatever Alpine areas they like.

Exciting, right? But trekking it was not a challenge to take lightly.

Even so, it was especially appealing, masochist that I am, since it was still fairly unknown to hard-core North American thru-hikers who're busy trekking the popular Appalachian Trail from Georgia to Maine or the Pacific Crest Trail from British Columbia to Mexico. It's one of the newer faces in the trekking world. It was just 2002 when partners from Alpine countries founded the Via Alpina to promote sustainable green development.

This Via Alpina is different, I kept telling myself, a road truly less traveled. If we accept the challenge to hike its length, we won't be the first, but we could be among the first handful to complete it.

And, Ötzi aside, who knows what we'll discover up there?

Okay, I'll admit I've long been fascinated by the Alps. Each snowcapped mountain has a tale to tell and personality all its own. The region still holds an inexplicable magic that's been lost or forgotten in our lives today.

It's a place of legends, of monsters, both real and imagined. It's a traditional abode to kings in castles, to dark forests with gnomes.

The range is also home to wild creatures like the steinbok, golden eagle and mouflon, hundreds of plants like the edelweiss and alpenrose, and marmots, the Alpine version of our North American groundhogs.

It's an area full of history and culture, as each passing civilization left their mark over millennia. It's also the bastion of a fiercely independent lifestyle that's becoming as threatened as the melting glaciers on its highest peaks.

Finally, and how could I forget, it's home to blonde, pigtailed, rosy-cheeked Heidi, my first boyhood crush. For a young kid in those days before Lara Croft, she was as sexy as it got.

I just knew there had to be something special in the alpine cheese.

However, the region's more than stereotypes, more than cheese and gnomes. We wanted to discover the real Alps, to share it with others who've never ventured far off the beaten path, or who view Europe with a jaundiced "been there, done that" eye. Wild paths lead you far beyond the staid museums and cathedrals, bridges and bars found on the city-a-day tour circuit.

Then again, exploring the Alps is much more than simply "bagging peaks." It's the unique people, culture and unforgettable day-to-day experiences along the way.

And most likely, it also means confronting your own personal fears and limitations on a daily basis.

What an adventure, I thought. If we trek the red route, we'll be in the high Alps moving from hut-to-hut for maybe five months—and that's not even taking into account any time off. Given the narrow window of opportunity in the high country between first and last snows, June to October, we'll be pressed for time.

For better or worse, it'll be similar to the challenge Cheryl and I faced when trekking across Tibet back in '92, always wondering when the first blizzard would hit. Even though the Alps aren't the Himalayas, it's far from a walk in the park.

Back in Tibet, we'd discovered the beauty of "slow, deliberate travel" as we hiked the high Himalayan plains from Lhasa to Kathmandu with Sadhu, our Tibetan horse. Besides witnessing an endangered lifestyle as we "chewed the yak" with former monks and farming families around their fire each night, we uncovered an added bonus. Total immersion.

Something happens to your perspective when you slow life down, when you wallow in your surroundings. You hear, smell and sense things you've never experienced before. You eat where locals eat. Sleep where they sleep. You see a side of their life that others miss. You share hopes and dreams. You learn tolerance and see how interconnected we are, even in distant cultures. You're transformed by rediscovering your childlike wonder.

Plus, there's a zen beauty to simplifying your life. Forced to carry everything you need for months on your back, your oozing blisters and aching muscles quickly convince you to travel lightly.

That's an important lesson on any trail.

I'd taken that style of travel to heart. It became my passion; you might say, "my sweet addiction." Over the next decade, I'd spent a month or more nearly each year trekking across Europe with a backpack on historic trails that include the Via de la Plata and Camino de Santiago (once with Cheryl) through Spain, the Via Francigena from England to Rome, St. Olav's Way across Norway, and then again upon a long-distance trail from the Italian Dolomites to Prague.

I probably tackled the most difficult one in 2006 with a French friend, as we hiked 4500 kilometers on a peace trek from France to Jerusalem. Originally walked by those Crusaders who became the first Knights Templar, we re-blazed what I called the Templar Trail, narrowly dodging missiles and jihadist fervor.

We survived, but just barely.

Still, I was hooked and after two years of facing the scary sameness of a so-called normal life, I was itching for a new challenge. And something told me the Via Alpina would be unlike any of the others.

After doing a little research, it soon became obvious that it'd be necessary to apply for visas, if for no other reason than to be able to attempt to complete the vast trail in five months. Nowadays with the Schengen Agreement, many non-Europeans can only stay in the entire European Union for ninety days at a time—not ninety per country, as in the days of francs, liras and marks. Stretching it into two seasons, a *hikus interruptus,* was out of the question.

Why not, I figured, use this opportunity to experience the Alps more fully? Why not live there?

That's the ultimate in immersion. Besides, after living off and on in Hawaii for decades, a change of scene was overdue. Mountains, four seasons, and evergreen were sure to be balm for the tropical soul. But where?

Ah, Grasshopper, that was the question.

Thinking back on all our travels, I remembered September 11, 2001, a day of infamy. With no idea of the tragedy which had just unfolded in New York City, Cheryl and I landed at Milan Airport and promptly caught a train to visit Siegi, a friend I'd met two years earlier on the Camino de Santiago. He lives in Brixen, a tranquil Alpine city in the Südtirol or Alto Adige region. Although now part of northern Italy, it was Austrian until the end of World War I and I was amazed by the way its mixed culture combines Tyrolean Alpine practicality with a refreshing sense of Italian *la dolce vita.*

Brixen, or Bressanone, as it's known in Italian, is a valley town of 20,000 in a storybook setting. Once it was the center of the south Tyrol bishopric and its low skyline is still dominated by an imposing cathedral, Gothic archways, oriel windows and Middle Age towers.

Yet despite its 1100-year history, it has an air of normalcy. It's not some fabricated, fantasy Tyrol-land. You sense the contentment as couples walk hand-in-hand down traffic-free, cobblestoned streets. Folks watch the world go by while sipping morning cappuccinos at outdoor cafés. People casually bike along the tree-lined Eisack and Rienz Rivers shouting a *"Hoi, Griaßti"* or *"Buon giorno"* as they pass friends in the easy-going, bilingual community. Why, even at the market, you can overhear one clerk gossiping to another in Italian, who answers in German.

There, in the shadow of the legendary Dolomites, the crisp mountain air invites you to breathe deeply. Not surprisingly, it's ideal for hardcore hikers. Locals take to the surrounding mountains for relaxing weekend walks on well-groomed trails and winter is anxiously awaited for the chance to ski, sled, and snowboard the Plose Mountain. Even Brixen's indoor pool and spa seem more designed for locals than its frequent visitors. There's certainly something special about that valley's water, the sweetest I've ever tasted, plus the food is equally super-natural.

Hey, you have to consider these details.

The region's vineyards and apple orchards offer fruit straight from their trees, not warehouse-stores, and supply a New England-like blast of autumnal color. Dairy farms produce fresh hormone-free milk, cheese and yogurt, and the valley celebrates its abundance with festivals featuring tasty smoked ham, apple strudel, breads, beer and wine served to an oompah beat.

Ultimately though, something impressed us even more. During that time of terrorist turmoil, we could never forget how sympathetic Brixners had been, welcoming two strangers far from home with open arms.

Consequently, it seemed like a logical (and did I say delicious?) choice. Its central location in Europe would make it so much easier for us to plan our annual treks without having to take out a second mortgage to fly halfway around the world. That never makes much sense when you're trying to live simply and lessen your carbon footprint.

Besides, I'd secretly hankered after a cool pair of *lederhosen,* or leather pants, to complement my annual Oktoberfest chicken dance outfit.

So, why not try Brixen?

That decision opened the floodgates on what could have been a logistical nightmare. Soon we were swamped with the details of applying for an elective residency visa and all its various stamps. Fortunately, Siegi came through for us in flying tri-colors, as he knows everyone and greased the wheels.

We also contacted Nathalie, the Association Via Alpina network's go-to person, explaining that we were interested in hiking their trails and in sharing our experiences. Although I vowed to write my usual warts and all account, bound to offend everyone in some small way, they made us official partners and provided a letter of introduction for officialdom.

Every little bit might help our case.

While the consulate deliberated on whether to let us stay for a year, there was no time to waste. We switched into phase two: gearing up and finding the absolute best and lightest equipment available.

There's an old Swiss joke. Every day the TV weather forecaster calls for the same thing: "Sunny with rain and a chance of snow." True. That makes it especially tricky to plan for all Alpine weather contingencies. Given the distance and workout of climbing 1000 meters (3200+ feet) up and then back down mountains every day, we knew it'd be suicide to carry more than seven or eight kilos (15-16 pounds) each. That truth had already been permanently etched in my soles.

So after careful deliberation, we decided to pack just the essentials: a change of clothing, extra socks, rain ponchos and pants, running shoes, lightweight hiking boots, gaiters to keep snow or gravel from our boots, hats, down jackets and sleeping bags, cameras, LEKI Nordic poles, and sachets of a powdered energy drink. We would divide a basic medical kit, compass, maps, and power cords among us. However, we decided against carrying crampons and ice axes. The trails would most likely be clear of snow and ice by June and they'd just add weight and take up far too much space.

Even though we were traveling techo-lite, I'd take a GPS backtrack gizmo which would supposedly allow us to retrace our steps if (when) we became hopelessly lost, if nothing else. Cheryl would also bring her trusty compact Mac iTouch that'd allow us to read a Via Alpina PDF for directions, since there was no English guidebook available then, and to possibly check our emails—if or when we ever found Wi-Fi coverage in the Alps. That was a huge unknown.

After hours of research into a dizzying number of innovative designs, we contacted GoLite to get their new lightweight packs, bags and clothing. I'd carried their gear on two former expeditions. Then Gossamer Gear, light-years ahead in their designs, supplied a tent weighing just a kilo that'd be handy in case of an emergency, if we were stuck in a blizzard, or tucked into a crevasse between villages. And finally, Omni Resources provided thirty precious topographic maps we'd carry a few at a time.

Meanwhile, to physically prepare, Upcountry Fitness, a local health club, mercilessly beat our flabby office bodies into submission with three months of strength and aerobic training. Although I sensed it might be "too little, too late" at the time, I have to admit their treadmill incline worked wonders.

Cheryl transformed from desk jockey into a mountain diva. Better still, I could see this challenge of trekking across the Alps appealed to her inner jockette. There was a little-disguised bounce to her step and refreshing sparkle in her hazel eyes.

Finally, we picked up our visa-required health insurance policy, which to be honest was little more than a security blanket. If we slipped off a 3000-meter peak, there wouldn't be much left to cart to a distant emergency room.

Nature gives no quarter. We were ultimately on our own.

Speaking of which, let me make this positively clear right up front: I have great respect for the mountains. It doesn't take much for them to shake you off, like a dog ridding itself of pesky fleas. Unlike some, I'm convinced there's no such thing as "conquering" mountains. With luck, you merely hope to survive them—and to reaffirm the value you place on life.

That said, the enormity of our journey didn't fully register until our topo maps arrived. One evening, Cheryl and I sat surrounded by them sprawled across the living room rug. As she called out each village name, I carefully traced a line between our daily stages. My orange marker went from valley to mountain summit and back down again, sometimes several times a day, before we reached a cabin. It wound around glaciers. It looped entire regions in crazy mandala circles, only to come back again.

We didn't say much, didn't have to. We'd been together long enough. One look said it all.

Dammit. Just what have we gotten ourselves into this time? We aren't mountain climbers, just trekkers. Sure, my last hike was across eleven countries. But as you know, it's not length that counts; it's the ups and downs, the backs and forths. A thousand-meter climb and descent every day, for months on end, would be harder than we'd ever attempted before.

Still, it was meant to be. The stars came into alignment.

The mail arrived one afternoon and we were so startled to receive our Italian visas that our screams left the bananas outside shaking from their stalks. Yet with one major hurdle crossed, packing up our lives was another daunting challenge. How do you sort through a lifetime of possessions to lighten your load?

For better or worse, about this same time, Cheryl was laid off her job and came to my rescue, pulling me out from under boxes just in the nick of time. Plants, furniture and cars all eventually found new homes, as well as far too many accumulated things. Did you know that kitchen cups multiply like bunnies when left alone in dark cupboards? It's true.

Our shedding continued right down to the garden gnome who was left, still smiling, at the simple wooden cottage. At long last, we carted our remaining worldly possessions to a shipping company where our boxes were so tightly packed a feather couldn't fit between them. Looking at the single wooden crate, we beamed like proud parents, satisfied to see our nomadic lives reduced to a more manageable size—yet shocked at the implications.

This time we'd definitely burned a bridge.

The days flew off the calendar like in one of those cheesy black-and-white films as we set off on a new chapter, the start of another trail. This one just happened to also be an exciting new path in life. We flew high on a surge of adrenaline. Mentally we were eager to escape paradise for a while, although I admit we were touched by sadness at leaving our circle of friends and family.

After saying *"aloha"* to them in Hawaii and on both coasts, we nervously flew to Munich and then connected by train to Brixen. Unfortunately, our arrival didn't provide the rest or reprieve we'd long anticipated. With the clock ticking loudly in our ears, we faced a deluge of nagging last minute details, especially applying for what they call the *permesso di soggiorno* with all its various stamps and processing at the local INAS (National Institute for Social Assistance), and then an added trip to the police station, the tobacconist for tax stamps, and finally the post office.

Although we already had visas, the *permesso* was our permission to actually *live* in Italy. Given the national backlog, we'd heard it might take months for them to schedule our personal appearance, at which time we had to produce more documents and have our fingerprints taken.

By then, with any luck, I figured our trek would be completed. We'd be back in our Tyrolean hideaway and overdosing on schnitzel and schnapps.

Before leaving Brixen, in one final stroke of genius, Siegi signed us up for the *Alpenverein Südtirol*. As members of their regional mountaineering association, we'd save 20-30% for a bunk bed at the alpine huts. Since this expedition was entirely self-funded, every euro counted. Unlike previous treks, we couldn't depend on staying in inexpensive hostels or *refugios*, and the anemic American dollar would put our budgets to the supreme test.

Then again, I thought, this is hiking. It's about as Everyman an activity as you can find. How much could it possibly cost?

Ultimately, our endless checklist was completed. Only then did we take time to mix a little pleasure with last-minute errands. On the way home from neighboring Bolzano, Siegi drove us to a quiet, shady park outside Vahrn for a brisk walk in a sluice flowing with icy water.

Kneipping, named after the Bavarian priest with the same name, is a teeth-chattering naturopathic treatment—and perfect for returning plane-swollen feet to almost normal size.

Too bad, I thought, I can't fit my entire body in this channel.

Until at last, we ran out of time. The evening before we left for Trieste to begin our trek from the Adriatic Sea, we drove to a neighboring village to launch our great adventure. The restaurant was traditionally Tyrolean from its sturdy handcrafted rustic furniture to the ceramic-tiled woodstove, from its unpronounceable menu down to the apple-cheeked waitress in her poofy *dirndl* dress with laced bodice and checkered apron.

It was perfect, just as I'd always imagined. Yet we ate in near silence, overwhelmed by last-minute doubts about the long odyssey ahead. However, I still remember that last meal.

Cheryl savored *speckknöderl* soup, a broth featuring floating baseballs of ham and flour that taste like Thanksgiving dressing, while I dug into the spinach ravioli and Siegi had gnocchi, all washed down with a local Magdalena red wine poured from an earthenware jug.

Afterward, the three of us shuffled out to the sun terrace just in time to catch an ethereal pumpkin light illuminating the jagged, snowcapped Dolomites, spectacular towers of ancient coral rising above us. At last, speechless, we relished our long awaited "whew" moment, topped off by a delicious dollop of Alpenglow for dessert.

Looking back, I optimistically took it as a good sign; there'd be clear sailing ahead. The Universe, well, had other plans.

Austria

Kötschach-Mauthen

Thörl-Maglern

Kranjska Gora

Trenta

Triglav
▲ 2864

Crna prst
Podbrdo

Vogel

Za Robom

Ermanovcu

Idrija

Crni vrh

Predjama

Slovenia

Italy

Razdrto

Matavun

Trieste

Premuda

Muggia

Adriatic
Sea

2

Get Lost in Slovenia

On the last day of May, our train lumbered from Brixen to Trieste, taking eleven hours to travel a few hundred miles. From the train station, it was just a short bus ride to the seaside youth hostel, a one-time manor in the dusky shadow of its former grandeur. After settling in, Cheryl and I climbed to the rooftop to watch darkness fall over the Adriatic and then we joined vacationers for their traditional Italian promenade along the boardwalk. With our stomachs in knots, we breathed deep in anxious anticipation, knowing that dose of salt air would have to sustain us far too long.

Then jet-lagged and train-weary, we shuffled upstairs: Cheryl to the women's dorm and me to the men's. Maybe it was wishful thinking, but we figured we'd catch up on sleep to prepare for our long odyssey ahead. As I knew all too well from past hikes, sleep can make or break you. Something so simple becomes crucial, especially on a trek that was shaping up to be a four-month marathon.

I was alone in the dark dorm room except for a cyclist who was already sacked-out. A lycra Milan jersey, Woody Woodpecker-like pointed helmet, skin-tight shorts, and those studded cyclist shoes that go clickety-clack when you walk were strewn across the floor. I silently climbed to the upper bunk and had just nodded off when suddenly the fella sat straight up, turned on all the lights, threw on his clothes, bathed in cologne, and went out for a night on the town.

All right, I thought, no worries. It's still early.

Well, he no sooner left than a 70-year-old Italian gent shuffled in, flicked on the fluorescent lights, and carefully removed folded clothes from his battered suitcase one by one—only to repack them exactly the same way. At long last, by the time he'd changed into his nightclothes and fell into mummy-like repose, the cyclist returned, repeating the drill.

That's got to be it, I thought. I can finally get some sleep.

But, no, just as we settled down for the night, the older fellow began a caterwauling to rival the groans of lovemaking hogs. His snores were so loud that Cheryl heard them down the hall from behind two heavy closed doors. As midnight approached and murder was clearly out of the question, I padded down to the front desk for sympathy, or a one-bullet solution.

The kid said "Sure," as if it happened all the time and sent me to a room in the basement to share with a cadaverous fellow padding around in hot pink pants and matching flip-flops. I didn't quite know what to make of his getup or stare, but at least I could sleep, albeit with one eye slightly ajar.

Daylight came too soon. Barely functioning, we went into town and began our first of many searches for a Wi-Fi (or as they call them a "Wee-Fee") area to access the Internet. A girl with purple hair and nose ring enlisted six perplexed others who led us to a café where we printed directions from a Via Alpina PDF for the trail's first stages. Then we hopped across the harbor to Muggia, a minestrone soup of Italian, Illyrian, and Slavic cultures just five minutes from the Slovenian border.

Carefully following those vague printed instructions, we set off trying to locate the trailhead from Marconi Square. No luck. Then we tried uncovering it from the castle. Nada. Having seen a visitor office earlier, we returned—only to find them closed for the day. Eventually, we climbed the stairs to a government office where fate smiled on us. Actually, it was more like a smirk. However, a lady working there warmly welcomed us and spent over an hour trying to help us find the mysteriously unmarked trailhead.

It was baffling. We hadn't expected a welcome banner or brass band. But why no sign, no X marks the spot for the start of a trans-continental trail?

"What do people do?" I asked. "How do they find the trail?"

"Oh, you are not the first to have this difficulty here," the woman confided, shaking her head in the calm resignation that comes from working at a bureaucratic office too long. "A Spanish couple had the same problem last year." She leaned forward. Then placing a finger to her lips, she whispered, "The trail exists on paper, but in practicality..."

Santa Patata!

That was the last thing we wanted to hear after coming so far. All the same, to her credit, the woman didn't give up. And neither would we. She doggedly called the local Alpine club and others to eventually discover the Via Alpina follows the older Muggesana trail marked in red and white stripes. It still didn't explain why it was disguised, but with another hurdle crossed, we thanked her and wandered off to find an unpretentious pension, or guesthouse, while vowing to hit the trail at sunrise.

As with many things, it looked great on paper. The next morning, according to our directions, we'd head up the steep hillside behind the pension and soon be on our way. In reality, we had to climb a steep road to neighboring Santa Barbara, hike around the village, and then descend quite a way to finally meet the Muggesana blue route. Initially, it looked like we were headed in the right direction, but then the markings suddenly petered out and we were forced back down the hill toward Slovenia. At one point, I swear we were within a hundred meters of the border, but I knew, according to the directions, we weren't supposed to cross until the next day. Reaching a pasta factory, we were given the ever-popular Italian, *sempre diretto* or "always straight ahead," and soon found ourselves at the edge of a regional park where villagers filled their jugs from a fountain gushing from a rock. Assured it was safe, and dripping with sweat, we gulped our fill.

It was hours before we loped into Premuda Refuge. I was glad we'd already reserved a pension room in the village. As it turned out, they'd left a key at the hut, which doesn't accommodate hikers anymore. After checking ourselves in, we searched for supplies, but everything was closed. So, we ended up walking back to Premuda for a carafe of cool white wine to enjoy with locals eating, drinking, and chattering away outside under giant umbrellas. Miraculously our frustrations and aches vanished as swiftly as the trail.

The first week on these trips is always the hardest as you work out the bugs, I kept reminding myself—and we've discovered an infestation.

The next day was another one of false starts. We left the village and sped off past surrounding limestone karsts, stone formations unique to the area.

According to legend, God had a few rocks left over after creating the earth. (I guess it's hard to plan ahead for such a big project.) He decided to put them in a bag and toss it into the ocean. However, the Devil, as always, had other plans. He cut a hole in the bag and the rocks fell out forming gullies, grooves, sinkholes and caves. They've been a mixed blessing ever since.

For 9 a.m. it was a breathtaking, heart-throbbing climb. Before long, we were in thick woods amid the laughter of school kids as our never-ending search for trail marks led us straight up the mountainside. Switchbacks, the clever invention that lays out trails on a gentle incline, are unheard of in Slovenia, an otherwise beautiful country. They're for flabby-assed city wimps. Why, a trail less than 45 or 50° is hardly worth climbing.

Given all that, it was nearly noon by the time we reached Pesek. To make up a little time, we detoured to Grozzana where we hoped to connect with the trail. Wrong. No one in the tiny village knew where the trailhead was, even the fellow who lived right next door to it. Two friendly dogs came to our rescue and attempted to lead us, but we failed to follow them and floundered awhile longer.

It took us another hour of climbing Mt. Kokos to accidentally arrive at Planinska koca na Kokosi Hut at 670 meters. Unfortunately, it was closed (too early in the season) and we couldn't even fill our water bottles. So backtracking down a tree-lined gravel road through stony pastures, we eventually stumbled upon the trail and made a steep descent to Lokev.

The village is near the famous Lipica stables where the world-renowned, high-stepping Lipizzani, or Lipizzaner stallion was first sired four centuries ago. But even more momentous for us was finding a faucet at a nearby cemetery of all places. Strangely, Cheryl was even able to connect with a Wi-Fi signal.

Grinning, she asked, "Think they have Internet in the Great Beyond?"

"Yea, but the roaming charges are gonna kill you."

Given the day's aimless meandering with a map, we sure didn't look forward to flying blind without one. And past those simple crossroads, there may as well have been a sign reading, "Beyond Here Lie Dragons." For four months we'd expected to receive new and improved Slovenian maps from a fellow we called "Map Man" and so we held off on bringing our own. Well, they still hadn't appeared. Consequently, we ran off our topo maps and his silence left us high and dry.

Now I readily admit, men aren't known for their eagerness to stop and ask for directions. But desperate times call for desperate measures. If we asked once, we asked twenty times a day in a hodgepodge of Italian, German and English— Getalish. It's one heckuva way to meet the locals. And to their credit, everyone did their best to direct us, albeit in different directions. Although the country folks were pleasant and many spoke a smattering of CNN-learned English, they'd never heard of the trail. Still, we held out hope.

Under the hot glare of the sun, we paused once again to ask directions from a man and his kids cooling in the shade of a large umbrella.

"We're trekking the Via Alpina," I announced in a glass half-full kinda way.

The big fella nodded approvingly and took a sip of wine. "Ah, you have good soles," he said, motioning to our shoes. I nodded. "But I have better," he said with a laugh and pointed to his car tires.

We had to appreciate his humor, but at that point, I couldn't help but wonder if he wasn't secretly trying to tell us something.

It was dusk by the time we finally reached Matavun, home to the famous Skocjan Caves. Although people have lived there since prehistoric times, their *zimmer* (bed & breakfast) was full, but they were helpful and booked us a room in the next village. By the time we dragged in, we were exhausted and dehydrated after a thirty-kilometer day. We'd pushed too hard, too far, too soon; the perfect recipe for sore muscles, strains and blisters. But what choice did we have? There were no other places to stop in between.

Then again, our room was comfortable and promised a good night's sleep, only interrupted by a crack of thunder at 3 a.m. At home, I'd sleep through it but on the road that can herald a miserable day. At the very least, it meant someone has to drag themselves naked from bed to bring in the hand-scrubbed clothes drying outside.

Groggy, we joined other guests at first light for what they promised was a special hiker's breakfast and I'd have to admit that eggs, smoked ham and bread never tasted so dee-lic-ious. It was a perfect excuse to take our time. Since it was still raining, we were in no particular hurry to leave. Besides, our innkeeper was a little more hospitable than he'd been the night before, even phoning Map Man for us. We made plans to pick up his maps the following night—then later learned his rendezvous point was a good twenty-kilometers off the trail. That's a logistical nightmare when you're hiking, but almost a step in the right direction.

Unable to postpone the inevitable any longer, we reluctantly threw on our ponchos and rain pants. Stepping outside, we ran into a Swiss couple who stayed there as well. They were headed south on bikes. With no bookstores or tobacconists in the tiny villages, they also shared our map problem, so we struck an easy deal and traded. Theirs would lead us through the countryside for the next two days, while ours would help them find their way south to the coast.

Pleased at our good luck, we caught the trail behind the caves and then slogged in rain over the next hour. Sure, we found the trail easier. But as we already knew by then, the path never took the most direct route from here to there. We chuckled about its odd diversions to allow you to admire the view and, as the PDF guide suggested, to "linger awhile." That's a great idea in perfect weather, but after wheezing up another mountain through mud in a downpour, I'll admit it was a little lost on me.

All afternoon we trekked through dark, moist forests carpeted in mulch, nature's insoles, and then down more gravel country roads. We paused at every crossroad to check for "O" markings on trees, since the trail was marked like that in that particular section. Sometimes we'd see them, but more often not. In that particular forest, bears were easier to find; but the intersections were the worst, often with no markings at all. It was anyone's guess which way to go. We'd set off in one direction for fifteen minutes on a goat track until we discovered our mistake, only to backtrack and try again.

Until finally, as we slogged into Razdrto after another confusing day, Cheryl couldn't help but sigh, "Who marks these trails, anyway?

"And what do they have against sharing them with others?"

The next morning when we awoke, Mt. Nanos, known as Okra (no relation to the much-maligned vegetable) in ancient times, was shrouded in fog.

"Look, instead of risking broken limbs," I suggested, "let's hike the bike path as far as Strane and connect with the Via Alpina there. Otherwise, it looks like another needless diversion for another vista. I'm sure it's wonderful in good weather. But it's impossible to see more than fifty meters in this mess. Maybe if this was a day hike and we weren't lugging packs it'd be different. But pacing is everything now. We need to conserve our strength for the long months ahead."

Cheryl nodded, reminding me, "Slovenia is training for the high Alps."

"Yea, and we can only hope the markings get better."

Even without the climb, trails were slippery and muddy and it was ten degrees cooler, a drastic change from 30° a few days earlier. As the day progressed, we passed a few rustic villages where people raised huge family gardens. Apricot and both red and black cherry trees overhung roads providing a moveable feast. Their red-tiled houses were well built. Many featured window boxes ablaze with red or orange geraniums, similar to their Austrian neighbors. Kids horsed around in haystacks. Cherubic ladies in aprons tended flocks of fowl, and there always seemed to be water fountains just when our bottles were empty. Garden gnomes, always a welcome sign, were spotted mischievously peering out of gardens or windows. We heard the comical cry of cuckoo birds from deep in primeval woods, which are even home to wolves, lynx and bears. Although we saw "Beware of *Medveds* (bears)" signs posted, we could barely be concerned.

Finally reaching Predjama, we stopped to warm up over a cup of soup at an inn. It lay at the base of an impressive castle built into caves by a local folk hero.

Legend has it that Erazem Predjamski, a well-known warrior against the Ottomans, fell out of the emperor's good grace and escaped to the fortress. Unemployed and bored, he began robbing wayfarers between Trieste and Vienna. Well, that wasn't good for tourism. Ultimately the emperor instructed the governor to capture Erazem, a task easier said than done. The knight had stockpiled supplies in the cave's secret tunnels, so a long siege proved futile. Still, there was no happy ending to the knight's tale. Treachery prevailed and Erazem was killed when one of his servants deceived him.

After gulping down my soup, I slogged over to the castle ticket office where a sympathetic lady called the Postojna hotel where we were supposed to meet Map Man. As he'd suggested, we mentioned the name of his friend, so they sent a van to pick us up. Things were looking up—or were they?

When we arrived at the inn so far off our trail, neither he nor his friend was there. We called, but he was suddenly unable to come.

Not a good sign, I thought, but not surprising. He swears he sent the maps. Will they arrive before we leave tomorrow? And how? Special delivery? Post? Marmot express? If not, how will we find the trail the next ten days to Austria?

That worried us, but if we'd learned anything from past treks, it's to believe that things work out for the best in the end. Usually, that is.

That evening we treated ourselves to a long, hot shower. I was just melting in its warmth when I felt a strange lump on the back of my leg. Thinking it was another clump of mud, I picked it off. Imagine my surprise when I glanced down just in time to spot a fat, blood-engorged tick, (a Slovenian woodland souvenir), swirling down the drain.

Ah, nature!

Our luck continued when we awoke to more dreary skies and rainfall. Then we received the good news/bad news. Yes, the hotel would take us back to the trailhead, saving us a five-hour slog in the drizzle. No, the maps hadn't arrived. Map Man had mailed them—the day before we arrived! On the van driver's suggestion, we stopped at a gas station and bought a better-than-nothing map to follow on and off in the cool drizzle to Hrusica.

As it turned out, we were alone again all day. That wasn't surprising given the weather. As usual, I trekked a little ahead of Cheryl, partially to find the trail. Besides, we'd vowed long ago not to be connected at the hip and to set our own pace as we'd always done on hikes and in life. In fact, she insisted on it. If anything, we were connected at the heart.

Trail markings altogether vanished once we circled Javornik Mountain at 1240-meters, and it was futile to take compass headings since our route changed direction every hundred meters. Still, a beautiful silence enveloped us as we hiked on trust: faith the trail knows where it's going (even if we don't). It was late afternoon by the time we came across a ski lift and were finally able to pinpoint our position on the map, and then begin a steep descent into Crni vrh, a speck of a village, where we easily found an inn. It was certainly more expensive than in the old Soviet days, yet the quality was far better.

Long ago, we'd learned to savor those small victories, not waiting for the giant triumphs along the way. So to celebrate, Cheryl and I splurged that evening on three types of pasta, *cevapcici* sausage, and *pivos* or beers. I already equated food with fuel on our journey—and if it was tasty, well, so much the better.

We slept a carefree trekker's sleep, at least I did. Cheryl bolted upright at the first boom of thunder, which then continued all night. The downpour eased as we loitered over breakfast, only to start again within thirty minutes of leaving the village. Then it changed into hail, forcing us to dart under the wide limbs of

nearby trees. Ominous clouds swept past overhead as if shot in time-lapse pho-
tography. In the Alps, we never knew what the next hour would bring.

"These weather patterns are diabolical," I muttered, wrapping up in my
blue cape-like poncho, "especially compared to the relative sameness of Hawaii's
daily forecast of 'sunny with the possibility of *mauka* (mountain) showers.'"

"Yea, anything's possible up here, especially in summer," Cheryl said, struggling into her rain pants.

We were resigned to follow our half-assed map, even though our path led
outside its borders. The roundabout route took us probably an extra three hours
or 12-14 kilometers out of the way until we finally reached Idrija, a former
Roman village encircled by a bucolic backdrop of towering mountains, steep
ridges and forests. Its claim to fame came with the lucky, accidental discovery of
the world's second-largest mercury mine in 1490.

For once, we were equally lucky to find the visitor office open. Strangely,
they have a habit of closing during lunchtime, on weekends, evenings, holidays
or generally times when travelers need them. A teenager who staffed their office
had never heard of the Via Alpina, even though a huge route map hung behind
him on the wall. Nevertheless, he was happy to sell us a map for the missing
Slovenian trail section and find us a room for the night.

No sooner did we step outside than the storm began anew, guaranteeing
we were soaked by the time we reached the three-story mountain pension. After
showering, we sure looked forward to finding a market and cooking dinner,
especially since the apartment had a kitchen with one of those behemoth
Gorenje woodstoves. However, it was Sunday and all the shops were closed, so
we settled into a local pizza joint.

It was run by a fellow who spoke perfect English like many Eastern
Europeans in their early 20s who consider it "cool." As we devoured a
Gorgonzola cheese pizza, he poked his head above the bar long enough to ask,
"Where are you from?" and then, "Is it true you get a flower lei when you arrive
in Hawaii?"

"Yes, you're leied if you're met by friends or you're on a package tour."

"And the girls? Are they as pretty as they look on TV?"

"Of course!" I knew a little about the subject. "The girls are a mixture of
Hawaiian, Japanese, Chinese, Filipino, Scots and other ancestry. That creates
some beautiful women."

He beamed. At least in his mind, he was plotting a future trip and we
hoped he'd make it some day. Fortunately, those islands don't have an exclusive
corner on the *aloha* market either. As we eventually stood to pay, he surprised us
by announcing, "Your last drink is on the house." Completely unexpected, his

small kindness made our day—or, considering the way things were going, maybe even week.

Rejuvenated, we were awake at dawn and stopped into a bakery, and then into the local bus station for coffee. For once, we had time to spare. The visitor office didn't open until later, but the manager called ahead to reserve a space at the next hut and they promised to open just for us. They'd also have food.

What more could we ask for? Markings?

Her news was wind in our sails and we flew from her office to cruise along the river on a quiet, sun-dappled path. Funny, we should have known things were going just too smoothly on that breezy summer morning. We were on a path—a great one—just the wrong one. That managed to put us behind schedule to start. After much searching, we eventually found the actual unmarked trail up a very steep road past the police station. Upon reaching a clearing, we only uncovered the well-hidden path with the help of locals who sent us marching uphill again through the woods for another hour to a pasture. Although the cows came over to greet us, they were no help with directions as the trail vanished in undergrowth and sharp thistles. I finally had to climb atop an old stone wall to spot and navigate the non-existent path.

Cheryl didn't fare as well. While grabbing onto whatever root she could to hoist herself up over rocks, she bruised her toes, wrenched her knee, slipped, and nearly took a header uphill.

"Dammit!" she growled. "How can they call this a trail?"

By this point, some folks might nitpick and complain the paths weren't well marked, but that's only because they weren't willing to spend an hour several times a day to find markings. When we did actually spot a marker, and believe me we feverishly searched, often they were 5-centimeters (2-inches) square. Plus it wasn't like you could turn to a fellow trekker. Over the first few days, a few bicyclists had passed from the opposite direction, but surprisingly we saw no other hikers. In fact, we'd seen no other Via Alpinists since leaving. Given the markings, I figured they were turned around and headed to Albania.

But we continued to ambush locals to ask directions as often as possible. We sometimes resorted to stopping drivers on the single-lane country roads, flagging them down with maps and mystified looks. Even if they couldn't speak English or German, we figured they could still point to our location on the map and possible routes. Once we even stopped at a secluded farmhouse to ask a family for help. They fetched their young daughter, maybe ten years old, who patiently stood in the middle of the road in tattered bear paw slippers. In broken English, she told us we could catch a gravel road and pointed down into the valley. That saved us hours.

Once there, we again asked directions to the mountain hut on the summit. There just happened to be several routes and we logically chose the one alongside the river, which took us straight up the mountainside. It seemed appropriate to finish the day just as we'd started, wheezing up another 1000 meters.

Our stop for the day, the hut at Ermanovec, is set on the watershed ridge separating Adriatic waters from those of the Black Sea. Historically an area of hot dispute, it was heavily militarized by Italy's Alpine Wall to the west and Yugoslavia's Rupnik Line to the east. In fact, bunkers once stood on Ermanovec. But you'd never know it these days.

When we arrived, the guardian or caretaker, a petite lady with glowing cheeks and curly black hair, was already inside the large stone hut cooking dinner for her two guests. Although she spoke no English, we got by with rustic German as we gratefully gobbled goulash she'd fixed to perfection. To make a fine evening even better, our hostess offered to call ahead to Porezen Hut in the morning to make sure they were open.

We didn't carry a mobile phone, a rarity for Europeans. We're not exactly Luddites. Quite the contrary. Even if we'd brought one from home, it wouldn't be compatible with their system. Besides, how often would we find a signal atop the Alps?

"Can you hear us now? Nope, didn't think so."

In the morning, we were disappointed to learn Porezen Hut was still closed. Seems they're only open on weekends in June, so we faced a dilemma.

Why climb a 1630-meter mountain, a hard, wet slog from the valley, when there's no place to stay after we summit? Sure, we could camp. We have our emergency tent. But since the site's known for its bloody massacre, it might be kind of spooky up there, if not disrespectful.

No, we'll go on.

After a small breakfast, we made surprisingly great time off the summit. Only then did we face another problem at yet another junction. For once, it had a sign, but nothing showing which of three roads to take.

"Alright, that's an improvement," Cheryl said. "But which direction?"

"Well, how lucky do you feel?"

"Not very."

We stopped a car and asked directions. The country fellow, reminiscent of the OZ scarecrow, said, "You could follow the path left to Cerkno." Then reconsidering, he said, "Or you could head right, past Mt. Skofje."

Hmm...left or right? Unfortunately, we chose the latter, which led us onto another mountaintop with no obvious way of reaching the bottom. Backtracking down to the crossroads, we found a vine-hidden trail leading straight down a creekbed marked with a sign to the old Franja Partisan Hospital. Hidden deep inside Pasica Gorge, Slovenian freedom fighters had run a hospital there. It went undiscovered by the Fascists throughout the long war.

It's amazing when you think about it. Then again, given the density of those dark woods and its vanishing trails, why didn't that surprise me?

The path led us off the mountain, through brambles, and at a 40° slope that looked unused since that war. Once in the valley, we filled our water bottles at the home of a tour bus driver who spoke excellent English. Although he suggested finding a room down the road in Dolenji, we were still determined to continue on the Via Alpina—as nearly as we could. So, we set off again. The trail, a country road, meandered up another mountain for two hours. Just to be on the safe side, at each junction we stopped drivers to confirm we were still headed in the right direction. With the thick forest, it was hard to tell. Heat and lack of water drained our spirits as we plodded a hundred meters apart in a daze.

There's no way we can make it to Podbrdo today, I thought. The only *zimmer* we've passed is closed. I doubt the farmhouse ahead is open, but we'll give it a try.

Za Robom was a big, rambling place protected by a relentlessly barking, pony-sized German shepherd. The guesthouse owner, a middle-aged, dentally-challenged woman, was about as receptive. When I asked if they had rooms, she grumbled, "No rooms, only beautiful apartment."

"I could sleep on this bench at this point."

"Forty euros."

"What? For the bench?"

"No, for apartment."

"With breakfast? *Frühstück?*"

She nodded, but really didn't want us to stay there. Truth was, she didn't want to clean the place and tried to convince us to trek another hour to a place she knew was open. We already missed the old days in Yugoslavia when haggling was a national sport and a pack of cigarettes could seal a deal.

At last, she relented and shuffled off to fetch sheets, saying, "Five minutes."

Before long she led us to a modern apartment where we savored a package of instant dry soup, the only food remaining in our packs with not a market in sight. As we rubbed our sore feet, too tired to talk, we watched a Slovenian television program, which looked like the early ancestor of MTV. Like something from the turn-of-the-last-century, it featured a hodgepodge of accordion groups, and then one woman played a comb while another jammed on a cow's horn. I couldn't wait for Lady Gaga to try that. With any luck, maybe she'd wear a black and white spotted cow outfit to match?

3

THE BEST LAID PLANS

OUR INNKEEPER WARMED UP THE NEXT MORNING, EVEN IF HER breakfast of bread, butter, homemade berry jam and mountain fruit tea left us hungry for more. For a while, we talked with her about the wild trail and then reminisced about our first visit to Slovenia when it was still part of Yugoslavia.

"It looks like so much has changed since then. That autumn of '89, Cheryl and I backpacked through Yugoslavia, Hungary, Bulgaria, and Czechoslovakia for months. In fact, we were in Gdansk, Poland when we heard that the Berlin Wall was falling. Talk about perfect timing. The next day we shot across to East Germany on the train just in time to help pound the wall into submission with a sledgehammer. You know, there wasn't a single hammer left for sale in all of Berlin. There was an amazing party with bands, food carts and television crews from around the world. Funny, I still remember the long column of East Berliners standing in front of the lingerie shops, waiting to get in. The line went on for blocks."

"My daughter was born that year and I remember it well," she replied with a wistful look in her eyes.

"We'd visited Lake Bled a few months earlier. I remember the ferryman carrying folks out to the island in the middle of the lake. He said he based his price on people's shoes. One look and he could tell their nationality. He bragged, "I have one price for Americans, another for Germans and West Europeans, and still another for East Europeans.""

She smiled knowingly—enough said. Learning we were from the States, she said, "Everyone is pretty comfortable here these days. Not rich, but comfortable. I have my mountain, my garden. I don't need much more," she added with a satisfied smile.

We had to admire that. Paradise is where you make it.

With that, we left and quickly made it down the road and then up to another summit and Cerkno Ski Resort. The roads and trails were better marked. The trail wound for the next two hours back down into another valley and along the swiftly flowing Zadnja Sora (River). For once, it was "all downhill."

I hiked a little ahead of Cheryl all day, pausing every thirty minutes for her to catch up. For me it was a leisurely pace, slower than usual. But her knee had been sore since her near spill and she limped, struggling to keep moving. So, I tried to choose gentler paths, but sometimes that was impossible. In the end, we decided to just make it a shorter day instead of continuing to Crna prst Hut.

Before long we reached Podbrdo, a hamlet of a dozen tidy houses set in a verdant valley where Tyroleans had settled a few hundred years earlier. It was easy to find the one guesthouse in town, a place run by a gregarious woman with curly, "Dance with me, Bobby," blazing scarlet hair. As we waited, her neighbor phoned ahead to confirm the mountain hut at Crna prst (1844 meters) would indeed be open the next day. That was a relief. Then we were shown into the lady's large house. She asked us to wait in her living room, and then brought cold beers while she and the neighbor's dutiful daughter cleaned our room. The little girl even wiped down the stairs by hand with a rag. Soon we were escorted to an upstairs apartment complete with a small kitchen and balcony. It was perfect. We could clean up, do some laundry, and have a good night's sleep after an easier day.

Rest was exactly what Cheryl needed. What I didn't need was to find another blood-engorged tick sucking on my leg.

Then again, what a difference a day can make. We got up earlier than usual thinking we'd beat the midday heat that'd slowed us down the past two days. Crna prst Hut was supposedly only three hours away, of course, straight up the mountain above the village. However, there was no place in between to get water and we were a little concerned about dehydration. Then again, our cheerful hostess plied us with plenty of coffee from a china service, along with meat, cheese and bread before sending us on our way.

The skies were clear and sunny. It had all the makings of a perfect day. We figured we'd take a leisurely stroll up the mountain. Who cared if it took us an extra hour or so? There was no hurry. Cheryl's knee was wrapped with an elastic bandage for extra support, buttered with analgesic cream from an elephant-sized tube I'd bought on my last trek, and we were using our Nordic sticks, so we thought we had our bases covered.

Think again.

The trail began in earnest once we reached Trtnik where it set off straight up the mountainside from someone's backyard. As I said, switchbacks aren't especially common in Slovenia and it was a lung-wheezer to climb. With pausing every ten minutes to catch our breath, it soon became obvious it was going to take longer than three hours, but we still weren't worried, as we enjoyed the abundant yellow, cornflower and violet wildflowers around us.

That was when everything suddenly went downhill.

Before we realized it, mist rolled in. Visibility was halved. We tried to quicken our pace, but the steep incline prevented that. Then we stumbled upon two memorial markers. Hikers in their 30s and 40s had perished on the same mountain. As the seriousness of our trans-alpine trek registered, fog sealed around us like a shroud. What had been a well-marked trail vanished. We were alone in a whiteout above the timberline. We couldn't see ten meters in any direction. No markings. No sign of a hut—only a field of scree that'd recently tumbled down off the ridge.

What do we do? Surely, we must be near the summit.

Conditions grew worse. The wind brought an icy mist. Temperatures swiftly dropped ten degrees to just above freezing. Cheryl and I became inseparable. Otherwise, it was too easy to lose track of each other. We stopped to quickly throw on our ponchos. We paused again to pull our down jackets from the bottom of our packs and put them on underneath the rain gear. Then we hunkered down behind low-lying pine scrub in a slight hollow waiting for it to pass. It was the only shelter the mountain provided at that altitude, except for the missing hut.

Cheryl started to shiver. Deep down, I knew we could be stuck there for hours or even overnight waiting for conditions to improve. Then again, they could always get worse. It grew cold enough to snow—even though it was June. Something had to be done, and done quickly.

Taking my chances, I left my pack with my partner. Then I slowly pulled myself straight up the mountainside to slightly better cover. Still, the slope was so severe it was useless to try and set up our tent. It was a long roll to the bottom.

I'd better go back down to Cheryl and bring her and the bags up. But where is she?

We'd lost each other in the dense mist and began to yell back and forth using a crazed locator call. Strangely enough, that worked and I stumbled back down. I checked my compass and then the map. As I threw on my pack, a small voice inside told me to head northwest, not north after all.

Psychiatrists be damned, I'd learned to listen to it long ago.

Yes, the hut should be northwest of the summit.

So on blind faith, we headed in that direction, slowly, deliberately, carefully placing each step among the scree to avoid a tumble. Call it dumb luck, or maybe our guardian angels were working overtime, because eventually in that muddle of a pea soup we stumbled upon what was left of the trail.

"Mark!"

"Woohoo!" Cheryl screamed back.

One marking led to the next as we slowly threaded through the white void. Suddenly, we reached a small snowfield. And then we spotted a rustic barn to our left. To our right, nearly on top of us but invisible until that moment, arose a two-story hut that'd been an Italian bunker during World War I. We'd made it!

Ducking inside, we were greeted by two lively Slovenian guys who were running around to clean and prep the cabin for its opening in a week, just in time for the local marathon. They claimed it was one of Europe's most famous races. Runners speed up the mountain and down to Porezen in 3-4 hours.

That'd be an incredible feat, I thought, especially in weather like this. Then again, the hut guardian has gigantic knee muscles that ripple like dancing doughnuts when he walks, so anything's possible.

We were just getting settled into the warmth when the hut door creaked open and in waltzed a young soldier on leave from Kosovo. Slovenians are a hardy bunch. He was only dressed in a t-shirt and shorts. He must have been right behind us on the trail, but we hadn't seen him. Then again, an army could have been near us and we wouldn't have known.

When we told the hut guardian we were trekking the Via Alpina, he shot us an enigmatic smile.

"We almost missed your hut because of the fog, plus we couldn't find any markers just a hundred meters away," I said. "They disappeared."

"Yes, we had a few posts wiped out by an avalanche last season. We haven't gotten around to replacing them."

"And Via Alpina markers are nearly non-existent," Cheryl added. "We've only spotted a couple in the past few days."

Hearing that, he went behind the kitchen counter, opened a drawer, and returned with a big grin. His hand overflowed with probably fifty Via Alpina logos, which should have been on the trail. That explained it. We'd also heard some Slovenians were taking down the markers. They thought it was an Italian trail simply because it had the Latin word "via" or "way" in its name. Obviously there was still some bad blood between them and they weren't keen on having an Italian trail run through Slovenia.

While we huddled drinking herbal tea and eating chocolate next to their woodstove, a downpour bombarded the hut. Lightning flashed the afternoon sky. Thunder reverberated across the valley.

After apologizing for their mess, the hut guardian said, "Of course, you can stay here tonight, but we're not officially open. Others heading up here have already turned back in this weather. I am surprised you made it." He gave a hearty laugh.

"Thanks." We were mighty grateful we'd reached it in time, even though we'd have to squat over a Turkish toilet, a porcelain hole in the ground, and shiver through a cold-water wash. It didn't matter. We were especially thankful they shared what little food they'd brought, since it still wasn't stocked in mid-June for the hiking season.

As for tomorrow, I thought, that's another story. We've been told it's a ten-hour hike to Dom na Komni Hut at 1520 meters. The trail's supposedly well marked for some of the way, but there are several junctions with other trails—and no one to ask directions. No villages. No places to fill water bottles. We'll trek down from 1844 to 1773 meters, and then up again to 1966 and down to 1520 meters. That's a lot of ups and downs. And this fella doesn't know if the huts on the trail after tomorrow are even open.

By then, we began to see our journey as one continual improvisation. Cheryl liked to call it "jazz." If this trail was music, the Via Alpina provides a basic melody, and we were forced to create our own tunes around it. That was the challenge. It wasn't the distance, although 2500 kilometers or more wasn't your usual ramble. It was the unknown we'd encounter while climbing at least a mountain every single day all the way to the Mediterranean.

We awoke at 5 a.m. to a magnificent view. We could clearly see all the surrounding peaks, in fact, and all the way to the Adriatic Sea. That much was a relief. The mountains to the south were impressive enough—until you looked north to the massive snowcapped summits. Magnificent! Those same Alps had called to me for so long and from so far away.

Still, out of the corner of my eye, I caught Cheryl wide-eyed, mouthing something that looked a whole lot like, "Oh, sh—ee—it!"

Anxious to set off while the weather was clear, we had two fried eggs with tea, bought the rest of last year's remaining bottled water, and choked down a 40-euro (55-dollar) tab. We set off at 7 a.m. carrying just two liters of water. It had to last 10 to 12 hours, depending on whom you believed.

Initially, our path was well marked for a change, yet we spent most of the morning tracing a narrow thread of a trail across scree crumbling beneath each precarious footstep. Each step promised a sheer thousand-meter drop to miniature villages below. One false step might be our last. At some points, we had to gently climb or lower ourselves via metal handholds or tied-in logs, fixed ropes like on a *via ferrata*. But those were few. More often, we were free climbing over huge rock faces. It can be great fun if you wear rubber-soled rock-climbing shoes and carry just water. But bouldering with full backpacks and slick hiking boots is courting disaster.

It all became more unsteady when our path was suddenly blocked at 3000 meters by wide, sheer icefields. Those took us totally by surprise. Again, since we weren't glacier hiking on this trek and figured the snow and ice would be gone by mid-June, we'd opted not to carry the extra weight of crampons or ice axes. So, we were forced to improvise. It was the only way we could cross. We'd have to make do. We dug toeholds by slamming our boots into the ice, and then plunged our Nordic poles as anchors at 45° angles to either side. It worked—to a point.

I had to admire Cheryl's courage to face all that, especially with a strained muscle and wrenched knee. Still, while crossing the first particularly steep ice-field, I heard her cry out, "I'm really scared." It was the first time in all our adventures, including climbing Mt. Kilimanjaro and trekking across Tibet, I'd heard those words from her mouth. But no matter what others might have you believe, trekking is a solitary challenge. We each face our own demons.

And as the philosopher Kierkegaard once said, "In fear, man finds himself." Given his logic, we were far from lost.

I could do little to help, except to yell, "We'll make it, just focus. Focus!"

Unfortunately, as soon as I'd finished crossing the icefield and wasn't look-ing behind me, she lost her footing. Slamming her knee into the rock-hard ice, for one scary instant, she perilously dangled by one pole from the mountainside. Not a pretty sight for sure, but far better than the option—sliding into the chasm. Ever the trooper, she didn't even tell me about it until later that evening.

I had my own testy moments. At one point, when lowering myself down a crevasse, I slid on scree and neatly sliced a hole through both the seat of my wind pants and shorts like butter. Other times, when the icy incline was too steep, we were forced to painstakingly descend rocks to cross below them and climb up over the other side. Those took total concentration to carefully place...each... step, keeping your balance. In a Zen-like way, it forced us to totally live in the moment. There was no past—and if we weren't careful—no future.

Seriously, we promised each other, if either of us lost our footing and slid to the bottom, the survivor would take a photo, no matter how painful it might be. Otherwise, it'd be too hard for a rescue team to find the body. And although I can't speak for Cheryl, I didn't want to end up as bear kibble.

Despite all that, five hours into our daily adventure, we finally topped Mt. Rodica's 1966-meter summit. While sharing an apple, we mentally prepared for another five-hour trek to Dom na Komni Hut where we hoped to stay that evening. The legend about how it had once been an Alpine paradise made it all more irresistible in my ongoing quest for mythical Shangri-La.

According to the fable, the Komna was once the rocky home of the guardian White Maids and Goldenhorn, a Billy goat, who was the means to a hidden treasure. One day a hunter from Trenta vowed to bring that wealth to a maiden. Tracking down the Goldenhorn, he injured it, only to see a magical herb, the Pink Cinquefoil, spring from its blood. By eating the plant, the Goldenhorn miraculously recovered. He charged his attacker, making the hunter fall into a chasm and die. Then filled with rage, the Goldenhorn ploughed up the pastures with his golden horns. Today all that remains is bare rock, although you can still see the ridged traces his horns left in the rocks. Paradise was lost when the White Maids, disgusted by the people's avarice, departed Komna forever.

We were just leaving Mt. Rodica when two hikers surprised us, climbing up from the other side. As they caught their breath, we excitedly told the local doctor and his wife about our plans to hike to Dom na Komni.

"You will never make it today," he warned in his heavy accent. "It is too far."

"But we were told it's only about five or six hours from here."

"We have never been able to hike it in a day. You are lucky if you can make it in twelve hours."

Twelve? His counsel sealed our fate. We knew he was right. Besides, Cheryl was injured and we'd already had an exhausting, heart-stopping day. We thanked them and descended to the Vogel ski area near the Lopata Forest Reserve, one of the Julian Alps' few remaining virgin forests. Renting a couple of bunks in its hostel, we were the only ones spending the night on the craggy mountain. Both the day-trippers who'd arrived via gondola and the workers caught it back down to crystalline Lake Bohinj for the night.

It was an odd kind of place. There were signs posted to conserve water, a noble idea. Yet when we went to take a shower and discovered no hot water, the guardian told us, "Oh, just let the water run for half an hour or so to let it get hot."

Later, as we appreciated a hard-fought bowl of spaghetti Bolognese, the dinner of budget Alpinists, I shared my concern with Cheryl about our day on the mountain and our predicament.

"I can't imagine anyone except an experienced climber doing this trek to Dom na Komni in a day. Twelve plus hours at this intensity is too much for your average hiker."

She wearily agreed, which led to an even bigger question. "If we actually made it to Dom na Komni tonight, then what?" she asked.

"The next hut is closed."

"According to what we've heard, the hut after it is beyond open. It was wiped out by an avalanche this year and is under heaps of snow."

"Short of camping on the side of these mountains with little supplies and no water, what can you do?"

"Then there's the chance of running into more snow."

Only a certain amount of luck and Providence had safely led us around the massive icefields today. Why push fate?

"It looks like we need to find a way to Trenta where we know the trail continues—that is, if the huts are open and stocked—and if the trail is passable," I said. That was a lot of "ifs."

She agreed. Finishing dinner, I half-jokingly suggested, "You know, in the future maybe we should take up a less life-threatening pursuit—like ice fishing. Sure, you have to sit out on some frozen pond all day, but all you have to do is drop in your line and wait."

"And if you're successful, you'll have a fresh meal."

"If not, at least your drinks stay cold."

Right on cue, our waitress appeared with a free shot of their tasty homemade apple schnapps.

That night, cuddled underneath a blanket in our tiny, heatless room, I grew discouraged while thinking about the unexpected turn of events and terrible hiking conditions for mid-June.

At this point, I thought, how many would simply give up and go home? This was absolutely one of the most difficult and dangerous days of hiking I've done in my life. But for us, retreat isn't an option. Our home's a storage crate. Beside, one of the reasons I wanted to trek this trail is to tell the tale of the Alps today. But so far, this trip's taken a different turn and we're along for the ride.

Will there be anyone left to tell the story?

That night we reached a tough decision. Since the huts were closed, our trail covered with ice and snow, and it was impossible to restock food or water, we decided to go to Trenta the following day where we assumed the hut would be open. That, of course, was easier said than done.

After breakfast, we wandered over to the gondola overlook, the same one with warning signs showing a stick figure tumbling off the mountain.

"Guess it's dangerous for fashion models to stand too close to the edge," I cautioned Cheryl, knowing I had nothing to worry about.

Nevertheless, its vista was breathtaking. It's undoubtedly one of the most pristine settings I've seen in all of Europe. The peaks of the Julian Alps frame Mt. Triglav, the tallest mountain in Slovenia at 2864 meters, and its national icon. Lake Bohinj, Slovenia's largest natural lake, lay in the glacial valley below: 4100 meters long, 1200 meters wide and 45 meters deep. It's a turquoise jewel; one I hope remains forever unpolished.

Cheryl and I caught the gondola down the mountain to the lakefront. If there was an actual trail down, and if it was marked, hiking could cause us to miss any connection to Trenta and we didn't want to risk losing a day or more. After trekking to the lakeside village, more than a little dejected, we eventually found their visitor office where we learned there are no roads or bike paths from Vogel to Trenta either. Sadly, we had to catch a bus to Lesce near Bled, and then on to Kranjska Gora. The following morning, if all went according to plan, we'd catch the once-daily bus to Trenta where we could begin hiking again.

Jazz, right?

The ride took us through verdant countryside, including Bled, an area transformed from an unspoiled village into a sprawling resort. After the splendor and solitude of the day before, this was one case where less would definitely have been better. Today it teems with throngs of visitors, t-shirt shops, and even a casino. Fortunately, its surreal alpine lake and mountains remain as brilliant as ever.

Before long, we arrived in Kranjska Gora, another mountain resort also flooded with visitors for its European Mountain Bike Festival. Ringed by sharp, snow-tipped peaks, it's in an inspired setting. We moved into the local hostel, a two-star former Eastern block hotel complete with kapok bedcovers, worn carpets and broken door locks. It was a blast from the past run by a friendly Serbian family, but the price was right.

Then we faced far more serious issues. As we settled down for the night, I grew more anxious about Cheryl's knee, pumped up like a bratwurst. She limped badly. It wasn't getting any better. I only hoped taking two days off the trail would help speed her recovery.

At daybreak, we caught a bus out of town. It wound steeply up a serpentine road of hairpin turns for over an hour covering the thirty kilometers or so to Trenta. By comparison, it made Maui's famous roundabout road to Hana look like a luge run. From the very start, we spotted patches of snow, not a good sign, as we slowly chugged to the summit. Along the way, we also passed many trails leading off into Triglav, Slovenia's only national park, born in 1924. Originally, 1600 hectares within the Valley of the Triglav Lakes were declared an Alpine Protected Park, until it was later expanded to over 55,000 hectares.

Maybe the most unusual sight was a tiny, intricately built Russian Orthodox chapel, a Fabergé egg made of logs. The Austrian army had originally built the high-mountain road using more than 10,000 Russian POWs to get supplies to the Isonzo Front. In the process, thousands died and then an avalanche killed a hundred in 1916. In memory of their fallen comrades, the survivors erected the chapel and stone pyramid containing their friends' remains.

For us, even by bus, the going was dicey. The driver blared his horn as we approached each blind turn, and then nearly drove over the edge before cranking his wheels hard to swerve in the opposite direction. When our bus eventually overheated, we sat on the crest for twenty minutes until the red warning light went out, and then snaked down the other side. At last, the driver announced "Trenta" and we were unceremoniously dropped off at a campsite—with a few more kilometers to trek uphill to the park office.

Triglav National Park information center is in an idyllic setting, a deep alpine valley carved by rivers and designed by glaciers. Gorge-like, its sheer rock walls rise from all sides with snow draping it like a wreath. It's a modern facility with museum, displays, gift shop, and a diorama of traditional alpine life. It was even showing a video of Kilauea Volcano exploding on Hawaii's Big Island.

Not aware that Soca Valley's Isonzo Front was the site of twelve major trench battles between the Austro-Hungarian Empire and Italy from 1915-17, we were heartened to hear about their new Walk of Peace running 109-kilometers through Slovenia. It commemorates those 300,000 soldiers who perished, while helping assure that nothing like that ever happens again in Europe.

The guides at the info center were sympathetic to our lesser plight, but their news was far from encouraging.

"Although the huts are open to the Austrian border, we had more than ten meters of snow last winter," the fellow explained. "Our trails are still blocked by ice. I called the first hut to confirm yesterday. Yes, they're open, but sorry, it is too dangerous to continue hiking from Trenta without crampons and ice axes."

Fine. It's time for Plan B. Or Plan C? But what are they?

We did have one bit of luck. There was still time to catch the 4 o'clock bus back to Kranjska Gora. In June, there's only one round trip a day on weekends, otherwise you end up stranded in Trenta for a day. There are worse fates. We had six hours to wander around the incredible setting. For a change, Cheryl and I attempted to take it easy, consider our options, and lick our wounds in private.

We found a secluded pool in the river where she could soak her knee while I chilled my attitude. Its pure glacial water cut to the bone and relieved any pain and swelling, at least for a while. At last, we flagged down our bus. Temporarily retreating, like ants trudging back to their dirt mound, we headed back down to Kranjska Gora. Hiking Triglav was just not in the cards.

Later, we emailed news about the current snow and ice conditions to Nathalie at the Via Alpina network basecamp, along with the need to carry ice gear in Slovenia until July. We hoped she'd pass along our warning to others.

As for us, it was time to improvise a new tune.

Germany

Weißenbach
am Lech

Oberstdorf   Ostbach· Lehne
Mindelheimer   Lermoos   Reit
Hütte   Prinz
Feldkirch   Luitpold   Coburger
                            Hütte
Gafadura   Schröcken   Innsbruck
Hütte   Sonntag
     Vaduz
Liechtenstein
Sargans

Switzerland

Bozen/
Bolzano

Schwaz
Kellerjochhütte
Rastkogelhütte
• Mayrhofen

Austria

Ginzling
Pfitscher Joch

Kiens
Innichen Kartitsch Kötschach-Mauthen Thörl-
Oberolang Liesing Egger-Alm Maglern
Brixen/Bressanone Zollernsee Feistritzer
Naßfeld

Italy

Trenta

Slovenia

**Adriatic
Sea**

4
But Do Ants Have Knees?

FTER BREAKFAST, THE SERBIAN INNKEEPER'S FRIEND VOLUNTEERED to take us a few kilometers up the road to the Austrian border where we could connect with the Via Alpina. He was a Montenegrin doctor who was equally concerned about the condition of Cheryl's knee. There was no use ignoring the problem with the hope it'd go away. Her limp grew increasingly worse; she struggled with every step.

While we easily found the trail at Wurzenpass, since there was actually a Via Alpina marker, we faced another 45° climb straight up the mountain. The Austrian trails were already better marked with hard-to-miss red and white stripes on trees, and sign posts even estimated hiking times to destinations. What a luxury. Still, we faced new, miniature adversaries.

That morning we trekked up and down forest paths fighting hundreds of relentless flies. Ten would land on my arm. I'd stun them—only to have them instantly replaced by another dozen. Then the blood-sucking mosquitoes joined in the feast. It was slow torture.

Not a liter too soon, we reached Dreiländereck Hütte just above a ski gondola. After stopping to flirt with calves who watched us with comical curiosity, we caught our breath over a peppermint tea and admired the views. All too soon, we headed down the other side, passing the monument at *Dreiländereck* or three-country corner celebrating the now-peaceful border between Austria, Italy and Slovenia, which was drawn after the bloody conflicts in 1918.

All afternoon we descended that mountain, an agonizing exercise for my partner. I'd trek five minutes ahead then wait another five for her to catch up. I even carried her backpack along with my own for two stretches, but it didn't help. Her knee grew progressively worse until she winced with every footstep. With her pained steps came an equally painful conversation.

"Look, I know how much this must hurt," I began. "Remember? I've been through a few knee injuries myself, even surgery."

"It's more than that," she said. "I'm hurt and disappointed and frustrated and angry and fed up. Each day after my knee was wrenched I hoped it'd get better. And it did feel okay for awhile after Crna prst, but the next day did a number on it and it was more sore than before."

"I understand and it hurts to see you in such pain. We both know you can't continue like this for months and risk permanent damage—even if you could tough it out. You've got nothing to prove to me."

We hugged tenderly leaving the rest unsaid, although I knew we needed to weigh our options that evening in Thörl-Maglern.

It was nearly 5:00 by the time we reached the tiny village after trekking ten hours to cover the short distance. It'd been slow-motion torture. Our only con-solation was sitting down to a hot Mother *schnitzel*, a batter-fried pork filet of baseball glove-sized proportions, along with hot potato salad and half liters of *hefeweizen*, unfiltered wheat beer, which was served in their dining room. It was great to return to Austria, a place near and dear to our hearts (and bellies).

Once back in our room, Cheryl looked at me with sad eyes and poured out a flood of emotions.

"I don't know which is worse: feeling pain, feeling inadequate, or knowing I'm holding you back?"

"Holding me back? Hardly. This has been tough going for us both."

"I try my best, but it's not good enough."

"That's not true. I'll tell you what," I said, pulling a map from my pack to study together. "You really need to rest your knee. Why don't you go ahead to Kötschach-Mauthen by train? It's on the route. Find yourself a room with a sweet Austrian lady to pamper you, get plenty of rest and join me in five days, on Saturday at Untere Valentinalm Hütte? It's just outside of town." With a kiss for luck, I added, "I'll hike there and meet you."

"It hurts like hell—the physical, the emotional. It's a double slap for me. It's bad enough I'm in pain. Now I have to drop out, wait and do this knowing you're still on the trail. I've seen some amazing sights and I hope it's not my last."

"It won't be," I promised as we hugged, but only time would tell. I hoped her recovery would be swift—for her sake as much as my own. Although I enjoy solitude, I didn't relish trekking the trail alone.

Then I added, "Hey, from past experience I know many of these little vil-lages have community spas. An hour a day in a whirlpool would really help your knee heal." I figured a doctor would prescribe the same treatment with rest, only probably for much longer.

She looked at me skeptically about the spa (What would she wear?), but was sold on the idea of getting off her feet. Besides, what choice was there short of quitting? She couldn't continue like that. We hoped rest was the answer.

If not, neither of us wanted to have that conversation.

Cheryl reluctantly left in the morning. The gastehäus owner's daughter kindly offered to take her to Arnoldstein where she could catch a bus to Kötschach-Mauthen. I left at the same time, only in another direction.

A steep two-hour climb out of Thörl-Maglern swiftly told me we'd made the right decision. The trail led straight up the mountain at times, well marked, but a challenge for someone in good condition—impossible for her. Funny, we thought we'd become stronger along the way, but I swore the opposite was true so far. We'd both shed weight and grew weaker with each passing day.

All morning I thought about the trail and our surprise at its sheer physical demands. It was already the toughest trek we'd ever attempted. Then again, I'd have to admit an equally difficult part was mental: getting up and climbing, usually in the rain, every single day. It wasn't like we climbed a mountain and then remained at that altitude between stages. No, each day meant at least one steep 1000-meter ascent followed by a tough descent of 3-4 hours.

While scaling the first pass of the day, I flashed on a possible solution.

Maybe it'll be better for us to trek a flatter, more southern path? Would the Via Alpina yellow route be easier? Would it be less physically demanding for Cheryl while letting us experience more village culture? Who knows? Years ago, we'd trekked paths from the Italian Dolomites through Austria to Prague, and I've hiked the Donau Radweg from Bavaria to Budapest. So, I know trails and *radwegs*, or bicycle paths, run through these valleys crisscrossing the countryside. I'll look into that option, if she's able to continue.

As for me, the route again circled roundabout—climb one steep mountain, descend and repeat. My so-called six-hour trek took eight. I wasn't in a particular hurry and stopped briefly at Göriacher Alm, or meadow, to fill my water bottle from a cattle trough, and then continued through narrow ravines on the Karnischer Höhenweg up Bartolosattel Pass.

It was near dusk and freezing with icy fog by the time I reached what I thought was the hut for the night. There was a fleeting sense of relief when I neared a few buildings on the hillside. But it was just a bar locked tight. It took another hour for me to reach the secluded village of a dozen houses and Feistritzer Alm Hütte at 1718 meters.

Inside, five locals tipped beers and I joined a fellow hiker from Salzburg. Even though it was mid-June, there was a sense of isolation and camaraderie up there, as if we were a team hunkered down to face a long winter together at the

North Pole. It was otherworldly, a place lost in time. The rustic hut was large and radiated warmth on that frigid evening. A wild black and silver boar hide and tiny, mounted deer skulls hung from walls. They encircled a woodstove in the dimly lit room. The food was equally rugged: either hearty goulash soup or wooden plates of sliced salami, cheese, thick brown bread and sweet, hot peppers.

The rain that'd threatened all day finally let loose at 6:45. As we hovered over our plates, an older Austrian hiker named Jäger and I compared our routes and they seemed to match for the next few days. So, I figured we'd be passing each other along the way. Although you'd never know it by looking at him, Jäger was a hiking superman. I decided maybe he'd make a good companion. At 75, sturdy and bald with owlish glasses, he carried a pack far heavier than mine. I was especially impressed to hear he'd left Thörl-Maglern later and arrived earlier at the hut than I did.

As the night wore on, the other fellows in the cabin grew curious about our trek and I showed them the Via Alpina map, tracing the route we hoped to follow.

"You know, Napoleon and his troops came through the same pass you crossed today," one fellow said.

Another nodded, adding in English, "Used to be a big hotel up here on the alm until the war. It replaced the old refuge. Mostly used as a spa for the rich."

"A carriage brought the nobles up here on a gravel road."

"Anton Achatz, the hotel owner, also had Maria Schnee chapel built. You passed it up there," he said pointing. "Well, he built it to overlook his grave. I guess to always be blessed, but the trees soon grew and blocked the view."

He snorted, as if to say, "Serves him right."

After a while, a Slovenian with American connections (he owns a condo in the Everglades) joined us. He bought me a glass of red wine and then told me an interesting story about national identities as we warmed by the fire.

"Slovenia has seen many changes the past century," he started. "Why, I know a fellow in his eighties who's lived in the same house near the border all of his life. He's changed nationalities six times. When he was born he was part of the Austro-Hungarian Empire, then he was Yugoslavian, then Italian, then German after the Nazis invaded, then Soviet-Yugoslavian, and now Slovenian!"

His great belly shook with laughter.

That's far too many national anthems to have to learn.

I was exhausted after the long day, yet there was no way to clean up. Even though my clothes were still damp with sweat, and my fly bites itched like crazy,

I was thankful to be in the snug room. Things would have been much worse if the rain had hit earlier while I was still on the mountaintop.

Although I said goodnight and turned in early, I awoke at 2 with my bladder ready to burst like a *piñata*. The only toilet I'd seen was off the bar. I ran downstairs in the dark to use it, but its door was locked. Outside? The front door was locked. No way out. I rushed up and down the dark hallway as quietly as possible, trying not to waken everyone, desperately searching for options. The window? Nah, too high. Balcony? Nope. Chamber pot? Nada. Empty wine bottle? You've gotta be kidding. Finally, hopping from foot to foot, ready to explode, I spotted a door with frosted glass that I hadn't tried, flung it open, and found a toilet, just steps from my bed.

I was mighty relieved—this is, until my zipper broke—fortunately (or not) in a permanently down position. Okay, now normally, you'd just pull another pair of pants out of your closet. But being a nomad of the trail, I only had this one pair with me. Cheryl had our sewing kit. And there were no stores or tailors way up there.

Time for a little improvisation again, I figured, channeling my inner Grizzly Adams. Until I found sticky pinesap or porcupine quills, I guessed I'd just have to watch how I sat until I found a safety pin.

In the morning, last night's fog still lingered on the mountaintop. Jäger and I set off at 7:30 in the cold mist, but soon parted ways as we set our own pace, promising to meet again that evening. Although there was a steep descent and several brief climbs, the path wasn't too grueling. For the first time, the surrounding meadows were filled with bell-toting cows who'd come up to graze (on summer vacation, no doubt) from the farms below where they lived the rest of the year. That's an old Alpine tradition.

Curious, I briefly stopped at one house and talked to the farmer. His house was over a hundred years old, and its rustic façade with its weathered wood and red geraniums in window flowerboxes perfectly complemented the landscape. The farmer also looked well suited to an Alpine meadow. With ruddy cheeks, glacial beard, and blueberry eyes, he could have just been sent over from Central Casting.

"Say, can I get water here from your trough?" I asked.

"Not a good idea." He grimaced. "Too close to the cows. Better to hike downhill. You'll find a carved spout looking like a man's head. Good water to drink there."

"Thanks. It's been hard to find. We're hiking the Via Alpina."

Hearing this, he excitedly shook my hand, saying, "I met two girls from France who were hiking it a few years ago." His eyes beamed. "They still send me Christmas cards!"

It was amazing he remembered them. The trail's so lightly traveled that locals recall every wanderer they meet. How special's that?

However, the region's been a traveler's crossroads since at least the 3rd century B.C. when the Illyrians met the Celts. Its iron goods were traded as far as the Med. In an attempt to corner the market on iron production, Romans occupied the region until the Teutons, Avars and Slavs had the same notion. Even today, some village names reflect its Slavic roots.

I headed downhill from his farm into a ravine on the Kurnisher Höhenweg where the trail intersects with a road. I expected traffic, but no one passed all afternoon. I did bump into a nuclear engineer and his wife on an outing. After making sure I was on the right trail, they took time to point out the small, purple Alpine orchid protected by Austrian law.

"All of Gailtal Valley is a living natural history museum," he explained in a professorial tone. "We have five 'Geo-Trails' with info panels telling its 500-million year history. Plus, people still find fossils of ferns, starfish and mussels from early times when it was an ocean bed."

We soon parted ways and before long I neared another alm lined by squat, weathered houses. Cows with basketball-sized bells grazed in the fields, joined by horses nibbling around the lake. Day-hikers wished me a cordial *"Grüß Gott"* as they passed, until I finally reached tranquil Egger Alm. Although there were two guesthouses, one was closed. The other makes a famous Gailtal alpine cheese, which I couldn't wait to try.

It's a family operation only open in the summer months, as few folks still live in the high Alps all year long. The weather's just too severe and supplies are as short as the warm weather. The manager, Ilsa, is the mother of two: a two-year old son and a daughter of four who's a real live wire. As I unpacked, the little girl pranced around the meadow wearing a cowbell strung around her neck, giggling and "mooing" to anyone who'd listen.

Two hours later, just as I began to think I had the dorm room to myself, Jäger poked his head inside, asking, "Okay if I share your room?"

"Sure!" I'd wondered what happened to him, considering his rabbit-like speed the day before.

He collapsed on the bed. "I've just hiked eleven hours in the sun." He must've become lost when the markings disappeared. Haggard, he apologized in German, "Sorry my pace was so slow."

"No worries. Have a rest and soon you'll feel like new."

While he took a nap, I made the mistake of heading downstairs where I innocently mentioned to Ilsa, "You know, I really need some energy."

Well, this set the gourmet gears into motion. Disappearing into the kitchen, she soon presented me with a huge platter. No, a feast. Since their specialty is cheese, I got four large servings of homemade soft cheese, a liverwurst pâté, another odd orangish pimento spread, Emmental cheese, fresh butter, homemade sausage, smoked *speck* (bacon or ham) complete with its rind of skin and fat, goulash soup with caraway, brown bread, and a liter of wheat beer. Then one of the villagers treated me to a shot of his delicious homemade apple schnapps. They hoped this was enough.

Were they kidding? I hadn't seen so much food in the last two weeks. By the time Jäger arrived, I'd made a pig of myself. It was painful just sitting there, but as he was just starting his feast, I felt obliged to stay. He was a fascinating fellow. The Alpinist went into detail telling me all about his past exploits, including climbing Mt. Blanc and Monte Rosa.

Then he hesitated, saying, "I am sorry. I have decided I will not hike the rest of the trail as planned."

I was surprised, but then again I realized the disappointment he must have felt at not being able to continue, especially with all his experience.

As if he needed an excuse, he continued with a shrug, "I am diabetic, have bad knees, and have had several heart operations. Once I was even dead for twenty minutes before they could revive me."

'I felt sorry I had no shoes, until I met a man who had no feet.'

The man was a walking contradiction. While we finished gorging ourselves, Jäger tested his blood sugar and then shot himself with insulin in his stomach and arm. Afterwards, he treated me to another beer and schnapps—while lecturing me about the amount of glucose in our meal.

He and I closed the café in that sleepy village at 9:00 and waddled up to bed, yet sleep was elusive. My stomach churned all night. Throwing it all up would have been the only solution, but it was bound to have awakened the entire house. Yea, they would've remembered this Via Alpinist for sure.

As it was, the kids brought down the house at 5 a.m. with demands for poor "Mama!" As penance, I only ate fruit for breakfast. The innkeeper snapped some photos of us, and then Jäger and I said heartfelt goodbyes. Only the elderly realize the permanence of some farewells.

I set a solitary path out of the village.

The day's trek was shorter than usual. There were just a few brief climbs and after one, I ran into a group of German hikers at Garnitzenalm Hütte where I'd stopped for water. From what I could gather from the handwritten note left tacked to the windowsill, the hut was still closed because of the long, nasty winter. They, too, had more than ten meters of snow.

When one of the trekkers asked about my journey, I told them, "My wife was injured and is resting her knee. Hopefully she'll rejoin me in two days."

"Doesn't that make it boring?" one lady from Ülm asked.

"Boring is not a word I'd use to describe this trail. Quiet, yes. Difficult, yes, but never boring."

I'd just briefly crossed the border into Italy before veering back into Austria within an hour. The old road dating back to the World War had fallen into disrepair, making the trail suddenly much worse and tricky to maneuver. After the saddle, I had to wend a narrow shale path along the edge of a mountainside. For once, I was grateful for fixed ropes attached to the rocks as added protection. As those hikers were heading the same direction, I felt I should caution them.

Pointing down the mountain, I warned, "The trails there are *scheiße*."

They laughed, as the word for "shit" was the only word in German I'd spoken, except, "*Morgen*." I figured my Deutsch was far from perfect and best left for emphasis.

As they stood to leave, a white-bearded older fella sporting a Tyrolean green hat with long feather and pewter pins stopped and apologized that he didn't speak English. Then, eyes sparkling, he tipped his fedora and wished me, "*AufWiedersehen*" in a touching moment of brotherhood transcending language.

After clearing one final hill, I had a clear shot into Naßfeld. The huge ski resort flows from the summit in the shadow of Gartnerkofel and Roßkofel mountains. Emerald pine forests cascade to a picturesque manmade lake far below. A stop along the Karnische Höhenweg, it's popular for day-hikers and I passed more than a dozen on my way down to the valley.

As usual, I stopped at the first inn I encountered, the Alpenhof Plattner Gästhaus. It had the look of a multi-star hotel, but I was lucky. They gave me a warm hiker's welcome, plus my first alpine club discount. Their manager was a friendly, talkative sort decked out in a Trachten green jacket sporting antler buttons. He went out of his way to spend extra time discussing my next day's route, which he reassured me was over a mostly flat terrain with possible snowfields, plus he forecast clear weather. Then he reminded me they'd recently changed the name of the refuge where I was headed from Dr. Steinwender Hütte to Zollnersee Hütte.

Afterward, I was shown the tidy dorm room downstairs, specially designed for trekkers and budget skiers. It was clean, warm and utilitarian with ten bunk beds and a desk. Hot showers awaited down the hall. Little did I know it then, but it was to become the benchmark for the rest of our journey. I had it to myself since they were between seasons. Following my quick shower, the manager went out of his way to load me into his car and take me down valley to the only market still open—or at least he thought it was. He eventually had to call someone to unlock the tiny shop just for me, but at least I could pick up a few supplies.

Now that's what they call "*Gemütlichkeit!*" or cozy Austrian hospitality.

Unfortunately, the next morning, the innkeeper's promise of no major climbs was wrong, so very wrong. Maybe it's a relative thing when you live at a mountain resort. I spent the first two hours climbing major ski runs only to continue with a long, hard climb up over the border again. What a heart-throbbing way to start a day!

The Italian section was especially difficult. The rugged trail was little changed since the First World War. Snowfields were thrown in as added bonus, promising a quick 500-meter drop to the bottom of a ravine if you weren't careful. As the wind howled, temperatures dipped, but I pushed on. Wearing hiking shorts is a powerful motivator to hike quickly, very quickly, in that kind of weather.

Just outside of Naßfeld, I trekked through World War I fortifications, trenches and memorials to the fallen. Those high mountains were the scene of a long trench-to-trench conflict, which began in 1914 after Archduke Ferdinand, heir to the Austro-Hungarian throne, and his wife Sophie were murdered in Sarajevo. It set off events that quickly snowballed into World War I. The harsh climate and hostility of the terrain up there claimed countless lives, especially those with little mountain skills who were forced to quickly build trails and shelters through backbreaking labor.

For me it was far from deadly, yet it was one of the longest stages to that point. There was no place to find water for the first six hours. Though someone suggested I could drink from the streams, I'd heard that advice before and suffered the consequences—even in unspoiled Norway.

Back when I was trekking St. Olav's Way, an ancient path from Oslo to Trondheim, Norway sizzled from a rare heat wave with temperatures above 30° C. Well, I quickly ran out of water without a house or shop in sight. But never fear. Before I'd left Oslo, someone bragged, "You'll never run out of water on this path because you can always drink from Norwegian streams. They're unpolluted and there's no need to worry about getting sick."

"No giardia here?" I skeptically asked. I'd already hosted those pesky parasites in Nepal and Tibet. They're a painful, sure-fire weight-loss plan.

"Lose twenty pounds in one week or your money back!"

"Nah, I drink from streams all the time," they assured me. "We have some of the purest water on earth."

With his advice in mind, I drank my fill. Oh, the bliss. Oh, the pain. It only took two days before I was bent double with cramps and gas to lay waste to wildflowers and wildlife. Of course, I knew instantly what it was and was eventually able to find a pharmacist with an understanding ear.

Yes, giardia is a gift that keeps on giving. And giving.

Warned of snowfields I'd encounter before the hut, I opted to follow a lower, drier path. Though it made sense, it took twice as long to hike the switchbacks followed by a tough trek straight up another mountainside. The rain that had threatened all afternoon did its best to hold out until I was actually a kilometer past Zollnersee Hütte. Since the hut's sign was down and covered with mud, I continued in a light drizzle to a neighbor's farm before realizing my mistake. As luck would have it, it was pounding rain and pelting sleet by the time I headed back down to the hut.

Although I was drenched and exhausted, it was another cabin with no hot water. However, it did offer over-priced food, the only game in town. There were no markets.

After all the cheese, I thought, maybe now's the time to fast a little?

That evening, Jacob, the hut guardian, warned us about the possibility of snow in the morning. In late June? His news had little effect on the Czech couples who also stayed with their guide in the hut. They had a van. They could quickly drive back down the mountain if conditions grew worse.

As for me, I had no idea how long it'd take to hike to Untere Valentinalm Hütte—only that Cheryl would be waiting—and the unpredictable weather would make a difficult journey more dangerous than ever.

5

IT'S ALWAYS
THE LITTLE THINGS

IT STORMED AND THUNDERED ALL NIGHT. THE HUT SHOOK DOWN to the bunk beds. It was little consolation "I slept with three beautiful Czech women," as I jokingly promised I'd tell Cheryl. One of them snored as badly as any man.

The deluge continued after I awoke. While the Czechs decided to cancel their hike to Naßfeld and linger over breakfast, I had a cup of peppermint tea and weighed the possibilities.

With the horrible weather, I decided to change plans, especially after Jacob confided, "The trail to Untere Valentinalm Hütte is no good. There are eleven icefields right now. And then it only gets worse."

No, instead of continuing to the hut in this muck, I figured, I'd head down the mountain to meet Cheryl in Kötschach-Mauthen where she'd been recuperating. She shouldn't be out trekking in the slippery mess with her knee, anyway. With any luck, I could make it down to the village before she started up to meet me.

It made too much sense. There was only one problem: I didn't have a clue where she was staying. Before we split up, I'd asked her to email the name of her *zimmer* to me once she was settled, but so far, there'd been nowhere to check my messages. Hearing my predicament, Jacob gave me the name of his friend, who was chef at a fancy hotel in Mauthen. He thought they might have an Internet connection. That was my only chance.

There are several paths off the mountain and I chose the one a little longer, but better marked. In that downpour, I couldn't afford to get lost—or slide down a muddy trail. So, I set off down a hard-to-miss, empty gravel road. Before long, I ran into a skinny fellow unloading hay from a tall tractor cart and we had a frustrating exchange.

"Going to Mauthen?" I asked.

"Where?"

"Mauthern?"

"Where?"

"Maffen?" I tried variations of the village's name in my best German commandant imitation.

He finally grinned and I realized he'd been kidding me. Ah, Austrian farm humor. Enjoying his laugh for the day, he agreed to give me a lift down off the mountain in twenty minutes.

Great, but I couldn't afford to stand outside in the freezing storm.

"Hey, will you just stop when you see me?"

He seemed to understand this perfectly well and nodded. Fine. I'd keep hiking at my brisk pace. Even though I had my down jacket on under a huge poncho, it was frosty. I needed to keep my core temperature raised.

Well, as his twenty minutes developed into two hours, I was glad I hadn't waited. By then, the rain had subsided and I'd covered ten kilometers or more. When he finally stopped and motioned me to climb aboard, try as I might, I found it physically impossible with a full pack to climb straight up the slick sides of his seven-foot high hay cart. Besides, looking in, he'd hauled his fair share of manure as well as hay. I didn't relish landing on my face in a botched attempt. So, I opted to balance on the wet hitch connecting the cart to his small one-person tractor—not a brilliant idea.

As I stood there, clutching on with half-frozen fingers, surfing hairpin bends on the gravel road, the lunacy of what I was doing struck. If (when) I lost balance, there was a good chance I'd be run over before he knew I'd fallen off. What a tragic way to end it all.

I could just see the headlines: "Shit Happens to Alpine Adventurer."

Screaming for him to stop, I leapt off.

Eventually, I wandered into town, found Jacob's friend at the hotel and he graciously let me use his computer to locate Cheryl. She was staying at a private house near the campground in Kötschach. With that news, the chef and I hopped into his BMW and he delivered me to the pension's doorstep. A jovial lady answered the door, and quickly making the connection between her recuperating guest and the apparition dripping on her carpet, she greeted me with a warm smile and hug. She rambled on and on in German and I was surprised to understand a good bit of what she said, even though I'd sadly never formally studied the language.

As Cheryl says, "Must be genetic."

Then her husband led me upstairs. As a gag, I pounded on the bedroom door until Cheryl gingerly creaked it open and peeked out.

"Oh, you're here!" she said, hugging me. "I couldn't imagine who it was. No one's knocked on my door in five days. I'm so glad to see you down here in one piece."

"Well, just thought I'd come down and surprise you. You shouldn't be out hiking in this mess today." She looked relieved.

As we celebrated our reunion over a bottle of the local white Müller-Thurgau wine, we explored our options. Even though her knee was better, it was still not up for trekking up a couple of mountains a day—even if her spirit was. In my absence, she'd made a trip to the local pharmacy where they measured her Q-tip like knee for an elastic knee wrap. The druggist stared at her in amazement, wondering how she still walked, then gave her the largest knee support they had in stock. Cheryl also picked up a lifetime supply of a tried-and-true analgesic cream. With those, she figured she'd be able to continue hiking, slowly at first, if there was less actual climbing.

Judging from her limp, I had to agree, so we decided to study our topo maps again to find a flatter bike route or *radweg* leading west through Austria until she recovered. As a bonus, trekking in the valleys would let us stay each night in villages for more cultural experiences than we'd seen so far on the high trail. There was more to discovering the Alps than just climbing mountains. Plus, they'd keep us out of the snowy passes, which could persist another month.

Given all that, I have to admit I had mixed feelings. I was reluctant to give up our goal of crossing the Alps solely on the Via Alpina red trail. Then again, I also didn't want to give up our lives on some icy, poorly marked path. I was sure we'd face snow by mid-October in the French Alps. Even if we could complete a stage each day, taking no rest days at all, it'd be mid-November by the time we approached Monaco.

More and more, I thought, there's just too narrow a window for anyone to possibly thru-hike the entire Via Alpina red route, all 161 stages, between June and October without running into ice and snow at either end. Realistically, someone would have to trek two stages many days to complete it in one short Alpine season—or they'd have to rely on having one very dry year—or have expertise with crampons and ice axes.

As a follow-up, I emailed our doubts to Nathalie at the Via Alpina network who confirmed others had faced the same dilemma. One fellow had already skipped stages and headed north to avoid the rain, while a lady Alpinist detoured south into Italy.

But were those any better? From what we'd heard, the northern passes were even more snowbound, while the southern yellow trail was in worse shape from rain and bad maintenance.

I had to remind myself: This trail's like jazz, right? It's not some inflexible 4/4 John Phillips Sousa march. It's time to improvise, create some wild riffs all our own.

To give Cheryl more time for recuperation, we hung out at the pleasant *zimmer* an extra day. Although it was sunny in the morning, threatening clouds formed at higher elevations. I was glad we weren't up there. Besides, both Kötschach and Mauthen were handsome little villages on either side of a river, nestled amid a patchwork of green and grey mountains. Birds chattered outside our window. It was serene as we ambled through the villages. Nearly everyone we passed greeted us with a traditional *"Grüß Gott,"* even the kids.

The next morning, a quick stop at the local visitor office confirmed we weren't lazy or too cautious in our decision to stick to lower elevations. Their staff called around and confirmed there was still too much snow in the mountains to continue hiking the Via Alpina red route.

While waiting, I was surprised to learn they, too, have their own special trail. As a peace walker, I was intrigued by what they call their Paths of Peace. Many old war trails remain and the Friends of the Dolomites and volunteers have worked to reconstruct and repair them. Their motto is: "Paths which once separated us, shall unite us today."

I like that idea. There's nothing like sharing a trail together and suffering the same blisters, soreness, sweat and thirst to remind us about how similar we are, regardless of our nationality.

With the ladies' help, we decided to follow a small country road west out of town toward Lesachtal Valley. It still offered its share of challenging climbs, but we could see how well Cheryl's knee fared and never be too far from a village guesthouse. It was the perfect compromise for the next week or so, until we reconnected with the Via Alpina.

All morning long, we passed interesting houses showcasing unique Alpine architecture, evident right down to their unusual barns where the outside walls slope in, instead of at right angles. Wildflowers, even purple columbine, brightened yards and windowsills. Tree stumps were painstakingly carved into curved waterspouts, caricatures or trolls. We passed many houses with beautiful wall murals, some of them religious, some featuring a local legendary knight, and others with simply their name and *"HOF"* or "Farm" plus its date of construction proudly painted above the door. Their houses featured a thousand variations of white plaster walls, green shutters, window boxes with red geraniums and an abundance of gnomes.

The Alps are well known for their gnomes, tiny creatures just about the size of a mushroom. Usually friendly creatures, they reportedly live in the woods and avoid human contact. Even with their long white beards and distinctive pointed hats, they're difficult to see as they blend into their surroundings. Leading quiet lives surrounded by animals and nature, folks say they can live up to 400 years. Some also adapt to life in villages and may be spotted in flower and vegetable gardens helping folks live peaceful lives.

And if the number of garden gnomes reflects the happiness of the people living there, well, I've gotta say Lesachtal Valley's one contented place.

By noon, we entered Birnbaum just in time to see a fellow rushing uphill. Dressed in a bright red vest, a fancy white shirt, and felt hat sporting two long, white feathers, he was moving like a man on a mission. Many folks in cars, musicians carrying drums or clarinets, and a procession of people on foot soon followed. They headed to a small chapel on top of the hill, but why?

As we neared the edge of town, we could just barely hear angelic voices and music wafting through the serene mountain valley for what we were later told was a traditional funeral.

Clouds threatened to erupt all day as we wended hills, crossed bridges over deep ravines, and tested the limits of Cheryl's fragile recovery. Finally, having trekked eighteen kilometers or so, we called it a day in Liesing.

One of those villages with a recent Slovak population, its name means "heavy woods." The standard of living is high in that part of Carinthia. The houses are large and sturdy, surrounded by great gardens or farms. The tourist information office found us a place to stay with a local policeman and his family who welcomed us like long-lost family.

As they served us homemade cake, he asked about life in the islands, while sharing details of his own. He was a former customs agent whose job disappeared when the European Union was born and border control became a thing of the past. He was then retrained as a policeman, but his passion was playing double horn in his spare time with the area's traditional musical group who'd recently cut their own CD and were highlighted at an international festival. Yes, he admitted his family also did some dairy farming, but not enough to make a living anymore.

As for us, relaxing around their dining room table, sipping chamomile tea, we felt like we'd just dropped by to visit friends. And after just one day hiking through a valley of villages, I'd have to admit we were feeling comfortable with our decision to be off the mountains for a while.

At daybreak, we set off with the warmest of goodbyes from our hosts in their front yard. They predicted no rain, but that was wishful thinking. It began before noon. Nevertheless, Cheryl already hiked a little faster. I was still loping ahead, but at normal speed. There's little on the Karnische Dolomitenstraße in the Lesachtal Valley between Liesing and Kartitsch, only rolling farms, bad weather, and snowy fields in the southern mountains. There were few villages and we were relieved to finally spot a cozy pizzeria tempting us to hang around—but not long, as it's always difficult to get moving after your muscles cool down.

It continued drizzling all afternoon. At one point, we stopped into Maria Luggau, a monastery whose Pilgrimage Church of St. Mary is one of Austria's most popular religious sites. They get nearly 40,000 visitors per year. We were eager to drop in, since religion plays an important part in traditional Alpine culture. In fact, we'd spotted roadside shrines and intricate crucifixes along the path for days. Many villages have small private chapels, and in earlier times it was customary to build at least one in each community.

However, on that drizzly day, we wandered through a deserted Baroque chapel; it wasn't a day fit for man nor priest.

Not surprisingly, Cheryl's knee began to throb in the frigid sprinkle and she earned her first blisters of many, but she knuckled down and we pressed on until we checked into the first *zimmer* we spotted in Kartitsch. By the time we'd showered and changed out of our wet clothes, only the promise of a hot meal (and our anniversary) could pry us from our cozy room. In retrospect, we should have stayed inside.

Heading to a nearby gastehäus, we were shuttled to a backroom to savor an pricey plate of *pommes frites* served by a harried waitress coping with a bus full of demanding diners. So, we left for a simple café across the street to celebrate.

And to all those other hopeless romantics who claim to enjoy "long walks in the rain," all I can say is, "Be very careful what you ask for."

We struck an earlier departure in the morning, but not before Cheryl sketched a drawing of a safety pin and showed it to our amused hostess who ducked into the kitchen and returned with a small gift. Her generosity kept me from flashing any more adolescent calves in my zipperless pants.

Then we swiftly headed down valley to connect with the bicycle path running beside the Drau River just past Möser. That single lane, asphalt Drau Radweg was hard on the feet, but a welcome trade-off. Getting lost was out of the question. It was perfectly straight for as far as the eye could see.

For once, we were far from alone. The elderly walked chubby wiener dogs or pushed baby carriages. Families promenaded and couples cycled east toward Linz. For a change, the rain mostly held off and it only sprinkled once we arrived in Innichen, a small Italian ski resort.

The village itself was minuscule. You could walk its length in fifteen minutes. Its jagged surrounding mountains were still partially covered with snow.

There was a beautiful Baroque church and streets lined with designer shops. I could imagine it must be packed with throngs during ski season, but the café waitstaff was anxious. There were few visitors in late June. Of course, the information office was closed, so we set off to find a place on our own.

However, that was the least of our worries. I'd discovered a swelling on the back of my leg, which had grown increasingly worse over the past four days. There was a purple ring and I didn't know if was a rash I'd picked up from a plant in the woods, a weird alpine poison ivy, or if it was from the first Slovenian tick bite. Although it looked almost alien, it wasn't particularly itchy.

Then again, we moved so slowly. Maybe I'd been "tagged" by gnomes.

Luckily, we also found the library where we read an email from Siegi, our friend in Brixen, telling us that we absolutely had to appear at their police station on June 29th. There was no chance to reschedule our face-to-face meeting, and our Italian residence depended on showing up in five days. Frankly, I was surprised. We'd heard those *permessos* could take months to process. Ours had taken less than one.

Then again, it couldn't have happened at a better time. If we'd been sequestered in the high Alps on the red route, we'd have found out too late. As it was, we could trek from Innichen and reach Brixen just in time.

Like they say, everything happens for a reason.

In the morning, the ring on the back of my leg bloomed hot and swollen. Maybe it was more than a poisonous plant, after all.

Our hiking continued down Pustertal Valley. The Südtirol's third largest valley community runs along the south side of the alpine ridge for about 60-kilometers west to the Brixen basin. Compared to the past week, we passed a village or large farmstead every five kilometers in the shadow of the Dolomites, renowned as some of the world's most spectacular mountains. Tolkien in design, they're unique for their bizarre shapes, needle-sharp peaks, and a hue morphing ability from day to day and season to season, from cool grey to glowing red.

Besides having those giants for company, cyclists passed all day on the *radweg*. In the bi-lingual region of northern Italy, we didn't know whether to say, "*Buon giorno*" or "*Grüß Gott*," so we settled on "Hallo!"

Although she gave it her all, Cheryl lagged all day. First, she had trouble with her other knee, then blisters popped up underneath her toenails. Ouch. Between the two, she was *kaput* by 2:00 when we rolled into Ober Olong, a tiny rural community set amid rolling hills and cow pastures. Wandering into its deserted center of town, we searched for someone, anyone, and finally found a gardener packing up his spades.

"Do you know where's there a good place to sleep?" I asked.

Bewildered, he turned to a passing elderly woman who assumed we were pilgrims hiking the Jakobsweg to Santiago de Compostela in Spain, since it also goes through there. Ragged, we must have looked the part. Without a moment's hesitation, she directed us uphill to a large building with a life-sized crucifix planted in its front yard. A billboard-sized mural of the Virgin Mary was splayed across the building's façade.

"Think they're religious?" Cheryl asked.

"Maybe it's a convent."

After a tenuous knock at the door, a lady answered and excitedly told us to sit on a bench outside while she hustled to prepare what they call *komfort zimmer*, an apartment with small kitchen and television, a rarity. It couldn't have come at a better time. We were tired, sore and famished, but still managed to head to the local market to pick up the ingredients for pasta along with local red wine, the perfect sleep aid.

Over the next two days, we continued trekking west to Brixen for our meeting. We passed through Bruneck where an elfin waif with blue eyes and braids at the visitor office tried to help us find the bicycle route to Brixen, but she knew nothing about it except to hand us a bicycle shop's map. We followed their route to Ehrenburg where we passed a railway station.

One fellow in its crew worked on the tracks in only a red, bun-hugging Speedo swimsuit with his gut spilling out.

We looked at each other chuckling, "Only in Italia!"

Finally, we ambled into Kiens, tired, dusty and feeling a little empty, like something had been lost on the trail. While waiting for a gastehäus room, we watched a schoolgirl innocently prance in her bare feet through a fountain. And that's when it dawned on me.

That's what we're missing—total immersion! So far the villages, guest-houses and restaurants treat us like we're package tourists, fresh off the bus. They seldom see hikers like us. It's true, we've seen more village life lately, but we've also been more sheltered. I hate that feeling. We need to change it and fast. It's definitely time to head back into the high mountains, back to the challenge, back to the adventure.

But it remained to be seen how far we could continue without running into snowfields again. Then, there was the climbing. Could Cheryl handle it?

The next day would give us the answer, when what was to be a short twenty-four kilometer day developed into one over thirty. It's a small difference if you're driving, but a long haul when you're nursing a bad knee. Before setting off that morning, we phoned Siegi to tell him we'd arrive earlier than expected for our meeting with the police. I figured it'd give Cheryl two extra days to rest, plus I'd have my rash examined at the hospital since the antibiotic cream I'd bought wasn't helping.

The trail led us down valley into a verdant region of vineyards and orchards. Apple trees grew in tight rows on wires, low enough to easily pick their juicy fruit. The corn was twice as high as those we'd passed earlier and gardens overflowed with produce. We continued hiking through Mühlbach, a charming village, and then down valley past a tranquil lake where Siegi and I'd relaxed a month earlier. Finally, we followed our view of the cathedral spires through the old city walls into stately Brixen. It felt like home.

Any anxiety we had about visiting the police station for our *permesso di soggiorno* quickly vanished. Siegi was there to translate the fellow's Italian. After we presented our paperwork, they measured us, took photos, and scanned our fingerprints into a machine. Finally, we were escorted into a back room where they inked each finger and whole palms for more prints.

"Need to ink this, too?" Cheryl chirped, pointing to her backside. The officer only grinned and shook his head.

I was relieved he had a sense of humor.

Suddenly it was over and much easier than anticipated.

Then came the unexpected. Cheryl and I stopped at the hospital. After fifteen minutes or so, I was sent to the emergency room where the doctor seemed baffled by my leg rash. Not the usual thing treated in an ER, I guess. After a short wait, Dr. Wenter, a kindly English-speaking dermatologist, examined my leg and confirmed my worst suspicions.

Yes, I'd picked up Lyme disease from the Slovenian tick. Just to be certain, a blood sample was drawn. Meanwhile, he ordered me to take oral antibiotics for three weeks. Test results would be emailed to me in ten days. Hopefully, we'd caught it in time. Its symptoms, many of which don't occur for a decade, include most everything: persistent pain, fatigue, impaired cognitive function, or unexplained numbness; everything except a desire to run for Congress (also known as temporary insanity).

What a cruel irony. I'd climbed Mt. Kilimanjaro in the dark, been shot at by Chinese soldiers as we trekked across Tibet, swum with a three-wheeler in the Arctic Ocean, avoided catching malaria or deadly bilharzia during seven months crossing Africa, and evaded kidnappers while trekking the Middle East. All to be brought down by a tick the size of a pencil eraser.

I was assured the antibiotics would do the trick. If not, I was to let them know when the hallucinations started.

Oh, right. Hallucinations? An unplanned trip to Strawberry Fields is *not* something I want to experience while hanging off some mountain ledge at 4000-meters. Yea, you bet I'll let them know.

And Cheryl? She again refused to have her knee examined by a doctor even though she knew we were headed back into the mountains. She's as tenacious as I am at times, both a blessing and a curse, and was afraid they'd bench her for the rest of the season. Try as I might, there was absolutely nothing I could say or do to change her mind. She was adamant about continuing, with the hope her knee would eventually heal and grow stronger over time.

Forcing a brave smile, she reminded me, "Hey, like they say, 'What doesn't kill us only makes us stronger,' right?"

6

OUT OF THE FOREST, NOT OUT OF THE WOODS

AT SUNRISE, WE LEFT FOR NEARBY STEIN SASSO WITH SIEGI, WHO decided to join us for the day's brief climb to Pfitscherjoch-Haus at 2275 meters. Since we'd continued trekking west through the valley to Brixen, it was the closest place to reconnect with the Via Alpina red route to resume our journey. Besides, a short day was better for my partner's knee.

Unexpectedly, the weather cooperated and it was a pleasant hike. It was actually warm when we set off and began our gradual climb through a pine forest and then up a swiftly flowing stream. Cheryl managed to easily match our relaxed pace. For once, we reached the remote refuge just as the fog moved in and the temperatures dropped.

Although empty when we arrived, the comfy dining room soon flooded with wonderful aromas from the kitchen, as well as with bicyclists and hikers who'd made the short trek from the lake below. They must have come for the hearty food, since the view was totally obscured. The mist continued to ebb and flow all afternoon, draping the craggy landscape in an ethereal mantle.

All too soon, after wishing us luck, Siegi sailed back down the mountain to return home. His friendship had helped us realize one dream. The next, crossing those formidable Alps, was one we had to face alone.

The dense fog was unyielding. The next morning it still brushed past the face of the mountain, far worse than we'd expected for the first of July. In that section, the Via Alpina corresponds with the Geraer-Hütte-Weg, so I knew ninety-five percent of our day's journey would be downhill. I also knew it'd prove dicey for Cheryl, since steep slopes were the hardest on her knee.

After fortifying ourselves with a typical Tyrolean breakfast of meat, cheese, müsli, bread, jam and coffee, we donned our heaviest clothes, our down jackets under our ponchos, and headed down the mountainside.

Fortunately, there was just enough break in the mist for us to see the trail markings for trail 524, the high-mountain path through Zillertaler Alpen Nature Park to Schlegeisstausee Reservoir at 1782 meters. Nearly just outside the cabin door, we crossed the border from Italy back into Austria, and then wound our way through a colorful mosaic of alpine meadows ablaze with wildflowers, including the pink alpenrose, a type of rhododendron. Waterfalls abounded to either side, cascading off sheer rock faces. Reportedly, on a clear day, we might have spotted eagles, chamois, a brown alpine goat-antelope weighing 50 kilos or so, or even the rare bearded vulture with its wingspan of over two meters. But given the dense fog, we were lucky not to trip over the young cows who'd been moved up to the high grass for the summer.

After two hours, it was jarring to unexpectedly arrive at parking lots jammed with cars and day-hikers. Then again, it was encouraging to see so many seniors enthusiastically trekking up to the hut we'd left that morning. It sure beat shuffleboard and pinochle for exercise.

An icy panorama unfolded around us as the snowfields and Schlegeisspeicher Glacier at 2800 meters became revealed. However, not even the magnificent setting could distract Cheryl from her constant throbbing pain. Wincing with each step, she put on a brave face. But her already deliberate pace deteriorated as the afternoon progressed, until we slowed to just two kilometers an hour.

At last, reaching Breitlahner after five and a half hours, I convinced her to hop a ride into Ginzling, the classic mountaineering village still seven kilometers away. As the bus wouldn't arrive for another ninety minutes, I left her at the stop and hiked the final bit into town. We'd arranged to meet at the visitor office and I arrived early enough to try and find a room for the night.

Not so easy. No one was home—or if they were, they were out working in their fields. After I'd called six zimmers four times each, Cheryl arrived and we set off to find one the old fashioned way by simply knocking on front doors.

Our home for the night bordered a field where several red longhaired Scottish Highland cows grazed in tall grass. They were the first of the breed we'd seen and I was surprised to find them, a long way from home. The calves were particularly personable. They'd approach and lick our arms with long black licorice tongues. I also particularly liked their roommates, the Tyrol Greys. With their great shaggy ears, they look like huge stuffed bears standing on all fours. They're a vital part of the alpine culture and landscape.

Grauvieh, or "noble cows" as the local farmers call them, have lived in the region over 3000 years. They're perfectly tailored to the harsh mountain climate and produce equally perfect milk for cheese and chocolate. In fact, they're far better adapted than we'd ever hope to be.

After cleaning up, I helped Cheryl rub more analgesic cream into her inflated knee while she popped another Ibuprofen, but I couldn't help thinking she'd been too optimistic about her recovery. It was clear we weren't out of the woods. Not yet.

The next day, our trek down valley went downhill in more ways than one. Before long, Cheryl's shooting pains began again. Then, although we set off on a *themenweg*, the track deteriorated to a cow path as it crossed dairy farms. Eventually we reached a suspension bridge crossing a swiftly flowing stream. It swayed so wildly that I suggested we cross it individually, yet we still had a helluva time, much like a legend I'd heard about another bridge in that area.

Even today, they call it the *Teufelsbrücke* (Devil's Bridge) over the Tuxerbach River outside Finkenberg. It all began when the farmers asked the devil to build a bridge and promised him the first living being to cross it. Well, when the bridge was completed, the wily villagers quickly sent a goat across. Furious at being tricked, the fiend grabbed it and rode off.

Eventually, after another sluggish day, we reached the controlled mayhem of Mayrhofen. Shoppers thronged streets, while others returned from day hikes, rafting or paragliding. Gondolas ran sightseers to the top of the mountain. Even a *käserei* offered cheesy tours. After the last two nights of alpine solitude, it was overwhelming. Cheryl and I rented an inexpensive room overlooking the slopes, went to a café for hot *wurst* and *schnitzel*, and then brought back a bottle of *most*, a traditional Austrian fermented apple juice, which we chilled in the hallway fridge.

Later, popping it open, we reluctantly sat down for another heart-to-heart.

"Look, Babe, your knees aren't doing any better."

She hesitantly nodded. We both knew we'd rushed her recovery.

"If you're going to continue, you have to get off your feet. You can't go on like this every day. I'm afraid it can cause permanent damage."

"Maybe, but what choice is there? I can't quit now."

"Nobody's suggesting that. Okay, you probably don't want to hear this, but why don't you visit a doctor, have it looked at, and rest a couple more days? According to the map, the next two days on the trail are going to be tough, especially with the condition of your knees. So why risk getting more injured? Pacing is everything—and we have several months to go."

"Thanks for reminding me."

"Here's a thought: Why don't you catch a bus to Schwaz? It's only 44-kilometers from here as the crow flies. And the trail passes through there. We can meet in three days."

"What'll you do?"

"I'll stay on the Via Alpina and hit two more mountain huts. Hopefully, it'll give you enough time to rest your knee."

"And then?"

"Then, we won't push it quite as hard. Together, we'll trek west down valley to Innsbruck on the *radweg*. It's flatter and it'll be easier on your knee. Besides, we haven't been there in years."

Her eyes lit up. "They do have good chocolate pastries."

"Even the Via Alpina folks recommend it, calling it the "Innsbruck option." It'd be a shame to miss the old city. As I remember, it can be fun."

Besides, I knew if we stayed on the northern route and skipped Innsbruck, our last hut-to-hut stage would be a grueling forty-kilometers over mountain-tops. That was the last thing my partner needed. We'd never make it at two or three kilometers an hour.

With a tender hug, we decided to hold off making a final decision until we checked the sky (and her knees) in the morning; but at dawn, it was drizzling again. The Universe had spoken.

For me, the morning began with a hike to Hippach along the scenic Ziller *riverweg* until I headed up the mountain via a long series of switchbacks. It was a tough climb from 633 to 2117 meters in one large gasp. I wended uphill in a light rain forcing me back into my poncho. As much as I appreciated its cape design, I was soon drenched in sweat, but I continued upward past a mountain full of zimmers far above the tourist hordes. Cars passed on the country road, but no one stopped except for a Volvo full of paragliders who asked where I was going—and then looked like they didn't believe me.

Oddly, I ran into them again thirty minutes later when I ducked into a small hotel to warm up. Friendly and inquisitive, they asked about our journey and then told me about a paragliding contest from Salzburg to Monaco over eighteen days. Wherever the gliders land, the racers have to carry them by them-selves to a mountaintop and begin again.

Not easy. Then again, it was over in eighteen days—not 118.

Although I enjoyed their company, I didn't dare to dally too long and cool down, as my shirt and shorts were soaked and I didn't want to catch a cold. Leaving, I followed the lower 302A that led to a steep gravel farm road. As I climbed ever higher through dairy fields, temperatures continued to drop while the rain picked up for a miserable combination.

By now, I thought, Cheryl's in a hot tub, melting her troubles away. It's a saner choice. I'm glad she doesn't have to go through this.

As for me, I was alone on the trail all day except for a German couple with their Australian sheepdog who I quickly passed as they tried to maneuver their pooch around a cattle grate.

Hours later, I spotted Rastkogelhütte on the summit. Wouldn't you know it? That was when the trail markings disappeared. I took the right fork, figuring it would switchback again. Wrong! The trail ended. In frustration, I pulled the electric fence post out of the ground, ducked underneath, and headed up the lush dripping wet meadow in the direction of the refuge. It was slow going and I managed to soak my only pair of dry pants, as well as boots and socks while climbing the steep alm. Eventually, I reached the road, only to look down to see the German couple and their dog following my lead. Sorry.

Well, from there it was only another thirty minutes until I arrived at the hut, worn-out, sopping-wet and dehydrated all at the same time. The woman and her daughter who ran the hut were hospitable and even swore my five hours hiking time was excellent. I knew better, but appreciated their encouragement. Every little bit helped.

While I re-hydrated, warmed by the stove, and admired the sunset from their photo-lined dining room, a weary couple in their early twenties dragged inside. They barely shuffled their feet. They were clearly spent.

"Where've you been?"

"We just came back from hiking Rastkogel Mountain," a curly haired fellow with intense dark eyes replied.

"In this weather?" It was 2760 meters high.

He nodded with pride.

"It must have been tough. Spending the night here?"

"We can't," his girlfriend sighed, hypnotically staring ahead.

"See, we're getting married tomorrow," he explained in a heavy Hungarian accent. "We still must walk down to Mayrhofen."

"Now? It's almost dark? You trying to kill her before the wedding?"

He laughed, but her glare told me she'd wondered the same thing.

"Maybe there's another way," I suggested, knowing a thing or two about exhausted women. "You could try to hitch a ride back down the mountain? There seems to be a little traffic when you get closer to town. Or ask the lady who runs this place."

Following an impassioned chat among themselves, they agreed and explained their dilemma to our guardian, who then spoke with her husband. Without a moment's hesitation, he offered to drive them all the way into town—at no cost. The sweet bride-to-be grinned ear-to-ear, relieved.

Yes, there are still some romantics in the world.

Austria's like that, truly a "kinder, gentler" sort of place. Before I went to bed, the innkeeper's wife offered to hang my sopping wet clothes in her warm kitchen so they'd dry overnight, and then shocked me when she stuck my drenched boots in her oven.

"For tomorrow's soup?" I asked with a grin.

After a good night's sleep in what became my own private dorm, followed by another hearty breakfast, I set off down the mountain on the opposite side and within ninety minutes arrived at another ski resort. Hochfügen was nearly deserted except for a few hikers heading up to Rastkogel.

That should make the innkeepers happy, I thought, as most had cancelled their reservations the night before because of the lousy weather.

From Hochfügen it's a steep climb up to Loassattel—no matter what path you choose. However, it's just a prelude to the Kellerjoch path. Kellerjoch mountain range has the highest elevation of the northeast Tuxer Alps. The Via Alpina gives hikers the option of spending the night at the lower gastehäus and making the ascent to Kellerjoch Hut in the morning, but it was still early and I preferred to climb in early afternoon.

I seemed to be the only fool making the lung-searing scramble, although a few folks passed me coming down the mountain amid wildflowers and bog. Once above the timberline, there was an eerie silence, flawless except for the constant buzzing of voracious flies. For a change, I was glad it was overcast and not hot and sunny. I sensed I was dehydrating again, even though I'd downed an entire liter of water fortified with a vitamin powder. There was an acrid taste in my mouth, my personal canary in the coalmine, but what could I do? Not a fountain or trough were in sight.

Well before arriving atop the mountain summit at 2237 meters, I spotted Kellerjoch Hut's Tibetan prayer flags fluttering in the breeze and could already see hikers enjoying drinks out on its sun terrace. Its vision spurred me onward over those last few hundred brutal, heart-bursting meters, until within an hour, I'd joined them. I'd made it another day.

Time to kick back and enjoy a breathtaking view across the Karwendel Massif and into Inntal Valley with miniature Schwaz.

As I began to unwind at a heavy wooden table inside, Jackie, the attractive hut guardian, greeted me in English. After asking where I was from, she said, "You know, I lived in Netherland, Colorado many years."

"In the boonies? We lived nearby in Boulder. What brought you up here?"

"I returned to Austria to operate this hut. Plus," she added with a sly wink, "to find a husband."

"And were you successful?"

"With both! Thanks."

Famished, I couldn't wait to ask what they had to eat, since I couldn't decipher the cryptic writing scrawled on their blackboard.

"Don't worry. I'll fix you food you'd like as an American."

"Thanks for your offer, but when I travel I like trying food I can't find at home." Besides, I knew I'd never find saimin up there, so I ordered the most Austrian food I could imagine: roast pork with sauerkraut and a huge *knödel* dumpling. It was a delicious choice, improved by the effort I spent to get there and the altitude.

As the sun set, Jackie invited me to join two couples from Schwaz, along with Katrina, her blonde barmaid, and their two visiting Nepalese cooks. For an hour, we had a lively conversation about the Himalayas, the Via Alpina and Jakobsweg. One of the women, probably in her early fifties, was a cancer survivor and the other fought the same disease.

As she put it, "We came up here to the mountain to leave all our problems far below.

Mountains are good for that. For me, a mountain is an island adrift in the clouds. You're removed, isolated, an observer on the rest of humanity and your own life.

And they did succeed at leaving their worries behind, as round after round of beers disappeared. As we relaxed together, they treated me to rare Alpine schnapps made from *vogelbeeren*, wild red berries found at those heights.

Toasting our good fortune, the blonde fellow explained with a glow, "The fruit must be handpicked because they ripen at different times. The berry itself is poisonous, but it makes delicious wild liquor. Yes?"

When we finally hugged goodbye, I saw a special something in their eyes—and it wasn't the schnapps. Why does it sometimes take a life-threatening illness to make us appreciate the fleeting moments, the smallest treasures of life?

As I retreated to my room, another group arrived. They were anxious to celebrate a friend's birthday, so it wasn't long before the accordion music began, followed by guitar playing and laughter lulling me to restful sleep.

The following morning was clear and cool, perfect for making the steep 1700-meter descent into Schwaz. For the most part, I met no other hikers except for one gnomish fellow. Compact, robust and bald with a flowing white beard, he approached and jabbered pleasantries. (At least, I thought they were.)

His Austrian German dialect was impossible for me to understand, so I only replied, "I've come from Kellerjoch Hut," and "*Ja, ja,*" before we set off on our separate ways.

As I neared Schwaz, more bikers, runners and trekkers headed up the mountain on that rare sunny day. I ran into a jogger who let me tag along as he sprinted down unmarked, nearly hidden Hobbit trails, straight down the mountain. No switchbacks or asphalt roads for us. No, Siree. My knees creaked in agony by the time we finally reached Schwaz, but I'd saved an hour of hiking, which was worth a little pain.

The visitor office where I was to meet Cheryl was just west of the Gothic church, so I headed in that direction admiring the beautiful architecture and quiet streets along the way. Even though most of the town was torched in the Tyrolean Freedom Wars of 1809, many buildings still reflect its rich silver-mining heritage.

With time to spare before our meeting, I stopped for a pizza on the walking mall and then ran into my partner milking a latté just a block away. She'd been off her feet and holed-up in a pension the past two and a half days, but unfortunately her knee was in no better shape. In the morning, we decided to make our way to Innsbruck. It was definitely time to have it examined at the hospital. Like it or not, their prognosis would help us decide whether she could safely continue.

At daybreak, like clockwork, we awoke to more rain. After a meager break-fast, we reluctantly set off hiking west along the *radweg*. As the downpour increased, I couldn't help chuckling at something a teenager had told us earlier.

"Here, we are used to rain. We say, 'Austria—three months of rain, nine months of snow! Bwa!'" He let out a typical local exclamation that's like laughing with a mouth full of milk. "The newspaper says this has been the rainiest year in 146 years! Still, if we're not hiking in the mountains, we're thinking about being up there." He shrugged. "It's in our blood."

Like ticks?

Too many long, wet hours later, we trudged into the Tyrolean capital and found ourselves dripping in the visitor office. There we met the angriest person we'd met so far on the trail. The *fonctionnaire* clearly hated her job and we were forced to play her childish game.

"We need to find a room for tonight," I routinely explained.

"How much are you willing to pay?"

Figuring a bigger city was bound to cost more, I said, "Fifty euros." That was nearly 75 dollars.

"We have nothing in the city so inexpensive." She sneered, as if scraping something from the bottom of her shoes.

"But we've traveled across Austria and have never paid any more."

She couldn't care less. Spotting an accommodations brochure on her counter, we entered her game in earnest. I'd pick a place. She'd say it was unavailable. I tried again. And again.

Finally, I asked, "Zimmer?"

"We don't book those."

"Hostel?"

"You have to call on your own."

"We don't have a mobile phone with us."

She shrugged, and then turned to take a call. We waited, refusing to budge. When she eventually finished, seeing we were still there, still forming pools all over her floor, she recommended a backpacker hostel.

Why didn't she suggest that long before?

"Try Nepomuks in the Old City. It's in *your* price range," she added with a condescending smirk. She was delighted to see us leave.

Hey, we didn't ask for much. Anything clean and dry was better than hiking in the rain or camping in it, and Nepomuks was a pleasant surprise. Our private room above the pastry shop was comfy and looked out on the boutiques lining the walking mall. Innsbruck, a handsome city framed by snowcapped peaks, was far busier than we remembered. Maybe it was our frame-of-mind this time around, our gnomish nervousness, but it seemed a little intense after the welcome solitude of the mountains.

After showering and hanging up our wet clothes, we ambled down the street to the Theresa Brew Pub where they craft micro-beers and fry a mean wurst with sauerkraut and roast potatoes. In its comforting ambience, Cheryl and I debated about her visiting the hospital, but she was still afraid they'd tell her to get off her feet for as long as a month and she refused to end her trek. So, even though I strongly objected, she decided against seeing a doctor. We'd continue to Scharnitz—and then, it was back into the high mountains—for better or worse.

All night long endless thunder rattled the windows. By morning, it was still cloudy but there was no rain. That was a small miracle. We wandered downstairs to enjoy wonderful cakes from the bakery, and then followed the river west out of town. It was encouraging to see Cheryl's pace had improved and her knees weren't as tender. It was anyone's guess how long it would last.

Upon passing the university, we were soon into neighboring villages where they harvested cauliflower, cabbage and broccoli. We followed the river path all morning until we arrived in Zirl where we made a steep uphill trek out of the village. Once, when the trail disappeared, we stopped a gnarled fellow on his way to gather shotgun shell casings from the ground where hunters had practiced.

He went out of his way to lead us to trail #10, which led 500 meters through the woods, back onto the highway, and eventually to tiny Reith where we'd tuck in for the night. Storm clouds gathered and we'd already trekked six-and-a-half hours. We hadn't covered much ground, but we'd pushed our luck enough for one day.

As it turned out, our timing was perfect. No sooner did we settle into a *zimmer* than the heavens lit up. A torrential rain flooded the streets. We waited until it paused and then hobbled up the road to one of the few places open that dreary night. It was filled with the blue haze of smoke and workers still dressed in matching overalls. As usual, there was no menu and we went through the familiar litany, "Do you have blah blah?" only to be told *"Nein"* again and again.

Finally, we resorted to the memorable old *When Harry Met Sally* film line and said, "We'll just have what they're having." Easy on the orgasm, please.

The morning fog burned off at sunrise. Without a moment to spare, we struck out on a quick trek to Seefeld in Tirol, once an Olympic site, and then another ten kilometers along Bike Trail Tirol to Weidach. Set at the base of the inspiring Wetterstein Mountains in green Leutasch Valley, it's absolutely one of the most inspiring areas I've ever seen.

In light of Cheryl's condition and anticipating another steep trail in the morning, we made it another short day. With good weather, we'd get an early start toward Meilerhütte at 2375 meters in the morning. Since we were only at about 1100 meters, it'd be a demanding day for my determined partner. Longer ones inflamed her swollen knees. But I promised myself, if we could finish it in five hours, maybe her pain wouldn't be too intense.

Hoping for the best, we stopped into Weidach's visitor office and they found us a room in Lehner, only thirty minutes away on foot. En route, we passed a Via Alpina marker showing where the trail intersects if we'd avoided Innsbruck, trekked north, and come down through Scharnitz instead. But considering the amount of rainfall and thunder the night before, I was frankly relieved to be in the valley and not standing like some idiot lightning rod atop those high peaks.

Fittingly, Pension Isabelle was as appealing as the valley itself. Our smiling hostess was as kindhearted as your favorite aunt and our room was one of the nicest so far, "well-appointed," as they like to say in brochures. Cheryl was especially impressed by what she called our bed's down-filled "tortellini pillows," puffed up and doubled like a giant's pasta.

On a more sobering note that evening, we again studied our maps and the zigzagging Via Alpina red route. By then, it was obvious we'd never be able to double-up on daily stages as once naively planned. In fact, if we stuck solely to the red trail, we'd be lucky to reach Monaco by mid-November—if at all. Most huts close in October when we'd also risk the likelihood of a major snowfall, obliterating any markers. (That is, assuming they existed in the first place.)

Considering all that, we decided to pick up the Via Alpina green route, otherwise known as the Swiss National Trail #1, when it intersected with our red route in Vaduz, Liechtenstein. We'd follow it across Alpine Switzerland and reconnect with the red route again in Adelboden. We'd take that to meet the Via Alpina blue route outside Larche, France until we rejoined the red route for the hop from Sospel to Monaco: red, green, red, blue, red.

Although it might sound roundabout, it was actually the most direct Via Alpina route. It was still over a hundred stages long, but it'd save us more than a month. That made it feasible to finish before the worst weather hit. We'd already seen more than enough rain, more days than not, over the first five weeks.

It was pure improvisation, after all, the jazz of trekking. Whether it'd work or not, well, remained to be seen.

7

WHAT'S THE SOUND OF ONE MAN FALLING?

THE DOGS CHASED THEIR TAILS ALL DAY. AS WITH ALL "BEST LAID plans," it began with good intentions. We had an early start from the pension and followed trail markings down valley to the trailhead for Meilerhütte.

I remembered looking at the map: After crossing a bridge, we'll head up the mountain following the same stream.

So we found a sign actually pointing the way to Meilerhütte and proceeded to slowly scramble up the narrow mountain trail from 1100 to 2375 meters. For the next two hours, we ascended a nosebleed path, slowly rising above the timberline, until at last we arrived at a beautiful alpine meadow.

That wasn't so bad, I thought.

Just about then, we were feeling mighty proud of ourselves. We'd made good time, Cheryl's knee behaved itself, and it was a spectacular setting. There was just one problem. 818. As I sat and caught my breath, my eyes focused on a faded and barely visible 818 scrawled on some rocks spread across the ground. My heart stopped.

No, that can't be. Yes, our trail's had the usual red and white stripes all the way up. Yes, it has led in the same direction. Yes, signs actually pointed to Meilerhütte. But no, this trail's led us to a valley on the opposite side of the mountain range from where we were supposed to land. It's the wrong path! Our hut lays over that sheer wall of impenetrable mountains to our right. Dammit!

I was upset by my own stupidity, especially after we'd put so much effort into the climb. I pulled out our topo map, hoping, searching to find another pass over those mountains. There was a faint jagged line. Sure, you could reach Meilerhütte in Germany from there. You only had to be a steinbok or Spiderman to climb the sharp vertical wall separating the two meadows. It was clearly beyond our capabilities, especially with Cheryl's injury. Our only options were to either retreat back down the 818 and struggle once again up the other formidable side—or continue to forge ahead a few hours and descend back into the valley. It was too late for the first and too hard on Cheryl. Besides, call me stubborn, but I try to make it a point never to retreat, so we did the only thing we could. We continued across the alpine saddle.

The meadow was remarkably inaccessible. We only ran across one other couple. Then again, maybe only one other pair was so mad. Right on cue, the weather grew teeth-chattering cold and foreboding—especially for two tropical trekkers. The wind slashed our faces. Temperatures dropped to 8°C, excluding wind-chill factor. What had begun as a pleasant four hour trek to the hut soon turned into an all-day slog in a giant loop around Gehrenspitze Mountain.

Out of a sense of survival, we joined the Austrian couple. (They had far better maps.) Together, we made our way past an enthusiastic dog and shepherd driving their sheep downhill with a "Who-eee! Who-eee!" A friendly old fella, he stopped to yell, "*Grüezi!*" ("Hi") to Cheryl as we inched our way past his inquisitive flock who came right up to us, as if to sniff their approval.

It was slow going in the frigid air, but we continued to pick our way ever higher over fields of stones, headlong into the bitter wind, until at long last we reached Scharnitzjoch Hütte at 2048 meters. From there, it was truly all downhill and it only took us a few more hours to stumble back down to Leutasch Valley—five frustrating kilometers from where we'd started seven hours earlier.

Sure, you can always philosophize and say, "It's the journey that matters and not the destination." And maybe that's true. We'd seen some magnificent scenery. We'd both successfully made a difficult climb, and we found a comfortable pension run by a Romanian family in Ostbach at the end of the day. They fixed us an enormous spaghetti casserole, and for once, I was stuffed like the Thanksgiving bird. True, we didn't make Meilerhütte, but I was certain there'd be others. In the end, the journey itself was unforgettable.

Right on schedule, it was already raining by sunrise—that is, if we could have seen the sun for a change. After breakfast, we set off on the Adlerweg (E4) through Gaistal Valley and soon reached a diversion through the woods, which delivered us to Gaistalalm. We were content to drop into a log cabin doubling as a family restaurant at the edge of the forest. It was a storybook setting. Their wood paneled walls were strung with ancient ski gear and homemade crafts. Its fire was crackling, the aroma of fresh cookies wafted from the kitchen, and a beautiful woman in long traditional *lederhosen* and braids served us fresh buttermilk and piping hot peppermint tea to lift our spirits on yet another wet day.

All too soon, we set off back on the trail and skirted past a lady with her gaggle of kids. It was freezing outside for mid-July. In her light t-shirt, she was a psychedelic shade of purple. As I turned to watch them, my foot slipped off the edge of the path into a ditch and my body followed. Crunch! I was thrown to the ground and only caught myself at the last minute on my palms and knee, bleeding pretty badly from all three.

Instead of slinking back to the restaurant as Cheryl suggested, (What do I say, "Duh, I fell walking down the road?"), I decided to skip adding humiliation to injury. Hobbling over to a nearby wooden bench, I threw down my pack, pulling out my water bottle and med kit right there. Then we began to clean the wounds.

Well, just as Cheryl poured water over my bleeding palms, a very inquisitive Palomino mare who'd watched from a nearby meadow decided to join us—nose first. It was hilarious. That blonde beauty was determined to check out exactly what was going on. She inspected my palms, and then stared with sympathetic brown eyes. She was face-to-face, so close I could feel her breath, but I needed room to work. I zigged. She zagged. I tried leaning against her to give us space. She barely budged. Cheryl nudged her away. She nuzzled back. I looked in my pack for bandages. The horse stuck in her head, too. I tried to rub antibiotic on my bleeding palms, but no. This horse was always just a fuzzy muzzle away, staring with curious saucer eyes. This went on for at least ten minutes.

Now, in case you think this was some odd hallucination of our oxygen-deprived brains, we weren't the only ones who saw it and thought it was weird and a little wonderful. Other folks stopped dead in their tracks on their way to the cabin just to gawk and chuckle at the overly concerned horse doctor. This continued until I was bandaged and we were repacked.

Why, even as we stood to go, she put one hoof up on the bench where we'd been fussing, as if she was ready to write us a prescription for the road.

"No, don't worry. I'll be okay," I assured her. Maybe it was just my imagination, but she actually looked a little disappointed to see us leave.

Still laughing, we continued into the valley where we rejoined the Via Alpina coming from the north. After five hours in light rain, we arrived at Drachensee. It's another gem of a turquoise lake surrounded by larches, rowan and pine trees at 1674 meters. Although Cheryl's knee had already had its daily workout, we managed to climb one last mountain to Coburger Hütte at 1917 meters. We arrived drenched, but elated by her progress.

Although eating kraut, knödel and wurst by the fire's glow has a way of making a day's difficulties disappear, our sleep was also the absolute worst. We shared the room with three older German hikers who insisted on singing until the wee hours. Once they finally turned in, their songfest turned snore-fest, interrupted only by frequent stumbles to the toilet.

As Cheryl blearily pointed out the next morning, "Too bad their beer consumption was bigger than their bladder size."

At dawn, after a breakfast of müsli and fresh fruit, a healthy change, we donned our warmest rain gear and then began a stiff climb behind the hut, picking our path around rocks in heavy fog and mist. It was slow, torturous going as we concentrated on carefully placing every step. After thirty minutes of facing a bitter wind and near-freezing rain, we reached the Biberwierer Scharte wind gap, a notch in the cliff face—only to begin our treacherous slide 1200-meters downward. It was another of those steep descents along a crumbling, sheer slate rock face where one misstep could send you plummeting to the scree below.

We were alone, a mixed blessing. The wind blocked any sound except the blood coursing through my body, "kabong, kabong, kabong," reverberating in my ears. Still, I couldn't help but wonder, "What's the sound of one man falling when there's no one around to hear?"

It took two tense hours to slowly, warily pick our way back down to the tree line. I was so pleased to arrive in one piece, especially with Cheryl's temperamental knee, I told her to scream, "Take that, Jack!" in memory of her jack-assed boss (and everyone's overlord who's laid them off as a human sacrifice to the bottom line).

"You made it! Never, ever let anyone diminish you or your accomplishments again. You're a strong, courageous woman."

She beamed.

More than anything, long thru-treks are much more than climbing another mountain. They're an exercise in concentration, focus and a chance to re-affirm your own worth and sense of self. They're empowering. Each day is a challenge. Some days, every step is one. As in life, it's important to celebrate the triumph of the little steps—and not to hold ourselves back waiting for the big victories.

Then again, reaching Biberwier was only a first step, the start of our day. From there, we connected with the Via Claudia Augusta, a route the Roman legions originally traveled through the Alps from Bolzano via the Reschen and Fern passes to Augsburg. It's even older than Brenner Pass, the second most important Alpine crossing. Paved before the birth of Christ, Roman legion cart tracks can still be found there. During those early times, the locals trained as skilled craftsmen in wood, metal and masonry guilds to service the armies. In fact, the valley continued to be famous for its craftsmen up until the 1800s when many left in search of work.

Our own arrival in tiny Lermoos came not a moment too soon. Storm clouds appeared over the Zugspitze and brought another heaping helping of rain. For once, we were already settled into our pension, comfortable another night. However, the next morning, we awoke to fresh snow on the surrounding mountaintops.

"*Ja*, it was three degrees on the mountain last night," the house *frau* warned with a wag of her finger. It was July.

"All the more reason I'm thankful we're here in the valley and especially not facing the tricky trek we made yesterday from Coburger Hütte. Can you imagine? Hiking that'd be dodgy today across the wet slate and scree."

Cheryl slowly shook her auburn hair, clearly relieved.

Considering the frigid air and relentless rain, we stayed in the valley and continued following the Via Claudia Augusta westward. It was more sane and we'd soon reconnect with the Via Alpina in Weißenbach am Lech. It again drizzled most of the morning as we wended through an abundant mantle of wildflowers. The gently rolling trail led us through Bichlbach and Heiterwang where we connected with trail 822, which led us through Klausen Forest in the shadow of Thaneller and Tauern Mountains.

Our trail was a picture of serenity. Black Labrador-sized ravens foraged in fields, while a flock of butterflies adopted us and fed on moisture on our backpacks. In Africa's wild, I'd marveled how the most beautiful and delicate butterflies are attracted to fresh dung. Did we smell that badly?

After reaching the quaint village of Rieden, it was just a short distance to Weißenbach on the Lech River in one of the Alp's most untouched natural valleys. It's majestic, even on the cloudiest of days. The river's the lifeline of a landscape continually at the mercy of the dynamic waterway and its fickle course. Even though Weißenbach hosted a bicycle race that weekend, luck was with us. We easily found a room at a local bed & breakfast thanks to the visitor office's computer that helps wayward travelers 24/7, without concern for their usual odd hours. The *zimmer* host even offered us a discount, which helped stretch our budget.

Already we found it surprisingly tough to trek the primitive trail for less than 65 euros (90-100 dollars) a day. To some folks, this may seem like a piddling amount. But we weren't on an expense account or your typical two-week vacation. It quickly adds up when your journey lasts four or five months. Sure, we'd save a bit if we bought all our food at the market, but that'd insulate us from an important part of Alpine culture—the food and local companionship.

Plus it's masochistic to eat cold food for months on end. Call us soft, but we figured one warm meal a day was money well spent, especially since so much of our challenge was to keep a positive outlook in the face of continual rain and freezing weather. That was worth the price. Then again, knowing Hulk Hogan, the massive American wrestler, stayed at that same *zimmer* only made our stomachs fantasize their breakfasts might be equally huge.

At dawn, we set off again amid threatening weather. The Via Claudia Augusta soon connected with the Via Alpina that led us for hours up Lechtaler Valley along the Lech River. It was another brilliant trek along shocking robin-egg blue water framed by alabaster rocks lining its banks. After passing Ghost Rock and its fountain, we stopped to admire pastel drawings on placards showing a knight (*Ritter*) riding an elk across a bridge.

It was hours later when the river trail ended and we caught the Schwarzwasser Weg west. Only then did we face the ultimate test of the day—and it was substantial. A stark mountain tauntingly loomed above us. Just as the enormity of the challenge sunk in, we were startled to spot five young climbers slipping down toward us. They were just as shocked.

"Have you just come down from Prinz-Luitpold-Haus?" I asked.

"*Ja*," the skinny fellow said, "but the trail is no good. It's badly marked. No markers from about halfway down to here."

"Really?" Why wasn't I surprised? "How long has it taken you?"

"Five hours! We make terrible time," he laughed, and the girls who hiked with him giggled in agreement. With his merry band of pranksters, he was obviously in no hurry, but we'd already trekked that long and I didn't look forward to facing another ten-hour day.

"Can you see the hut from here?" I asked, hoping for a visual reckoning.

"No, it is on the other side of the mountain. You just go straight ahead and head for the gap up there," he said, pointing. "There are no marks, but it's very nice."

"Nice" wasn't a word I usually associated with sheer, unmarked trails.

At that, he wished us luck and they continued their happy-go-lucky scramble down the mountainside.

Cheryl and I looked at each other, as if to say, "Well, where do we begin?" and then decided to hop the electric fence. That's a tricky maneuver when you're soaked, the grass is wet, and your nether regions are "this close" to a Guantanamo experience. Then we began our tenuous 800-meter climb. It was hard enough to face late in the day, but when the trail suddenly vanished, all we could do was follow his advice and head for the gap.

Up we climbed on a 60° slope over rocks and meadows carpeted with wildflowers, until I unexpectedly spotted the silhouette of another climber far ahead. Appearing just as lost, he was wedged below dense, low-lying bushes fronting

Bergwachthütte. Impossible to climb and tricky to maneuver around, he was stuck on a razor-sharp, scree-covered slope.

Upon spotting us, he frantically cried out in English, "Where is the trail?" It was anyone's guess. We were wondering exactly the same thing.

Based on our "head for the gap" instructions, I yelled, "To your left!" (I think.)

While he gingerly picked his way across the face, Cheryl and I dug deep, tapping the last of our reserves. I took the lead and eventually discovered the thread of a trail just where I'd imagined it might be to the left of the scrub. I called out for Cheryl to join me, but she only made it a few steps in my direction before her knees gave out! She collapsed, swearing at herself and the so-called path. Only a boulder prevented her tumbling off the face of the mountain.

Seeing she was in trouble, I scrambled toward her as fast as I could. Meanwhile, she picked herself up and painfully crawled on hands and knees in my direction. As she finally reached safety, I helped her to her feet and whispered the one phrase I'd repeated nearly every day since we'd started.

"Almost there."

"Promise?"

The other climber, a hefty fellow in his 20s carrying a huge pack, soon joined us. Panting, dripping with sweat, and half-dead on his feet, Alex introduced himself as an Iranian student.

"This is much harder than I thought," he said. "I've already lost my sunglasses pulling myself across those bushes. But at least I'm only hiking four or five stages, and then returning to my studies in Munich. And you?"

"We left from Trieste 45 days ago."

He gasped. "Is every day like this?"

"No. Many days the weather's worse." Then I wondered, "How'd you hear about the Via Alpina, anyway?"

"Oh, on the Internet. I entered 'hiking + challenge' and this came up."

"That it is—and you picked one heckuva place to start!"

After sharing my water since his canteen was dry, the three of us made the final ascent toward the ridge at over 2180 meters. It continued to be dicey, but we took full advantage of fixed ropes and metal steps attached to the rocks, until we finally made it to the summit and took celebratory photos.

It's true; a mountain is always highest when you're climbing it.

Yet there was no time to relax, until we had made a steep descent to Prinz-Luitpold-Haus, which lay beside a small alpine lake on the other side of the crest in Germany. The classic stone cabin is a golden eagle's nest ringed by snowfields of feathers.

While darkness fell, we checked in and ended up sharing a room with a dozen others who'd arrived from the other side of the mountain. How'd we know? As Cheryl said, "They look far too rested—and smell too darned good."

When we awoke, the sky was clear for a change. After breakfast, we left genial Alex as he headed north and back to school. I felt optimistic about our climb back down the mountain. But wouldn't you know it? As soon as we set off on the Via Alpina, within minutes, a dense fog moved in and cut visibility in half. It was just our luck.

Since the mist made the trail slipperier than usual, we were forced to cautiously pick our way across the face of several mountains. We even crossed two snowfields, although they were nowhere near as intimidating as Slovenia's. The fog didn't dissipate until we crested the mountain and found ourselves standing amid a patchwork quilt of wildflowers, the most we'd seen so far on our journey.

It was noon by the time we arrived in Käseralpe, a café surrounded by cattle, ducks and rabbits, where we stopped for a drink and to sample their homemade herb and pimento-flavored cheese. Lucky for us, dairy farming is particularly important in that region, especially the brown Allgäu cows. Small and stout, they produce milk into old age.

(Maybe they're the mysterious source of powdered milk?)

From there, we trekked another ten kilometers along a quiet, tree-lined *weg* down valley to Oberstdorf, Germany's southernmost spa resort. We couldn't arrive in the Bavarian village soon enough, as we were sapped, sunburned, and weary from the intense humidity. All afternoon, sweat from my shirt and shorts had drizzled down my legs, filling my socks.

Consequently, our tiny room overlooking the imposing mountains where we'd begun our day became an unlikely setting for an unsettling experience. While alone and stretching out, I suddenly found both my inner thighs cramping like they were in a shark's jaws. A hot flash flooded my face. I screamed and doubled over in pain. Heaving myself from bed, I dragged my body on bended knees to the sink and drowned my pounding head in cold water until it passed.

I could only imagine it was dehydration; but it was unnerving to be struck and vulnerable by something out of nowhere. Only once before did something similar happen when I trekked alone in extreme heat. First, there was an acrid taste like ammonia. Shortly afterward, without warning, I was unable to move either leg. I was frozen stiff in a wheat field. I finally had to allow myself to fall and then haul my body with both arms to a nearby stream to drink.

What if it happens again up there?

Thank God, breakfast was a feast. There were five kinds of sliced meat and as many cheeses, fresh baked whole-grain bread and hot pastries, creamy butter, fresh-squeezed orange juice, fruits, and strong espresso. It was an Alpinist's fantasy; my mouth still waters at its memory. We made an extra effort to load up on liquids and bananas for potassium and then set off again, hoping the cramps had passed.

Although I'd vowed to increase my fluids, we soon ended up wetter outside than within. It began drizzling shortly after we left Oberstdorf on the hiking trail, passing the pilgrimage church of Loretto Chapel. As usual, we were alone. Any sane hiker (or pilgrim) stayed home in that mess. For hours, we followed the Stillach River facing a downpour forcing even the cows into shelter. We continued toward Schwarze Hütte, figuring it'd be the safest place in foul weather. No doubt, the *panoramaweg* lives up to its name on a sunny day, but when you can't see fifty meters ahead, there's little vista to enjoy and always the chance the weather will change for the worse.

By 1:00, we arrived at the hut, treated ourselves to a drink, and then continued trekking up the ultimate steep and slippery slope to Mindelheimer Hut. Picking our way over boulders, we made sluggish and deliberate headway, fighting both the effects of three rigorous days and gnawing dehydration. Nonetheless, our 800-meter climb went smoothly, especially after the clouds cleared, the humidity subsided, and Mindelheimer, perched on yet another cliffside, at last came into view.

The Germans know how to build them right. The hut was modern, complete with a sundeck and a drying room. We pulled off our boots and unwound. Sunlight glistened off fields overflowing with a vibrant collage of yellow, blue and pink wildflowers.

Best of all, we were swaddled in a serene silence, the still and soothing solitude of the Alps. It had already won me over. By then, I cringed each time we entered a village of any size—and looked with a little pity at those who could escape only for a hard-fought day or two to explore those craggy monoliths.

What better way is there to discover nature, to find peace, or one's true self?

Often on our journey, we'd stayed overnight in a hut and found we had to pry ourselves from bed and out the door the next morning. It's only natural. Although its cozy comfort, tasty food, or hospitality would tempt us to stay a while, we'd press on. There was still too much ground to cover before October.

And so it was. All too soon, we left the serenity of Mindelheimer Hut, scrambling across the mountains and back down into the valley. As usual, there was much more climbing, a tricky trek across smooth snowfields, and then a startling encounter.

Shortly after inching our way across more ice, we spotted six steinboks relaxing atop nearby cliffs. They were the statuesque, horned, brown antelope we'd seen so often in photos, paintings, or with their heads mounted on Austrian pension walls. Regal, they're the wild, independent symbol of the Alpine high-country. These creatures, unfazed by our presence, nonchalantly watched us pass. Then cresting another hill, we found another five lounging atop a rise. Even the family trekking with their loud kids behind us didn't disturb them. Why? Maybe they've seen too many hikers pass that way before to become perturbed. We were hardly hunters. Somehow, even minus a hunting calendar, they knew we meant them no harm.

Before long, Cheryl and I shot downhill to connect with the *wanderweg* into Schröcken. There were several routes and we, of course, stuck to the most difficult one, the Via Alpina. It led us through dense woods and across a hillside with barriers set up to hold back tons of snow in the avalanche-prone region. In the Alps, that danger remains a very real part of life. The worst occurred in January 1954 when about thirty out of the eighty avalanches in the Große Walsertal Valley hit villages, causing eighty deaths and enormous damage.

That path eventually led us to the main highway, down switchbacks, over a high bridge, and through a tunnel. Arriving in the tiny village of Schröcken, we'd left Germany behind and were again back in Austria. Rooms were hard to find that time of year. Ours was nearly the most expensive of our journey so far, even though we were far outside of ski season.

However, I thought, prices may remain high, as we'll soon leave Austria. Then it's a quick pass through Liechtenstein into Switzerland, never known as a budget destination. I just hope August brings us better weather.

The Alps are like love. You can have sun, rain and snow all in the same day.

That harsh reality was driven home the next morning. We awoke to showers and dreaded having to climb another mountain and circle around the other side to Buchboden. It was drizzling when we left, so we stopped at the edge of the tunnel and donned rain pants and gaiters, our sauna suit, in a futile attempt to keep the body parts dry that our ponchos otherwise missed. As hikers know, that's wishful thinking. Rain gear may keep out the showers—only to make you sweat so much that you get just as drenched.

Outside the last tunnel, we discovered the trail to Biberacher Hütte where we enjoyed a chat with the young cows in their pasture and a sudden, sunny break in the weather. Then we set off around Glattjöchlspitze Mountain on another one of those shifting scree paths at 1900 meters, just a half-meter wide, which drops off to a chasm below. Although we were certainly used to them by then, we ran into a German couple out for a day-hike. They were a disaster waiting to happen.

It was obvious the woman was bothered by heights. Not a mild fear, but an "OH, MY GOD, DON'T LOOK DOWN" bloodcurdling terror. Her poor, chivalrous husband had to lead her by the arm past the most difficult section, and then return to fetch his own pack—just as the heavy rains hit once again.

That downpour turned our path into a muddy slip & slide. The large rocks littering our path were slicker than snake spit and we maneuvered the best we could, using Nordic poles as anchors. Still, it was slow going as the winds howled and the rain grew in furor. Eventually we reached Ischgamelalpe, an old Celtic settlement, and ducked into a barn for cover while the other couple continued down a steep path toward Buchboden in hammering rain. For once, we were in no particular hurry. We waited until it let up before continuing more sensibly down a gravel forest road.

All along the way, we passed prime examples of what they call the traditional "three-step agriculture" used throughout the Große Walsertal Valley. For centuries in the spring, families and their cattle moved up from their lower valley farmsteads to the "Maisäß" for about three weeks. Then their cattle continued up to the high alms in the summer while the family subsisted on dairy products. Unfortunately, due to mechanization and easier access to summer farms, this style of traditional farming has virtually disappeared in Walser areas.

Long, wet hours later we arrived in Buchboden, a few houses without even a market. Why was it a Via Alpina stage? Did we miss its hidden charm? A night in their only pension is out-of-the-reach for most trekkers. Besides, how would they house dozens of hikers at a time? A little dejected, with gritty resolve, we pressed on for one more hour into Sonntag, the neighboring village.

Six kilometers made a world of difference since we found a cozy, affordable *zimmer* with a family who epitomized Austrian hospitality. They made us feel like we were home, despite looking ragged, unable to take another step, with our morale at its lowest point in weeks.

At dawn, we awoke to freezing rain and fresh snowfall on the surrounding summits. It was a sign. Without hesitation, Cheryl and I decided to stay put for a day, running outside just long enough for a trip to the market to restock supplies. And why not? It'd been almost three weeks since I'd had a day off the trail. I'd lost my edge. Anyway, there was plenty to do indoors. We needed to re-jigger our itinerary to catch the Via Alpina Swiss green route. We finally had Wi-Fi access for two entire days and were able to communicate with the outside world, especially our friend Pete, who we'd planned to meet in Linthal. All was good.

Then again, it was anyone's guess when winter would arrive. By the looks of the fresh white powder that morning in mid-July, it could be any day.

Finally the rain passed, if only for a little while. It was simply cloudy the following morning. Much of the recent snow had already disappeared. For once, we took our time enjoying a huge breakfast of prosciutto, seeded rolls, yogurt with chocolate, hard-boiled eggs, fresh cheese and butter from their farm, coincidentally the same place we'd ducked into at Ischgamelalpe two days earlier. Their bountiful *frühstück* was fitting, since the entire valley's what they call a Große Biosphere because of its wealth of plant and animal species.

All too soon, we left the warmth of their house to trek west down valley to Feldkirch with renewed vigor. We flew along the gradual slope and it only drizzled for a short while. It was Sunday. The only sound in the valley was the pealing of the church bells, a not-so-subtle reveille to get sleepy-eyed villagers dressed and off to services. We were alone all morning until we reached St. Gerold where we were heartily greeted by a dozen uniformed men of varying ages having a smoke by the roadside.

"What's the occasion?" I asked.

"It is the eightieth anniversary of the local fire department," said one beefy fellow, his chest sparkling with medals like a Korean general. "Villagers from all around will come here to celebrate."

That explained all the passing fire trucks. Young musicians hurried by carrying brass horns and woodwinds. Decked out in ruffled white shirts, flowing black coats, hats and knickers, they looked like they'd just stepped out of an old Dutch Masters' painting. Winsome ladies, their hair wrapped in buns high atop their heads, dashed from doorways in ankle-length green Trachten dresses with laced bustier tops.

More than ever, I wished we could hang around and join in the festivities. However, we'd arranged to meet Pete the following Saturday, so we had a schedule to keep. It felt odd: a real to-do list. ("Wait, let me check my planner.") Then again, we looked forward to trekking Switzerland with a Swiss, and he promised to reveal how locals hike those legendary Alps.

All day we followed the river as the valley widened into a flat patchwork of farms, orchards and the first vineyards we'd seen since Brixen. Those same rolling hills had been inhabited since at least the Bronze Age, maybe even during prehistoric times, so they had plenty of time to get it right.

Feldkirch appeared sprawling at first compared with all the hamlets we'd crossed the past month. Yet, it offered a subtle romantic charm with its Schattenburg castle and medieval section of town. As we knew by then, the downtown visitor office would be closed on Sunday, so we went straight to the *Bahnhof* where a woman at the train office called the *Jugendherberge* or youth hostel for us. Of course, the town has a camping area, but we opted out. All too often, some bureaucrat's idea of camping is to park one trailer as close as possible to another on a concrete pad. That's roughing it. I could just imagine our tiny grey tent, vibrating, and sandwiched between two behemoth trailers as they ran their generators all night.

On the other hand, Feldkirch's hostel definitely had character. It was located in a converted infirmary dating back at least to the 1300s. Back in those days, it was far outside the city—for obvious reasons. From 1350 to 1689, the Black Death or Bubonic Plague ravaged Europe. In fact, as much as half of Feldkirch had succumbed to it. To save the rest, the ill were sent to Siechenhaus, the present-day hostel. When the Black Death disappeared after 300 years, the same building became a leper colony, a mental hospital and then a poor house. Beautifully renovated and reopened in 1985, it's somehow appropriate to now host budget travelers, another dying breed.

As we unpacked, I thought, "Oh, if these walls could talk. Then again, it's probably better if they don't."

● Bern

Switzer

● Lausanne

Adelboden

Grie
Bunda

Lenk   Kan

Lauenen
Sanetsch

Bietsch

France

Dents du Midi
3257

Le Godey

La Vare

Weisshor
4505

Ref. Tornay-Bostan

Chateau Neuf
Vernayaz
Cabane de Susanfe

Salvagny

Champex

Matterhorn
4478

Trient

Bourg-St-Pierre ▲

Ref. Moëde-Anterne

Montroc

Mont Blanc
4810 ▲

St. Leonard

Monte
46

▲

Luzern

Sargans

Linthal

Engelberg

Klausen Pass

Elm

Altdorf

Meiringen

▲ Wetterhorn 3701

nelwald
Grindelwald

▲ Finsteraarhorn 4272

ngfrau 4158

Italy

8

Beware the Föhn

NO CHAINS DRAGGED DOWN THE HALL. NO BUSTY COEDS WERE chased in slow motion across lawns. No tortured messages appeared scrawled on bathroom mirrors. Surprisingly, it was all too, ah, normal.

We left the hostel after a huge buffet breakfast and walked the short distance into town to mail our completed maps and gaiters back to Brixen. This lightened our backpacks by more than 2.5 kilos. So by then, we carried an absolute minimum, especially considering the probability we'd run into nasty weather again before our trek was over.

As we'd learned way back in Muggia, it's always hardest to find the trailhead in cities. After stopping at the visitor office for last-minute hints, we caught a path from the center of the old town headed toward Liechtenstein. It led us up a steep forest trail past the Tashi Rabten Buddhist monastery, a refuge of Tibetan culture with its own peace stupa. Then we silently wended through sleepy villages, passing no one as we climbed ever higher.

For once, the sun shone brightly and we were soon flushed with sweat. Still, I'd take that over rain any day. Before long, we started passing signs for Feldkircher Hütte, one of the last huts in western Austria. However, wouldn't you know it, the rare, sudden abundance of signs only confused us. They pointed every which way. It wasn't until we'd found the trail straight up through the forest that we were certain we'd found our path.

(Note to self: The direction is UP, always up.)

At last, gasping for air, with our hearts pounding a polka, we summited. The valley unfolded in more than breathtaking grandeur. From high above Feldkirch, we could see all the way back to Sonntag, still wrapped in snow-capped peaks. We arrived at the hut shortly after noon, just in time for a drink. I was glad we hadn't attempted to reach the cabin the night before. We'd toyed with the idea, but now I was certain it was one mountain too far.

From the little hut, we began another 400-meter climb past a satellite tower up a forest road. Alone with our thoughts in the alms, we didn't come across any other trekkers until we reached a saddle in the shadow of Drei Schwester (The Three Sisters), a mountain with its own fascinating fable.

One day, as three arrogant girls were out gathering berries on the Holy Day of our Lady, they came across a beautiful woman.

"May I have some fruit for my poor sick child?" she asked.

"Those who want berries must gather them themselves, beggar," they snapped back.

Well, this was certainly the wrong time to cop an attitude.

Surrounded by celestial light, the woman transformed into The Holy Virgin saying, "You have defiled my holy day, you have denied my request; you have stones for hearts. And as stones shall you stand here for all eternity." Bam!

In view of those same rocky sisters, we hung a sharp right and soon found ourselves at the border pass, simply marked by a small metal sign. We were suddenly in Liechtenstein, one of the world's smallest countries. Like many Alpine passes, Sarojasattel has its own turbulent history. The Swiss marched to battle via the pass during the Swabian War of 1499, and it was fought over again in the French war of 1799.

Crossing it, we made a steep trek down the other side of the mountain and had just about given up finding Gafadurahütte when Cheryl spotted smoke swirling to our east. The cabin, built by Prince Johann II as a hunting lodge, sat perched on the edge of a meadow, serenaded by the constant konk-a-donk of cowbells. Its bucolic setting was such a startling contrast to Vaduz, capital of the pocket-sized country, which lay spread out in Rheintal Valley far below.

The harried guardian swiftly led us inside where we left our boots in a special mudroom, standard in most of the huts. Then we picked out wooly grey slippers from a dozen neatly stacked on wooden racks, and were shown to the dorm where we were assigned bunk beds. Although easily accessible by road from the city, the hut wasn't crowded. Quite the contrary. At that point, only one family already shared the room with their kids, along with a couple of singles.

Listening to the guardian's odd lilt, I was intrigued by her accent. While only a valley away from Feldkirch, her speech was close to gibberish for me. She spoke the nearly extinct dialect of German Walsers who'd settled there around 1300. Even though those high Alps helped preserve their ancient dialect for 700 years, only 20-40000 Walser speakers remain in all of Europe.

Still, I had to laugh. Here we are, after weeks of intensive language study in Austria, once again like family dogs, understanding nothing, wagging tails in ignorant bliss. Plus now, everything will be priced in Swiss francs instead of euros. That'll stretch our meager budget to the breaking point.

Already we'd seen how some huts provided a bunk bed at a reasonable price and then charge as much as a fine restaurant for food. But what choice do hikers have other than to bring their own, which many huts don't allow? Don't get me wrong. I loved many of the mountain huts and appreciate all the guardians' hard work. We absolutely looked forward to arriving at the end of a long day, especially to those with a cozy ambience, camaraderie, warming fires, steamy showers and working toilets. No complaints. Hands down, they sure beat sleeping on the ground in freezing rain.

Then there are the others—places where you spend a bundle for the pleasure of sleeping side by smelly side, crammed into bunk beds with two-dozen snoring strangers in an unheated cabin with no shower, hot water, or way to clean up.

Either way, they're culturally revealing. To the question, "Boxers or briefs?" we can now categorically say, "Black briefs" for both men and women Euro hikers.

Although we left the hut at 7:00 under clear skies, it was already thundering by the time we'd made it midway down the mountain. I was glad we decided not to scale the Three Sisters in the threatening weather. Believe me, we considered it. Instead, we hit a series of switchbacks and swiftly descended into the valley until we were just outside of Vaduz. Small shops extended as far as the eye could see. Since we knew a *Jugendherberge* was nearby, we dropped into a café to see if they could give us directions. We were surprised when the clerk insisted on leading us outside by the arm and pointed down the street to a pink building.

That was easy.

Wrong, again. The hostel was closed for seven hours. On checking closer, we were shocked to find their rooms cost 58 euros (88 dollars) a night—for a youth hostel. No doubt, for youths with gold cards. By that point, we were bushed, still grimy from the day before, and fresh out of patience.

So when one of the receptionists arrived and poked her head inside, I asked, "Can we at least take a shower while we wait for you to open?"

With a look you might give a stray dog, she said, "Why don't you go next door to the swimming pool and bathe there?"

Seriously? In a pool? In Liechtenstein? What, with soap on a rope?

"Are there private rooms in town?" Cheryl asked.

"No, we don't have zimmers in Liechtenstein."

"One-star hotels? Inns?"

"They're $150 and up. Look, you could always catch the bus back to Feldkirch. They have a hostel. Austria is cheaper, you know."

We knew. We were flummoxed. (Not unusual these days.)

Never retreat, I thought. Don't go back to Feldkirch. We'll only have to catch a bus back here in the morning and it'll cost as much as our room. What to do?

Sulking down the streets of Vaduz, a sleepy bourgeois-burg, we found an information office staffed by a sympathetic woman who also ran a textile-weaving program for the disabled. She patiently called several inns for us with no luck, until I finally spotted a camping place listed in her brochure. It wasn't far and it promised bungalows. She called. The cabins were already full, but they said to come anyway. They'd find us a place.

Thankful for her help, we hiked west on the *radweg*, past the Prince's impressive castle, visible atop the hillside on a steeply sloping terrace.

"Can't we just drop in there to spend the night?" Cheryl asked.

"I'm sure they have plenty of room—if they're home."

I'd read how the royal family has only lived there since 1938 in an interesting twist of history. Some say, back in the 17th century, the Liechtenstein family sought a seat in the Reichstag or Parliament. However, they couldn't qualify since they didn't hold any territory directly under the Imperial throne. To do so, they had to buy lands without any allegiance other than to the Holy Roman Emperor. After many years, the family arranged to purchase the Lordship of Schellenberg in 1699 and Countship of Vaduz in 1712. After which, (Tah-dah!) Charles VI, Holy Roman Emperor, decreed Schellenberg and Vaduz united. Liechtenstein became a sovereign member state of the Holy Roman Empire. The Princes successfully bought the seat, but then didn't set foot in their new principality for over 120 years.

Vaduz is far from a bustling metropolis. It's more like a large village surrounded by vineyards, woodlands and fields set along the Rhine River. We soon found ourselves tracing the waterway past rustic dairy farms and fields of hay. With their simple lifestyle, it seemed even more out of place to pay first-class prices for basic rooms. I'm sure local farm folks would howl at the extravagance.

Campsites are well hidden in Liechtenstein. Although it wasn't far, we had to ask directions several times. The site sat camouflaged at the base of Mittagspitze Mountain. Since most people stayed in campers, we had the entire dorm to ourselves. It was hardly luxurious, but the showers were hot and it was quiet. Better still, it promised a fantastic night's sleep in a loft cooled by a mountain breeze under an open skylight.

Nodding off, Cheryl whispered, "Let them keep their overpriced rooms."

I could hear her wide grin even in the dark.

Breakfast was compliments of a coffee machine hit shortly before we set off tracing the *radweg* west. Before long, we found a market and dropped in for a local treat, a slice of *Leberkäse* (AKA a hot bologna loaf) spread with mustard on a Kaiser roll, while Cheryl enjoyed a nut and honey roll. After our al fresco feast, we soon rejoined the Rhine and followed it to the border.

Admittedly, Liechtenstein certainly has its good points. How many countries can you hike across in a day?

Breezing across the bridge into Switzerland, we passed a row of fluttering red flags with white crosses, and then caught a path along the opposite side of the river as it meandered through the rolling countryside and Rheintal Valley for another hour into Sargans, a pleasant village under the watchful eye of another castle. First mentioned in 765, Sargans played an important role on the trading route to Italy and Austria.

The trail led us right to the door of an outdoor shop where we bought a topo map to cover our route for the next two days. That'd take us to Linthal where we'd meet Pete, who'd promised to bring a few with him.

Then, there just remained the daily question of where to sleep? Few visitors overnighted there. A travel agency doubled as their tourism office. After we shared tales of our adventure with its manager, he called Lizabeth who runs the village's one and only bed & breakfast. A brief ramble through the old city led directly to her door.

Lizabeth was everyone's stereotypical grandma, right down to her rosy cheeks, engaging smile, sparkling blue eyes, and white hair tied up behind her head in a bun. The lively 70-something made us feel right at home, fussing over us with fresh coffee and chocolate cake before leading us to a beautiful bedroom.

So, imagine our surprise when she announced an hour later, "I have been invited by my grandchildren to '*Schlafen im Stroh*' or sleep in the straw tonight."

"What's that?"

"Oh, many people in the countryside no longer keep cows, or their animals are up in the alm for the summer. So they clean their barns, bring in fresh straw, and let people sleep under blankets."

"And people enjoy this?"

"Yes, at least I think they do," she said with a chuckle. "I've never done it before, myself." Then she hesitantly asked, "Would you mind if I join them?"

"Mind?"

Even though we'd just met, the sweet woman gave us the run of her home. Handing us her keys, she said, "Help yourselves to whatever I have in my refrigerator." Then, as an afterthought, she added, "Since I will not be here to take care of you, I will cut your rent in half, if that is okay?"

Who were we to keep a grand lady from spending quality time with her grandkids in the straw?

She proudly showed us her garden, along with her bunnies and a cat who remained well hidden. Then she insisted I grab a bike and join her for a short ride down the street. She wanted to show us exactly where we should catch the shortcut out of town in the morning.

Lizabeth, a very special lady, reminded me why I like to do these treks. It's not so much the places you see; it's the folks you meet along the path. Traveling simply, you throw yourself out into the universe with abandon, depending far on fate and the kindness of strangers. Simply put, it means trusting, letting go, and letting life unfold in a natural and beautiful way. It's a remarkable exercise.

Would we find Lizabeths in our own hometowns? Probably. Or at least I like to believe so. Maybe we all have moments to be like her—to extend a hand to strangers—if only we listen.

Cheryl and I left her place early the next morning, figuring we had a long day ahead. Were there any short ones? Her shortcut saved us valuable time. The *weg* heading straight up the hills to Mels was a real lung-burner for that time of day, but it allowed us to avoid the long switchbacks on the village road. For us, it signaled the start of a valley trek down shaded roads to Weisstannen. I hiked, lost in thought, and it wasn't long before we entered the little mountain village at the very back of the valley of the same name.

According to legend, Weisstannen hamlet got its name from a silver fir, which stood in the square where the parish church was built in 1665.

After finding the trailhead, we immediately caught an uphill path wending west, continually climbing until we reached a small cabin. At first, I thought it was the usual food hut, typically closed. But this one made fresh cheese and sausage right there, so we took advantage of the opportunity and bought meat platters to gain energy for the long climb ahead.

That was when the weather decided to take a radical change for the worse.

All of a sudden, deck chairs rearranged themselves. Farm implements flew across the yard. We were nearly lifted off the ground. A dry, down-slope south wind, or *Föhn*, began howling with a vengeance.

Now this is not your normal strong wind. No, Siree. This warm wind can blow for days at a time. This is a monster wind called a "Snow Eater" for its ability to cause avalanches and make snow melt and temperatures dramatically rise in just a few hours. This wind makes brave men weep, or, according to some psychiatrists, even go insane. Its reputation is fierce, and for weeks we'd been warned to "BEWARE THE FÖHN!"

Great, I thought. Timing's everything. All we have to do is climb this 1000-meter mountain—and descend the other side—in one piece.

We gobbled down lunch and I tucked my hat into my pack. No way was it going to stay on my head in that bluster. I tied my red kerchief over my head in a white guy's dew rag, and then Cheryl and I scurried off, passing the cabin's pigpen kept just out of sight. As tiny, pink piglets curiously poked tender snouts to the fence, we felt a little embarrassed by our latest pig-out.

I warned them, "Run! Run like the wind!" And if ever the phrase was perfect, that was the day.

As for us, we began a several hour struggle to the base of that formidable mountain. The sun and *Föhn* beat our faces raw. Nonetheless, we persevered, mimes walking into the wind, one labored step at a time until we finally reached the end of the valley. Then we wound steeply upward between still snow-clad peaks. Inching higher, we grabbed fixed steel cables secured into the face of the mountain. Facing a gale-force wind, we counted on them to keep us anchored to the ground as we pushed higher and higher, until we eventually reached a sheltered meadow.

There we paused only long enough to gulp down some energy drink, and then continued toward Foo Pass at 2223 meters. It was a slow-motion struggle. Finally, after one last determined press, we reached the crest, hugged, and wasted no time in scurrying down the opposite side.

Although we'd already summitted, I was worried. Ominous clouds sailed past at cartoonish fast-forward speed, blanketing nearby peaks. Still, this was trekking. We'd only had two speeds: slow and slower.

The thousand-meter descent added hours to what became another ten-hour trek. By the time we reached the valley floor, I ached from every muscle, plus a few I never realized I had. Ten hours was just too long for any one stage; worse when you combine several similar days back-to-back.

The village of Elm lay beneath the towering summits of the Piz Sardona, Piz Segnas, Hausstock, and Kärpf Mountains. After arriving at the edge of the small village, it only took us one look at what they comically call a campground, a toilet cabinet nestled in a mud bog, for us to decide to find a room. One kind elderly lady phoned several private zimmers for us, but they were filled. So, she called the visitor office who agreed to stay open late.

Still, it was an awkward dance. Even though they were a stage on the Via Alpina, Elm had no facilities for budget backpackers. Hotels were expensive, B&Bs little better. The dorm was chock-a-block with kids in a summer sports program. Hey, we were even tempted to sleep in a pint-sized log cabin in their playground, but decided against it at the last minute, not wanting to be roused at midnight by some over-eager night watchman. Eventually, we decided to hitch to Matt, just off the trail down valley where rooms were a little more affordable. Finding our hotel was another matter.

On our way there, we passed a rundown *zimmer* with an Elvis GRACE- LAND MANOR sign tacked outside. They had a sense of humor. We knocked on the door. A grizzled, chubby fellow decked out in long underwear answered. The only thing missing was the banjo pickin' boy from the film *Deliverance*.

"DUNKA-DUNG-DUNG-DUNG."

"Gotta room?" I asked.

He scratched his chin, chewed it over for a long moment, mumbled to his wife inside, scratched his stubbled jaw again, and then slowly nodded.

"Take 50 euros?"

Sight unseen, it was probably twenty too much, but we were beat.

He tilted back his head as if lost in thought; he didn't say a word, only shuffled off to show us the room. It was pitch-black inside, yet warm and it didn't reek, all that mattered by then—except his price which was pure fantasy.

The fat fellow refused to budge off his equally robust price of more than a hundred bucks. Odd. We'd seen it before in small villages that get few travelers. It baffled us. Why would folks, who look like they could use the business, rather see their place sit empty than rent it at a reasonable price?

Dejected, we finally arrived at our own falling-star hotel, just in time for the daily thunder and heavy rains to commence once more.

The next morning we caught an easy ride back into Elm. After stopping at their market for breakfast, it was late by the time we finally hit the trail. Cheryl wanted to hike along the road that morning, but we'd agreed to catch the mountain path if the weather was good, an unlikely occurrence, but stranger things had happened. So, after a little grumbling, on near-empty bellies (and no, it wasn't the cheese talkin'), we set off up another steep trail and reached the ski resort and its gondola restaurant in slightly over an hour. Since we moved in slow motion, we had some soup and split a sandwich. Then all too soon we were off on another climb up yet another mountain with little to differentiate it from the last dozen.

Surprisingly, switchbacks were already less common than in Austria and there weren't as many huts, but their horseflies were more ravenous.

We continued our climb all morning. It was early afternoon when we finally reached a summit. Now normally, this was the occasion for a brief cele- bration. However, we soon realized this was not Richetlipass as we'd hoped. Crestfallen, we still had to climb down the mountain into a caldera, cross it, and then climb back up the other side. To make matters even trickier, our final climb to 2261 meters was straight up out of a meadow minefield of manure.

Ah, the murky, messy, untold story of hardworking Swiss cows.

On the crest, we ran into the first hiker we'd met in a very long time. Jesse, a friendly Dutch kid with a large pack, also trekked the Via Alpina green route but just for a week or two. While comparing notes, he said he'd also had trouble finding affordable places to sleep each night.

"In fact," he admitted with a chuckle, "I slept in a kid's cabin in the Elm playground last night."

I liked the kid already.

"Hey, good for you. We eyed the same one."

The path leading down off the mountaintop was a knee-crunching slide through a pasture of sheep dung. It was the bucolic home of a hundred wooly wonders, along with a few newborns whose mothers grunted menacingly as we neared. Plus it held a mosaic of multi-hued rocks promising to end your fall—head first, if necessary. The recent rains had made it precariously slick.

And the only thing worse than arriving to your room soaking-wet is arriving soaking-wet and reeking of sheep manure.

We no sooner left the sheep-patties than they were replaced by sharp slate that seemed even more slippery after all the rainfall. Even though we carefully picked our way down the mountainside, at one point I heard a muted thud and muffled yelp. Cheryl took one misstep and landed spread-eagled with a face full of thistles, her ego more bruised than anything else. At least, she hadn't tumbled off the mountain, or plopped an hour earlier in the poopy pasture.

Our thousand-meter descent ended two hours later in the village of Linthal at 662 meters, just as the deluge struck once again. I expected to see an ark floating down the street. Our legs were jellified. Our bellies were empty. We hustled double-time to a hotel where they gave us a room up in the attic. It was filled with immigrant workers in cubbyholes reminiscent of those I'd seen in photos of the Underground Railroad. But at least we were safe from the storm; plus their restaurant served an excellent meatloaf with sauerkraut, potatoes and soup, which silenced our grumbles once again.

After a big breakfast and under perpetually cloudy skies, we set off for the train station where we met our easy-going friend Pete who'd finally arrived. Although he'd promised sunny skies for weeks, some things are outside our control. With one look at the foggy, drizzling weather, he quickly suggested a practical alternative to more glassy trails.

We'd begin our trek from Braunwald, a scenic non-motorized ski village overlooking Linthal. Starting there allowed us a more level and drier trek to

Urnerboden, especially wise considering how much more it'd rained during the night. After stopping for a quick drink in Nüssbuel, the three of us trekked the high road along the Fätschbach River for the remaining two-hour stretch to Urnerboden, a miniature village set at the base of Klausen Pass.

Upon entering, we noticed the oddest statues of roosters throughout the village, even one high atop a pole. If it were Africa, I'd say they're into cock worship. But as it was Switzerland, there had to be a more rational reason.

Then again, maybe not.

They say that long ago, back when it was time to set the canton's border between Glarus and Uri, the villagers made a wager. At the first rooster's crow, one runner from each of those villages would take off along a path. The border would be set at the point where they met. Well, the crafty people of Uri starved their rooster, while Glarus made sure theirs' was well fed. As a result, Uri's ravenous cock crowed at the crack of dawn, while the Glarus rooster slept in. So, Uri's runner covered more ground and claimed much more territory, including Urnerboden, before their runner even woke up. I can imagine this was a little upsetting. In fairness to the Glarus sprinter, Uri's contender agreed to let the other fellow carry him back uphill as far as he could. That'd become their border. Today, the present boundary is set where the Glarus runner collapsed—dead.

Like I said, maybe it wasn't so sensible after all.

Even with more territory, we couldn't find a place to stay in town. There was no room at its sole inn, so we opted to head up Klausen Pass and sleep on its 1955-meter summit. It was a smart choice. Otherwise, it would've taken us several hours in the morning to reach the crest, only to have to continue to Altdorf, back down another valley.

The humble two-storey inn is a landmark, although an unusual one. Take a hotel with a turn-of-the century décor and chamber pots, and combine it with the stumbling funhouse tilt of the *Titanic*. Heavy winter snows have shifted the hotel on its rock foundation and its hallways run downhill into the front rooms. So much so, its old-fashioned beds should come equipped with seat belts (instead of life preservers).

Ah, but the vista and sunset were heart stopping. You could see forever. That is, until dense clouds swiftly encased the mountaintop and promised still more rain.

Miracle of miracles, it cleared just in time for our morning chocolate croissants! Maybe we should credit Cheryl. The day before, she'd made a bet with Pete, who insisted it'd be sunny (yea, a sucker bet) and she easily won.

He shrugged it off, chuckling, "Oh, no, I meant tomorrow." So maybe he'd brought sunshine after all.

For once, we set off in glorious sunlight along a gentle *Höhenweg* running along a terrace above the same valley as the Via Alpina, only higher, offering a more panoramic view. The trail undulated along a mountain ridge covered with wildflowers and wild seniors out for a Sunday hike in the country. Everyone wished us "*Grüezi*" (another version of "*Grüß Gott*"), with a smile to all they passed. We even met two women yodeling to their husbands up ahead. If it was a gentle reminder to "Pick up milk at the alm," it's the sweetest way to give a "honey-do" list ever invented.

For once, we took our time on the trail and frequently stopped without worrying we'd arrive too late and find the visitor office closed. It was Sunday. That was a given. We even paused to share silly, intimate moments with young, grey, fuzzy-eared cows.

"Is that milk I smell on your breath?"

Rushing was out of the question. Pete's backpack, holding enough food for weeks, weighed twice as much as ours. Consequently, our friend taught us to take more breaks, which we dubbed "Mini-Merzs" in his honor. Then again, he also reminded us to slow down and appreciate the scenery—and especially the many quaint mountain restaurants along the way.

"It's the Swiss way of hiking," he insisted with a contagious smile, and who were we to argue? At one hut, our tow-headed friend introduced us to a Swiss soda, practically the national drink, made from milk serum. Whatever that is? Then we shared a wooden platter of sliced sausage and dried, smoked beef similar to prosciutto that's sliced as thin as the Dead Sea scrolls, as well as a variety of fresh, creamy alpine cheeses served with sweet gherkins, brown bread and dark mustard.

Now that's what I call 'culture,' a delicious one at that.

By late that lazy afternoon, we arrived beside a pond with yet another restaurant. After catching our breath and some long-missed sunshine, we discovered time was tight after all, since Pete needed to make his train connection back home. So we left in a rush to catch the Eggbergen gondola down to the tranquil lakeside village of Flüelen. Earlier, he'd phoned its campground to reserve a room for us in their trailers, but they'd claimed to be full. Imagine our surprise when Cheryl and I appeared on their doorstep and were ushered to a bungalow for the night. It was pure serendipity.

Then again, we probably looked so bedraggled they felt sorry for us.

Either way, before he left, the three of us unwound in a café beside picture-perfect Lake Lucerne, where verdant mountains plunge to placid water.

Before leaving, Pete left a parting gift: his practical ways.

"See Switzerland like the Swiss do," he suggested with a sly grin. "If there's a gondola, we take them up to the trailheads to save time."

Although we were reluctant, that made too much sense. It just might keep us off some of the busiest roads. In our case, maybe it meant we could avoid more ten and twelve-hour days. Why, even the Via Alpina PDF guide suggested catching gondolas or chairlifts to connect some stages.

Besides, I thought, there are no hard and fast rules on this trail. After all, this isn't a pilgrimage, a thousand-year-old path marked every 50 meters with a scallop shell or arrow. There are no places to have your *credencial* stamped each night to prove you were there. This trail is walking jazz, wild and fresh each day.

Improvisation. Yea, we need to remember that.

9

WHEN COWS FLY

ETE HAD BROUGHT THE SUN WITH HIM. WE WOKE TO ANOTHER clear morning, yet it was tough to get our bodies to leave the campground. The past week of overlong hikes had drained our strength and only pure willpower kept us moving westward.

After grabbing a sandwich and coffee, we headed across town to Attinghausen then up to Brusti. From there, the five of us, two bicyclists, an older hiker, Cheryl and I, began our steep continual climb toward the well-traveled Surenen Pass at 2291 meters. Traveled since the 1200s, it has its own unique fable.

A young shepherd was so fond of his lamb he decided to baptize it. (No doubt, he'd been in the mountains far too long.) Much to his obvious surprise, doing so transformed it into a monster Greis that killed the kid, townspeople, cattle, and made the alm uninhabitable. Well, you can't have a monster mucking about your meadow. As these stories go, a passing student heard of the creature and told the locals to raise a silver-white bull. During its first year, the calf was to be fed milk from one cow, in the second from two and so on. On its ninth year, it was led by a Waldnacht virgin to the pass and released. The massive bull charged and met the Greis at a stream. A hideous fight started. The earth trembled. When the dust cleared, the terrified farmers returned to find both the monster and powerful bull sprawled lifeless at the brook. In memory ever since, that water has been called Stierenbach or "stream of the bull."

Without a single Greis in sight, we couldn't help but feel revived by the sun and crisp mountain air. All went well until we reached the saddle just below the pass where we ran into another massive snowfield amid boulders. Since I could clearly see trail markers on its other side, we forged ahead and continued up the left side to the summit where we ran into Jesse, the climbing Dutchman. We hadn't seen him since Linthal and knew he'd soon head home.

So far, that was one major difference with the Via Alpina. Many folks didn't hike it as a thru-trail in the tradition of the Appalachian Trail, as we'd originally expected. It was more a path they'd sample for a week or two, and then sensibly return home to nurse aches, pains and blistered feet.

From its crest, we began a four-hour descent through a stunning Alpine landscape. Although snow-capped peaks glistened in the sun, water was always in short supply. We were often tempted to refill our bottles from its many streams, but hesitated. After spotting a flock of camouflaged sheep grazing on a nearby snowfield, I was glad we'd held off. Like I said, giardia is not your best hiking companion.

As usual, it was late afternoon by the time we reached Engleberg, a ski resort with a 12th century Benedictine cloister. Assuming they'd updated the original plumbing, we thought it'd be interesting to bunk there as I'd often done on earlier treks to Jerusalem and Rome. They're guaranteed to be quiet. But no such luck. The nuns politely shooed us two scruffy backpackers off, and we ended up trudging across town to a private hostel.

It appeared normal enough from the outside, until we poked our heads through the door. A bizarre wailing echoed down the shadowy corridor. We sneaked around the corner and spotted a group chanting in some mystifying tongue. They swayed from side-to-side to a primal music, amid tambourines and drumbeats. To me it all looked a little Indiana Jones-ish. I half-expected the curtains to part to reveal the sacrificial bonfire. In fact, we were ready to dart out of there when a dark, mysterious man approached, disarming us with a smile.

"Is the manager around?" I hesitantly asked.

"We haven't seen him for hours," the Sri Lankan explained. "But if you need a room and don't mind, you can sleep in one of ours.'"

That's bighearted of him, I thought.

My partner and I glanced at each other and quickly agreed. Besides, at that late hour, what choice did we have? After showing us to the group's spare room, we were equally shocked when he said, "Come, have dinner with us. We have fixed plenty."

"No, that's okay," I said, and he genuinely looked disappointed.

Reluctant to accept any more of his generosity, we trekked to the village market to stock up on supplies. Then later, relaxing with the group in the dining room, we gave them some of our nectarines for all their help. In return, we were pleasantly surprised when they brought us a plate of fried chicken and rice (not monkey brains).

Kidding aside, that's another aspect of trekking I enjoy. Even though we have different nationalities, languages, culture, politics, and sometimes-odd cuisine, the simple act of sharing food at the end of a tiring day creates bridges and allows us to see each other simply as fellow travelers walking this path called life.

By morning, Engleberg was draped in a dense fog. At least, we told ourselves, it isn't raining—not yet. We expected another tough hike to Trüebsee Lake and were not disappointed.

Squinting to view it for the first time through the clinging mist, Cheryl sang out, "It must be bee-yoo-ti-ful on a clear day."

Given the string of bad weather, that was our running joke.

"Yea, maybe we should stay and linger awhile," was my classic reply.

We continued our steep ascent to Jochpass at 2207 meters. Once we cleared it, the skies did as well, revealing sparkling Engstlensee. From the lake, we decided to sail straight down the mountain to Meiringen, or so we thought.

If ever there was a time to "linger," this was it. The valley was magnificent, otherworldly, an emerald Rivendell, and likewise it drew us like Gollum to "My Precious." At one point, we counted fifteen sets of waterfalls. But it soon became apparent we'd picked a bad time to color outside the lines.

It took us hours to arrive at the valley floor and then several more along a mountain road to reach the village of Innertkirchen. For far too long only its beauty sustained us, until we eventually limped into Meiringen. We were in sad shape. First, our knees had been pummeled by the steep descent off the mountain, and then our feet felt like they'd been pounded with bamboo rods by the asphalt trail. Town was a reprieve.

Meiringen was popular with travelers as early as 1234. Nowadays, its identity is more linked to the tales of Sherlock Holmes and death of Moriarty at nearby Reichenbach Falls. It swarms with Arthur Conan Doyle groupies. Pubs serve authentic English breakfasts—or so the signboards claim.

"Two Sherlock Scrambles with Watson Waffles to go, please."

A scramble out of Meiringen is a heart-pounding way to start any day. Even though the trail began just steps from our room, we traipsed all the way back into town from the albergue or hostel to the visitor office to find out. With the detour, we had a late start heading toward Grosse Scheidegg, passing the famous waterfalls along the way. After yesterday's long stretch, Cheryl grumbled under her breath at the prospect of slogging another eight hours up another mountain to Grindelwald. Of course, I shared her pain, but there are few villages in between to make a shorter day.

Then again, we couldn't have asked for a more beautiful summer morning. For as commercial as the village had been, the mountain was wild and pristine.

While the trail wended farther into dense, dark forest, an exceptional panorama gradually unfolded. Schreckhorn Mountain, the canton's highest peak at 4078 meters, was jaw-droppingly revealed.

It was about that time we ran into a fellow-trekker, a Belgian with a crusty, well-seasoned look. Hugo was a gregarious Irish wolfhound of a fellow with a scraggly beard and piercing blue eyes. Gaunt and all legs, he was also trekking the Via Alpina and left Trieste just a week before us. I was surprised we hadn't already met him after nearly two months on the trail.

The three of us hiked together all day, laughing and swapping stories, especially about our life-changing experiences on the world's trails. Hugo knew adversity. He'd hiked the difficult Pacific Crest Trail from Mexico to British Columbia through the Rockies and across Death Valley.

Like us, he was baffled by the lack of signage at times on the Via Alpina and difficulty in finding affordable places to bed down. Unlike us, he preferred wild camping, just pitching his tent in a meadow or forest whenever the mood hit. Although its bohemian sound appealed to me, we'd already been warned. Camping's highly regulated in the Alps. Maybe sometimes we could pitch our tent at dusk, but we'd have to strike camp at daybreak. That'd be a hassle. Plus we'd have to carry all our food and stove fuel, too.

Then again, we'd miss the huts, the villages, plus what culture (mostly drinking songs) we discovered at those altitudes. And to be totally honest, I could think of few things so depressing as camping in the driving rain for forty plus days. Call me spoiled, but I'll readily admit I looked forward to a hot shower at the end of the day.

Hugo, the eccentric mountain man, swore he preferred to bathe in cold streams or lakes.

"Good for my legs," he claimed, pointing down to sinewy limbs sticking out of skintight mini-shorts that'd be ruled obscene in certain southern states.

The three of us eventually reached Grosse Scheidegg summit at 1962 meters. Its hut swarmed with hikers, mostly folks who'd arrived by bus, since we'd seen few on the trail. I still had a hard time getting used to that unique form of mountaineering. Maybe it's just my tick talking, but it sometimes got under my skin.

On one hand, I figured it opened up the "mountain experience" to anyone who could afford to step onto a bus and fork-over a hearty fare. On the other, it's exasperating to slog up what you think is a primeval mountain, pick your way across scree for hours, often in the rain or fog, and to endure gnawing hunger and unquenchable thirst—only to arrive to the smell of diesel; to find a secluded hut inundated with a hundred bus passengers who've come up for the day, who eagerly pay a small fortune for a cheese plate or kitschy pen with a sliding gondola, and who look aghast at your sweaty appearance.

After a quick snack we began our rapid descent to Grindelwald, a village that's hosted travelers since the 17th century. As we put our knees through their grinding paces, Hugo demonstrated his unique way of descending steep passes—his "seductive duck walk," as he called it. He lowered his center of gravity into a half-squat and turned out his feet. Then with a giggle of glee, wiggling his butt side-to-side, he waddled down the trail.

All afternoon the three of us sexily duck-walked down lush hills in the shadow of a glacier rising before us. For once, we had the foresight to reserve beds at a "*Schlafen im Stroh.*" We figured it'd be similar to the place where Lizabeth met her grandkids. Besides, I was eager to discover the Swiss fascination with bedding down in a barn.

After arriving in the busy tourist center of Grindelwald, we called the young woman running the straw hotel who came to pick us up, as her place was far outside of town. As it turned out, her bunkroom with straw mattresses was already jam-packed for the night, so she led us downstairs into her modern dairy barn. The stalls appeared to have been recently washed and clean straw was thrown down in frames on the concrete floor. Nevertheless, there was still a faint, unmistakable, head-clearing aroma.

It's Switzerland. Why can't it be chocolate? Or fondue?

Since it was already nearly dark and it'd be impossible to find another place, the three of us surrendered to the experience. We rolled sleeping bags on top of the straw and then hung wet clothes across a line used for tying up the cows' tails so they don't "soil" themselves.

(Episode II revealing the secret lives of dairy cows.)

Then we took a shower and ate outside on picnic tables before calling it a night—when the flies feasted on us.

All in all, I have to admit it wasn't a half-bad experience. True, our eyes watered from the faint l'eau de urine as we tossed and turned in the straw, but sleep wasn't entirely elusive. Besides, it was an authentic bit of culture for today's jaded travelers—all for the price of a pension.

The next morning, looking around that farm, I couldn't help but notice the hubbub of frenzied activity in Grindelwald below. What a contrast to the quiet alms we'd grown to cherish. We'd already seen it far too often across six countries. For decades now, the self-sufficient mountain family who's survived centuries of harsh winters, hunger, disease and disappointments has left their pastures behind and moved into villages for a better life. Or, if they stayed, many have seen their village transformed from a collective of farms, a community, into another Alpineland where residents sell magical marmot oil elixir to tourists. They've turned from herding cows to herding visitors.

I realize some will think this is an economic necessity in today's world. They'll say, "Good riddance" and embrace the so-called easier life. But how much has been sacrificed in the name of progress? Maybe it's just my tick talkin', but it seems something integral to Alpine life has changed and been lost forever: a traditional lifestyle, a fierce independence.

After a filling farm breakfast, we were fortified and headed up the mountain to soon rejoin the Via Alpina. We left Hugo back at the barn to take care of last-minute details. Besides, with his meter-long stride, I figured he'd soon pass us in a cloud of dust on the trail.

One helpful feature of Swiss trail signs is their approximate hiking time to summits, huts, and villages. It can make you feel mighty satisfied when you actually arrive ahead of when the sign predicts. That is, until you remember their times are formulated using an exacting Swiss formula based, we were told, on the hiking times of Swiss grandmothers. Then again, if all Alpine grannies were as fit as Lizabeth, we shouldn't feel bad.

Reaching the top of Kleine Scheidegg ahead of schedule for a change, I was pleased our ascents were finally getting easier. Then again, they should after sixty days of climbing every day. Hugo arrived shortly after we did. Following a break to wolf down fruit and chocolate beside its out-of-place train station, we began our swift descent.

The surrounding mountains and their glaciers were clouded over and I expected the nagging daily rain to hit again, but it passed and before long we reached the car-free mountain village of Wengen.

Abruptly stopping, Hugo said, "I want to stay behind here a while."

"Why?"

"Because my mother has a towel from here," he said, as if it made all the sense in the world. Given his logic, I guess a personal visit to China was long overdue. But that was Hugo, an enigma wrapped in a cotton towel.

After making plans to meet him that night in Gimmelwald, Cheryl and I made a swift descent to Lauterbrunnen, nestled in a deep Alpine valley. The village drapes both sides of the Weisse Lütschine River. It's an exquisite setting bound to inspire writers, both the famous and more obscure. In 1779, Goethe was so impressed by its waterfall that he wrote his poem "Song of the Spirits Over the Waters." How could I compete with that?

At the end of this vale, up on the cliffside, lay the even smaller community of Gimmelwald where we planned to overnight. Staring face-to-face with the Mönch, Eiger and Jungfrau Mountains, Cheryl and I had stayed there off and on for a decade or more. It was our refuge from the world—even from the excesses of travel. After a quick stop at the market for wine, pasta and tomato sauce, Alpine essentials, we trekked to the end of the valley along a quiet, shaded pedestrian *weg*, and then caught the gondola for the short ride up to the mountain hostel.

Sitting outside on its deck, surrounded by the incredible panorama, I once again felt the energy, a stoic invincibility, emanate from the rocky triumvirate. No, I wouldn't be climbing it this time, but felt fortunate just to witness its power once more. Actually, the first ascent to the Eiger's 3970-meter summit was made in 1858, but its north face was impenetrable until 1938 when Heckmair, Vörg, Kasparek and Heinrich Harrer succeeded.

After a few hours, Hugo arrived in the dark. Having trekked up the mountain, he missed Gimmelwald altogether, and then came back down the path from Mürren. However, his persistence was rewarded with hearty leftovers from folks who'd cooked far more than even they could eat at one sitting.

Gulping it down it on one breath, he smiled in canine satisfaction.

As for us, Cheryl and I decided to take our long-awaited time-off up there. We spent the next day hiking to tiny Mürren through steep, terraced pastures to stock up on provisions. The highest Bernese Oberland village populated year-round, Mürren has long been a skier's dream, but maybe it's best known for the James Bond film *On Her Majesty's Secret Service* shot atop the mountain's revolving restaurant. For a change of pace, we poked around the relaxed car-free village. I even took advantage of their sports complex and melted for an hour in their whirlpool, a soak making everything all right again in the world.

Just one incident marred our visit. I'd left my best pair of hiking socks hanging to dry in our dorm room. When we returned to the hut, they were gone. Vanished!

"Now, who in their right mind would want to nick my smelly socks?"

Cheryl shot me a look as though the answer was obvious. "I'd guess one of these girls was grossed out by the odor and just tossed them out when no one was looking."

Really? It remains a mystery to this day. If anyone happens to find a pair of green wool hiking socks that appeared in their backpack quite by accident in Gimmelwald, please send them home. No questions asked.

The following day was a holiday. Swiss National Day commemorates the founding of the Confederation in 1291. In that year, a historic alliance was reached between the cantons of Uri, Schwyz and Unterwalden against the Hapsburgs who tried to take the strategic region leading to Gotthard Pass. Men from those cantons swore eternal allegiance to one another and Switzerland was built over the next 500 years around that genesis. And in typical Swiss fashion, we celebrated—by climbing another mountain.

From Mürren a trail leads straight up to Gimmela. I'm sorry to report our day off had the opposite effect of what we'd hoped for. Instead of feeling reinvigorated, our legs were lead weights. I nursed a hyperextension running through the arch of my right foot, yet plowing forward, always forward, we left Gimmelwald before our frisky friend and met again only briefly at a trailside café. All too soon, Cheryl and I set off again to begin a long, steep slog up crumbling slate to Sefinenfurgge Gap at over 2612 meters. While we took our time to warily place each footstep, Hugo bounded past only to meet us again on its summit.

There, high above the clouds, we also ran into two young Frenchmen who'd hiked the Via Alpina for four days. Switzerland with its higher-than-usual peaks, had to be the toughest place to start. One already lamented not bringing Nordic poles.

"I used to laugh at people who use those sticks," he confessed. "But no more. On this trail, people two and three times my age pass me like I'm standing still. And they're all using sticks. I'm going to buy a pair when I get home—if I make it that far."

All too soon, they set off in the opposite direction while we began a slow, deliberate climb down across shifting scree. Even though Hugo trotted down the mountainside like a horse headed back to the barn for dinner, we actually arrived in Griesalp village before he did and easily found the *Naturfreundhaus*.

It's a practical tradition to take off your boots at the door and slip into house slippers, so I donned the largest, robin-egg blue, Papa Smurf plastic clogs I could find and clopped into the cabin. The cozy place was already nearly filled and Cheryl and I were awarded their last bed in a room just large enough for a mattress and window. But it did have an interesting theme. Bovine sheets matched the milk-makers grazing just outside. Then again, what the room lacked in size was easily made up for by the big doings planned for the evening.

They'd prepared a sumptuous buffet of ham, cheese, grated salads, pudding, and *rösti*, the hearty Swiss dish of grated potatoes similar to hash browns, sometimes prepared with cheese, onions or apples. We were hardly alone. Hugo dragged in at dusk since he'd stopped just outside the village to soak in an icy stream. The entire village was there as well, decked-out in their finery, filling every seat on the terrace overlooking the valley and opposite hills. There was even an oompah band playing accordions, horns and drums—in-between making the rounds to joke and drink with friends in the audience.

Well, for half-starved hikers, the buffet was beyond our wildest fantasy. While I was certainly no shirker at the buffet table, Hugo helped himself to five plates of food, which grew more inspired as the evening wore on. Once he even topped a heaping plate of sliced ham and potatoes with pudding and whipped cream, which he ate with gusto.

It was nearly 10:30 before the fireworks began. Huge bonfires blazed on the surrounding hillsides. Some say they celebrate the expulsion of foreign bailiffs in the 14th century when fires spread hot news in those days before CNN. However, I liked another person's more passionate version: The fires symbolize the burning of the remaining French and Austrian noblemen's castles.

Although clouds already gathered the next morning, the *Naturfreundhaus* guardian predicted it wouldn't rain until afternoon. Unfortunately, she was wrong, so very wrong. As we set off on another steep climb to Kandersteg, dark clouds swarmed in. We were in for another rough trek.

By 9:30, we reached a gastehäus and enviously peeked in as diners still enjoyed their casual *frühstück*. Little did they know a tempest grew outside. Still, ever optimistic, we hoped we could make it over the mountain and down the other side before it struck, so we continued racing up the narrow trail toward the summit. Even after it began spitting rain, we still held out hope that it'd pass. It had happened before. But after finally throwing on our ponchos, we only continued a short distance before the first flash of lightning lit the sky and a crash of thunder shook the ground.

"Dammit, that was close."

Suicidal to continue, we rushed 150 meters back down the mountain to a farm, figuring it wisest to wait it out there. Just as the full-on pummeling began, we ducked under the dairy's front awning. We'd just made it. Within seconds, the rain turned to sleet. In August!

Inside, Cheryl and I joined others waiting out the storm as the hours crawled by. The fog would burn off and we thought it was clearing, only to see it turn black again. Shortly after noon, it was clear we were stuck there for the night. Even if the storm did pass, by then the trail across slate and scree would be dangerously slick. Who knew when the rain and fog would return? When we were on the summit? During our descent from 2700 meters? No, we opted to stay at the farm where we rented mattresses in a dorm above the stables.

As it was bitter cold outside, for hours we shared a snug room with a group of kids. They'd come from cities to work at the farm for several weeks and experience country life. Some led the cows to pasture, others milked them, while a few mucked stalls or cleaned the outhouse, since there was no inside toilet or shower. They received little pay, yet that wasn't important. From their enthusiasm, you could see they simply enjoyed life up there.

The day wore on. Out of boredom, we retreated upstairs to the mattresses for a bizarre symphony. With eighty cows directly below, a nonstop cowbell cacophony bombarded us like a berserk Balinese barong orchestra and sleep was impossible.

The evening picked up after we joined the family sitting around their kitchen table in the warmth and glow of their woodstove. As we shared the story of our journey so far, they served homemade meringues topped with cream. Eventually they asked if we'd like dinner and Cheryl and I were eager to sample the delicious products made right on their farm: Emmental cheese, ricotta, several types of herbed goat cheese, salami, a pimento loaf, and homemade butter and bread. Soon we felt like we were just friends dropping by on another stormy night. We read their old newspapers, checked on the weather forecast, and practiced our mangled German, less perfect than ever in the secluded valley with its singsong dialect.

Eventually we hesitantly climbed the stairs to the dorm expecting more of the same, but were relieved to find they let out their cows at night to graze. During the day, the flies are too relentless, covering their faces in a black fluttering mask. So, our room was peaceful. Our only challenge in the dark was to sneak past ol' wild Willy, their amorous bull, to make it to the outhouse.

We packed up at dawn, anxious to climb the mountain before it sleeted, hailed, snowed, or rained horny toads. Only more lightning would deter us. The early hour allowed us to tour their cheese factory, or *käserei*, with its large copper cauldron, and then watch the family and city kids as they rounded up eighty head of cattle from the pasture.

It was a study in controlled chaos. Their tiny orange dog ran the show. He nipped at the cows' heels as he drove them back into the barn, helped by yelps from the others. One quiet city kid with a crew cut particularly impressed us. He strutted across the yard like a major-domo in his rubber boots, waving his stick as he herded the cows into their proper doorways. When one particularly headstrong calf hopped the rope barricade and threatened to sit on the family car, he wasted no time in letting it know who was boss. And the ear-to-ear grin on his glowing round face told us he'd found his calling.

It was far from sunny when we finally began our rushed ascent and we were only halfway up the Hohtürli Pass, the highest point on the Swiss Via Alpina, when fog abruptly rolled in. That complicated things. The scree-littered trail was difficult to find, so I frequently turned around to make sure Cheryl was still behind me, but she bravely plowed forward. The final set of a hundred or so slippery stairs carved into stone were particularly daunting, but within two hours, we hugged on its breathtaking summit.

Imagine our surprise when we heard a familiar voice and turned to see Hugo and two fellow Walloons he'd met headed our way.

"Hey, where've you been?" I shouted.

"After that huge dinner, I slept-in at the *Naturfreundhaus*," he said with a laugh, "and didn't leave until two in the afternoon when the weather cleared."

"Timing's everything. We were worried when we didn't see you. Thought you were stuck in that mess."

"No, I spent a comfortable night up here in the hut," he said, pointing across the scree to the stone refuge.

"With that lightning, I'm surprised it survived."

"Yes, we heard that a house down in Griesalp was hit," Cheryl added, "and burned to the ground last night."

Life is just that tenuous in the Alps.

Although we were above the timberline, we were far from out of the woods. We no sooner cleared the summit than it began to rain again, light at first, then strong enough to force us back into our dreaded ponchos. This turned the already wet trail into a muddy mess. Each step had to be carefully placed. Otherwise, you'd fall on your butt, as I managed to do anyway. Waterfalls gushed in furious torrents. We leapt on stones across pools at the base of each one.

At one point, seeking warmth, we dropped into a hut for drinks and ran into a group of friendly English Scouts who were in the high country for a day hike. Even though they were drenched to the bone and trekking without ponchos or sticks, they were in seventh heaven. We ran into them later scampering down the trail, oblivious to it all.

That afternoon we skirted Blüemlisalp Glacier, which according to fable was once a meadow so fertile that its cows gave milk three times a day. Each summer a young farmer moved to the mountain with his large herd. One day, to prevent his new wife from walking over rocks, he built a pathway of cheese from the hut to the storehouse. It was paved with butter and rinsed clean each day with milk. When the farmer's mother learned of his odd building project, she visited to scold him. Arriving thirsty, she asked for a cup of milk. Well, the son, egged on by his wife's laughter, only gave her a mug of whey—worse than skim milk in those days—and then they mocked her. She left outraged, but not before cursing the alm, willing it to be covered by eternal ice. She'd hardly left when part of the glacier slid off the mountain, covering the meadow, people, cows and huts under ice. Even today, some claim the son's cries and mooing of his cows can still be heard.

At the base of the mountain, we passed huge Öschinensee Lake. It's surrounded by an interesting open-air museum of statues crafted by local artists. "Must be beautiful when the sun's shining," we sighed in unison, but it was invisible in that blinding fog.

For once, it was surprisingly early when Cheryl and I arrived in Kandersteg in Kandertal Valley. Back in the Middle Ages, cattle were driven through there on their way to the Wallis region, while salt was brought from the other direction. I didn't envy them. It'd taken us two days to do one stage in the foul weather. The five of us, Cheryl, the Walloons, and I spent the night in a dorm room next to a campground. At least, it was warm and protected.

In the morning, we gathered our clothes from the drying room and left to find breakfast before continuing through the clouds. Although we loaded up on liquids and even had our last treasured energy drink, we were forced to stop again. Cheryl's leg cramped from dehydration, so we downed a liter and a half of soda before continuing our climb up a field of razor-sharp scree.

Temperatures plummeted to 4°C, which spurred us on—especially me in my shorts—and we summited by noon. It was blood-freezing on top. The mist had risen with us, obscuring the Lohner Mountains at 3000 meters. Given the weather, we opted not to hang around too long before beginning our tricky descent through a sea of clouds on the opposite side.

Now, I have to admit, when I first glanced over the ledge, it looked terrifying. The path fell right off the mountain. And it was a long way down. We had no idea how far that drastic descent continued, but there was no time for second thoughts. We pressed on. Initially the scree field was so dense we had to take our time carefully picking our way through. Then those rocks were replaced by oozing mud and cow dung, an awful combination. At one point, I spun 360° in an uncontrolled twirl. I caught myself only at the last second by thrusting my poles into the ground, just as my skull headed for a boulder.

For an hour, we continued down switchbacks past interesting stacked rock formations.

"Early burial mounds."

"Yea, Ötzi the Iceman slept here," Cheryl replied, although we both knew the 5300-year old mummy lives a sheltered life these days in a Bolzano museum.

Eager to find some rest ourselves, we landed late that afternoon in Adelboden, another ski resort. Even though they've hosted winter guests since the early 1900s, there's no budget accommodation. No zimmers. No *schlafen* in any straw.

The camping area was packed with Scouts. Other villages were out of reach by that late hour.

As we eventually unpacked in an over-priced hotel room, I said, "You know, Cheryl, it's time for hotels at each stage to get behind this Via Alpina. It's bound to grow in popularity and can be great for off-season business."

"True, most of these villages aren't exactly packed this time of year."

"Besides, they just need to offer basic rooms at hiker prices."

"A simple dorm room will do."

"Like back in Naßfeld. Hikers don't need a TV or bath in their room."

"Just a clean bed and a place to hang wet clothes."

"No mini-bar? Yea, I guess we're not big partyers after ten hours of climbing mountains."

She grinned. "It's like I always say. We're in this for a long time, not necessarily a good time."

With that, she tore off her clothes and darted for the shower.

After a lean breakfast, we fled down Adelboden's main drag of wooden-faced buildings and left before the locals were out of their beds. Although there were no banners or fireworks to mark the occasion, we'd reached the end of the Via Alpina green route and connected once again with the red one.

We followed the trail as it led through woods and up to one gondola station circulating empty cars and then another. No, it certainly wasn't busy. We passed nobody on the trail to Hahnenmoos Pass until we stopped to chat with an older lady walking her black and brown Bernese pups. It was a relief to find the path down the other side of the pass was not nearly as slick as the day before. However, as it snaked into Lenk, we approached it with growing apprehension after Adelboden's pricey welcome.

Long before it was a spa resort, Lenk was the first stage on Bernese soil for merchants bringing wine from the Rhonetal Valley. Back then, we'd heard, the Bernese and Wallis people frequently fought. Once, when the men of Lenk left for military service, the Walsers climbed the pass and stole their cattle. Upon clearing the other side, they celebrated with quite a party, but the people of Lenk were wise to them. They quickly tracked them and reclaimed their cattle. Removing their bells, they kept ringing them until the cows were safely home. Outraged, the Walsers planned revenge. Hearing this, the brave Lenk women armed themselves with pitchforks and scythes and met the Walsers on Langmatte Meadow where they beat them into retreat.

We arrived early for a change and knowing our own history, I half expected something would force us to move on. Cheryl's knees were faring better. Things were going too smoothly. Of course, their visitor office was closed for lunch, but after we finished a baguette and cheese wheel, we returned and they found us a room. It was in their sports center where about a zillion teenaged athletes attended a training camp, so they warned us it might be noisy. No problem. As long as they didn't hold a football match around our bed, I figured we could handle anything.

As it turned out, it was one of the better places we'd stayed at in awhile. They offered Internet, there was a huge all-you-could-eat breakfast buffet, and their office even called ahead to book us a room in Lauenen for the following night. It was at a Berghütte, a mountain cabin with an address in the same small village.

For a change, we'd made a reservation like locals do. How very civilized we'd become. We considered the matter finished.

We awoke to another sunny day. That made two in a row. At first, there was nothing else remarkable about the trail. We climbed another mountain pass, ascended another ski run, trekked through more forests, and crossed along another river. Then all that changed. We saw cows fly.

A helicopter swooped low and landed nearby. After consulting with farmers, they took off again into the hills. It returned a short while later dangling a dead cow from a long steel cable like a worm at the end of a fishing line.

How'd it die? Did it slip on dung and tumble head-over-hooves in a blur of black and white down a mountainside? And where are they taking it?

The farmers patiently waited with their trailer to cart it away, perhaps to give it a proper burial.

"Ah, Gertie, we knew ye well."

After all, it was Switzerland.

It only took us six hours to arrive in Lauenen; a half-day's trek for us. Upon reaching their visitor office, we were shocked to discover the room we'd booked in Lenk was actually a three-hour hike south—in the wrong direction. Just our luck. Fortunately, the sympathetic lady at the office knew a local woman who rented rooms nearby.

Sonja graciously welcomed us into her home. It was a *zimmer* in the finest tradition, complete with a cozy bed covered with a down comforter, a round dining table where I could write, embroidered wall hangings, a sink with mirror, and windows looking out to flowers in her yard. There was even a friendly family tabby cat who poked her head through the window to check out the new guests. Sonja couldn't do enough to help us relax. After warning us not to put our stinky boots outside overnight (maybe because the foxes would make sweet love to them?), she called ahead to find us a room outside of Gsteig where we'd stay the following night on our way to Sanetsch Pass.

It meant we'd cover a stage and a half, so it'd make the next day a little longer and the following one shorter. There was just one problem. While studying the maps that evening, I realized we'd either be in small villages or huts for the next four or five days. Our euros would never last that long. So we had to find an ATM machine, today's equivalent of the old "Psst... Change money, change money" guy who'd once prowled European city streets. Since tiny Lauenen didn't have any, at the last minute we had to go to nearby Gstaad, the chic ski resort. We'd already missed the last bus, so we were forced to hitchhike.

Well, luck was with us for a change. It only took us ten minutes to catch a ride and another ten to reach the ski area. Not knowing exactly where the bank was, the driver dropped us off at the train station at the far end of town.

So far, so good. However getting back to our room was trickier. Folks don't hitchhike in Gstaad unless their Maserati's in the shop. Car after car zoomed past without slowing down.

As the sun quickly slipped away, I said, "We'd better start walking, but not too quickly."

That had to be better than just standing there, since I figured folks would assume we were heading farther than the next designer boutique. Still, we were invisible to them. We'd almost resigned ourselves to hiking all the way back to Lauenen when a lady with a Fiat stuffed with groceries swerved and skidded to a stop. Relieved, we crammed inside amid her sacks as she sped off.

Along the way, with a friendly smile, she quizzed us about our home, what we were doing out there, and how we liked the Alps. Then she did the most remarkable thing. She drove right past her own home and continued down valley to drop us off at our doorstep.

Believe me, on a day when we'd already seen cows fly, her lift was a far greater miracle.

Happy Austrian gnome home (though the tree doesn't look pleased)

Alpine wandering is celebrated on this home's outdoor mural

Predjama Castle, not your typical cave dwelling, Slovenia

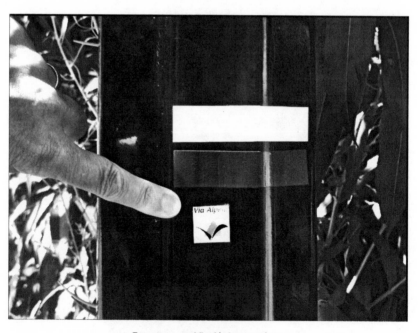

Easy-to-spot Via Alpina markers

Breathtaking Dolomites near Brixen

Farsighted cows often mistake humans for salt licks

Unexpected mid-July icefields

Our Rivendell had 15 waterfalls, near Meiringen, Switzerland

And *you* thought life was tough?

Steinbok, one of a dozen encountered above Schröcken

Another scree scramble, Bundalp, Switzerland

Typical Swiss dairy house with award bells across façade

For every breathtaking "up" there's a knee-crunching "down"

Reaching an Alpine village is a sight for sore eyes (and feet)

Marmot awaits fava beans and a nice Chianti

Alpine wildflowers brighten even foggy days

Austrian Road Department humor ("You're too young to die.")

Memorable *Schlafen in Stroh*, La Vare

Lauterbrunnen, beneath the Monk, Eiger and Jungfrau

Home of Queen Cow winners, France

Time stands still on cloudy Alpine days

Alpine salamander, Michelin Man of amphibians

Beneath Aiguille de Chambeyron, 3411 meters, France

Don't eat the yellow snow, near Bousieyas, France

Mirror Lake above Lac Ste-Anne, France

Not your typical Alpine image, Pas de la Cavale, France

Nothing beats reaching the summit, overlooking Mt. Blanc range

Long, lonely path to La Vare, Switzerland

Unsurpassed views from atop Col de Brévent, France

Rugged mountain hut atop Grand St. Bernard Pass

Exceptional refuge hut awaits, near Col de Anterne

Josephine Baker fondly remembered by the Blue Devils

Col de Demècre with stone man (note hut on left), Switzerland

Desolate ex-border outpost near Archeboc Refuge, France

Rare standing-still moment

Agony of de feet

10

MR. MOUSTACHE & HIS SNAILS

WE AWOKE TO ANOTHER BEAUTIFULLY SUNNY AUGUST DAY, the kind we could easily get used to. It was a quick climb back into meadows and woodland, and then onto what we thought was the turnoff to Sanetsch Falls. Since there was no marking, a Swiss rarity, I stopped an older fellow who was out for a drive on the dirt road.

"Can you show us the trail to Sanetsch Pass?"

With one of those unique French facial shrugs, a contortion like you're sniffing year-old goat cheese, he pointed us in the right direction, then warned, "Be very careful up there. It is a steep and very dangerous climb."

One fleeting look told us that was an understatement.

He continued, "I have walked it many times, and..."

His expression seemed to ask if we really wanted to tackle it.

"Why not take the cable car?"

Of course, that was always tempting, but not in such perfect weather.

"No, we'll hike."

We appreciated his concern, but didn't worry. We'd faced tougher ascents. Besides, they seemed to be getting easier. Cheryl's knee had almost shrunk to normal size again and my gasping for breath less resembled a death rattle.

"As you wish." Before driving off, he left us with a familiar, "*Bon courage!*"

I hadn't heard that expression of "Good luck" since my last trek across France and still found it encouraging. Then again, the fact he'd spoken French instead of German told me we'd stepped across another invisible barrier in a tiny nation boasting four languages—five, if you count English. The area's affectionately known as the "*Rösti* Trench" after the beloved staple of the German-speaking Swiss side. Now we could be equally illiterate in a new language for the rest of our trek.

"Slowly" referred to more than our hiking speed as we struggled to recall vocabulary from high school French class (or *Pink Panther* films). I still remembered how to ask, "*Où est la bibliothèque?*" ("Where is the library?") in case we ran out of reading materials. Or Clouseau's "Do you have a leecense for zat minkee?" The rest lurked somewhere in the dark recesses of our addled minds.

We slid down to a small bridge leading over a stream at the base of the falls. A sign promised another three-hour climb to the crest, so there was no time to waste. The trail zigzagged across the face of the mountain as we wended our way up another crumbling path to the 2048-meter summit at the top of Sanetsch Falls.

There wasn't much on top: a former mountain hut boarded shut, a weathered cross, a stone chapel, and a restaurant resembling a Mexican cantina. Waitresses in blue, frilly dancehall-like dresses scurried from table to kitchen, while a pompous fellow swaggered back and forth, decked out like a pirate in a cocked hat, black vest and a kilo-worth of pork chop mustache. He directed and starred in the opera.

"Ah, we called last night and have reservations in the dorm," I said.

"Room is not ready," he gruffly replied. "One hour."

Okay, no worries. We took advantage of the frenzy of day-tripping diners on the terrace and took off our packs to dry our clothes in the sun. While waiting, we also checked our route for the following day, splaying maps across a table as we milked overpriced beers.

There's an unwritten law of pricing in the Alps. The higher you go, the higher the price. It doesn't matter if it's a short drive on a road down to the village store, or they have to use a team of elephants to bring up the pasta and brews. It's all the same. In fact, it was worse at their so-called hut, since they likened themselves to a gourmet bistro amid the clouds.

Hungry as ever, we looked at their menu. After a hard day on the trail, how many hikers salivate at the thought of escargot? Maybe I'm the exception, but snails just don't get my juices flowing.

So, we waited and waited, as we sat on tree trunks converted into stools. Once I made the mistake of shifting on my seat. The next thing I knew, it broke off and I lay sprawled on my butt on the sundeck. The other diners pretended not to notice, (after all, this was polite French company), but it was a cruel irony to think I'd climbed all those mountains only to fall off a barstool—especially after only one drink.

Just when we were about to give up, a dark Basque girl with curly hair appeared and led us upstairs to our dorm bunkroom. When full, it slept thirty or more on foldable mattresses on the floor, but at that point, there was just one other fellow staying there. Good thing, since there was only one toilet and shower, and we were delighted to be first in line—all the more likely to find hot water. For me, there's a simple thrill to taking a shower at the end of a long, sweaty day. It ranks as one of the great pleasures in life. You can have your bathing in cold mountain streams—been there, tried that. A hot shower is more than washing off the mud and crud. It's a renewal of the spirit; it's a fresh start for another day. And when I miss it, well, it's like wearing the same underwear for a week.

I stripped down, ready for the warm goodness to flood over my weary body. I turned on the water, jumped in, screamed, and leapt five feet sideways. This water was beyond cold. It was glacial. Still, desperate times call for desperate measures. Holding my breath, I dunked just my head into its icy spray and washed it as fast as humanly possible, quicker than I did back in that Tibetan stream.

Yet, I had to wonder: Do brain-freezes cause permanent damage? Or do they just make you want to grow wild mustaches and wear pirate outfits?

That evening it rained, no large surprise, and everyone expected more in the morning. At least, we were already at 2048 meters. One climb was out of the way. The next hurdle was dinner. Since we'd already ruled out eating snails, Cheryl and I studied the menu in the now-empty restaurant and were stunned to discover dinner at the "hut" would set us back more than our daily budget without wine. Ouch.

So, when our waitress arrived to take our order, I suggested pasta. They didn't have any. I tried sandwiches. Sorry. We did see fondue for 17 euros (25 dollars) on their menu and thought we'd split it. Why not? It fell under the category of Swiss culture. It was our duty to sample the local heritage.

"Good choice. And for you?" she asked, turning to Cheryl.

"Oh, we'll just split one."

"Sorry, but there is a two-person minimum on fondue."

Like a two-drink minimum? Maybe it's just the tick talkin', but it was hard to rationalize spending fifty dollars on cheese and stale bread cubes, no matter how famished we were.

"Well," the waitress said, nervously looking around, "we normally don't let two people split one pot, but since the chef is not here..."

With that, she gave us a sweet wink and left for the kitchen. No more than a minute later, we heard the most awful screaming coming from behind its door. Through the small window, we saw Mrs. Mustache sternly lecturing the poor girl. I could only imagine she was driving home the rigidity of their gooey cheese policy. Clearly, one cheese did not stand alone. Honestly, I felt more sorry for the waitress than us when she sheepishly returned to break the news.

"That's okay, we'll just have one soup and an ice cream."

At 24 euros, we figured mustache wax doesn't come cheap up there.

We moped back upstairs to our room. The shower was still like bathing in liquid nitrogen. The sink floweth over. Storms began again. We ignored our hunger and turned in early. Tomorrow was another day. At least, we'd have a good night's sleep in our quiet room, snug and dry while it stormed outside— or so we thought.

At one in the morning, a family of six with four dripping young girls appeared. Flashlights blazing, they proceeded to put sheets on their beds amid giggles and loud whispers. It wasn't easy in the dark. It took what seemed like an hour before they eventually settled down.

We managed just a few hours sleep before we cranked open our eyes and joined the rest of the guests still in various states of slumber outside the front door of the restaurant. The cute Moroccan waitress showed up in her poofy dress, but she too had to wait outside in the near-freezing fog. The front door was locked. There was no sign of Mr. Mustache.

To take his mind off the weather, a Frenchman asked us, "How'd you sleep?"

"Fine, until some idiot and his family stumbled into our room, waving their lights around at 1 A.M.," I said. "Can you imagine having a bunch of kids out on a night like last night?"

"*Oui*, they woke us up, too."

The man beside him fidgeted, until he finally admitted, "That was us."

He was the same fellow we'd seen in our room on our arrival.

"If you were in the room that early, why didn't you make their beds," Cheryl asked, "so they wouldn't have to do it in the dark?"

"And why were you out in the dark on the mountain?" I wondered.

"I was taking pictures of the lake illuminated by the night sky."

"In the rain? And fog?"

"You can't just come waltzing into hostels so late," Cheryl scolded in her best firm, motherly tone. "Besides, huts are usually locked by 11:00. Hikers are trying to get a good night's sleep."

"Sorry. Like to see my photos?"

We looked at him like he must be crazy.

"Here's my card and web address, if you'd like to order one."

He just didn't get it.

The rains began again in earnest. It'd been tough shivering outside in the cold, but enough was enough.

"Where's the chef?" Cheryl asked. "Where's Mr. Mustache?"

The waitress giggled at the name and hesitantly pointed to an apartment attached to the restaurant.

Cheryl walked over to it. "Here?"

The girl nodded.

Cheryl tapped on the window. Not a rustle.

She pounded harder until someone snorted, "*Très bien!*" and we heard stumbling around inside. Eventually Mr. Moustache flung open the restaurant doors, seated us, and in a less-than-cordial mood brought each table old bread, butter, jam, and a couple slices of cheese. The rest must've gone into the ill-fated fondue.

"Kaffee? Arr! You want kaffee?" he asked, then shuffled to the kitchen.

The weather, like his breakfast, was miserable and cold for August. Eager to leave, we climbed into our raingear and trekked in fog around the frigid man-made lake. It was still a long, steep climb up to Sanetsch Pass in a drizzle that grew to a downpour. As I slogged along, I enviously thought about the clueless photographer.

About now, he's "lingering" around the hut's cozy woodstove with a hot coffee, smug and snug, still trying to justify it all.

Reaching the top of the pass, long used for trade and warfare, it became impossible to find the Via Alpina until we dropped into a dairy farm for directions and found a sympathetic ear. The farmer, dressed in her white cap, matching clogs and a lab-like cheese making outfit, even stepped outside in the pouring rain to point us toward the disappearing path.

"I have told them several times the path is not well marked," she warned. "If I were you, I would not walk it today in this weather. Besides the rain and fog, you have to pass steep crevasses. One bad step and you can break a leg. Plus, you will need to cross some sections using fixed ladders and ropes."

"We have no choice but to continue. We can't spend another night at Mr. Moustache's."

"Is it that bad?" Our pained looks left no doubt. She shook her head and asked, "Do you have a..." She searched for the word. "A compass?"

"Oh, yes," I assured her, though it was nearly useless on trails that meander every hundred meters in different directions.

Even though she stared at us as if we were out of our minds, we'd continue.

The path immediately wound along a stream and into a valley. Then it continued over the hills and wet rocks, a giant's jigsaw puzzle spilled over a carpet of meadow. Each chasm was just large enough to snap an ankle if you stepped slightly wrong. That was bad enough. Then came the bouldering. Slowed by my cumbersome pack and, by then, worn-slick boot soles, I inched across a huge, slippery rock, stretching spread-eagle to wedge my hands into crevasses to yank my body up. It's not easy being born with less than orangutan-length arms, but eventually I made it to the top. Cheryl wasn't so lucky. She was stuck halfway, four-meters up, unable to pull up or slide back down. I had to scoot back toward her, pass her the end of my Nordic pole, and virtually pull her to safety. That earned me a grateful kiss.

For hours, we continued in the rain and mud and slick rocks over the pass and down the other side. A distant dam and village eventually rose in the mist. Just when we thought we'd survived the worst, the trail turned treacherous with a sudden straight vertical drop of about 1000-meters.

I can admit it now. I was worried. Scared shitless.

Today, of all days, in the rain. This makes our toughest climb in Slovenia look like a school outing. How're we going to pull this one off?

Sometimes, it's best not to just stand there debating the challenge. It only allows time for the seeds of doubt to grow in your mind. You have to act. You can't go back. You can't see what's ahead. You can only move on.

And as the German philosopher Nietzsche once said, "And if you gaze for long into an abyss, the abyss gazes also into you."

Something told me that neither of us liked what we saw.

We grabbed a secured rope with pruned, half-frozen fingers. Then we eased and slid our way down the slippery slate trail. Think of it as "controlled falling." With ponchos wildly flapping in the wind, we slowly descended two metal ladders—only to continue snatching more nylon swimming pool-type frayed blue ropes, as we traced a precipitous trail along the mountain's craggy face. We hung on for dear life. Each step promised to be our last. At one point, I grabbed a rope to gently lower myself down the cliff—only to find it unfastened at the base. All of a sudden, I swung Tarzan-like above the chasm below!

"I didn't come all this way to die on this trail!" Cheryl shrieked in terror.

"Focus!" I called back, trying to calm her, but I secretly felt the same. That path, especially in foul weather, was a tough if not deadly challenge for long-distance hikers who aren't by nature expert climbers (or sky-divers). There had to be a better way to go between those stages.

Steeling ourselves for the final 100-meters down, we scrambled to a dry ledge. Then we slid down the mountain face on switchbacks through wet scree and mud with the rain our relentless nemesis. Several times, I heard Cheryl cry out in pain as her knees were constantly pummeled.

Maybe, I thought, we should make contingency plans to head back down into the valleys if this weather continues. It's a possibility. But this isn't Austria with handy *radwegs* connecting villages. How far will we have to go out of our way to circle a mountain rather than climbing it?

Even though the slope was torture, hours later we made it down to the village of Godey in one piece. For that, I will always remain truly grateful. As we shared our story over dinner with the couple who ran the cozy guesthouse where we landed, they claimed to be amazed at our accomplishment, or dumb luck, in that weather. Their dog was less fortunate. Seeing him limp around the dining room, we assumed he'd broken his leg.

"*Non*," the lady explained, "he was bitten by a viper!"

"A poisonous snake? Here?"

"*Mais, oui.*"

The most terrifying thing we'd seen all day (other than the monstrous mountain) was a black Alpine salamander, a pumped-up Michelin amphibian on steroids. Maybe there are worse things than falling off mountains, after all.

Otherwise, if someone was to ask, "How was Switzerland?" I'd have to say, "Delicious!" even though we already noticed a big difference in its French-speaking west. As much as the dinner cuisine improved, breakfasts were puny. No more meat, cheese, yogurt and müsli for *frühstück*. No wonder they called them *petit déjeuner*. With few villages between hiking stages and no trailside cafés, we'd have to learn how to survive ten hours on bread, jam, butter and coffee.

Mon Dieu!

At dawn, we left after breakfast under clear skies. It was a short hike up to Derborence, which lay beside a deceptively still lake. Back in 1714, one of the southern rock towers of Diableret peak collapsed, bringing fifty million cubic meters of scree and boulders onto the valley floor. It buried fourteen huts along with fifteen inhabitants and their cattle. One man was making cheese at the time. Lucky guy. After being buried for three months and surviving on cheese and water, he emerged alive. It was a miracle, right? Not quite. Adding insult to injury, he wasn't accepted back into his village until the local priest exorcised him. Wonder if he ever considered moving?

From Derborence we scaled another mountain and then crossed a meadow to Anzeindaz. Since the weather was atypically good, we were far from alone for a change. Many hikers had already arrived at the restaurant hut. Although it was the official stage stop, Cheryl and I decided to continue to Pont de Nant. Since we could never rely on two clear days in a row, I was all for hiking a little longer under sunny skies. After joining the others out on the sundeck for a tasty bowl of local creamed herb soup, we began our ascent to Col des Essets at 2029 meters.

The afternoon's trek was picturesque as we crossed a rustic meadow enclosed by peaks on three sides. As is true for the rest of the Via Alpina, this particular stretch corresponds with another long-distance route, the Tour des Muverans. All was going too well for a change: good weather, full bellies, renewed vigor, optimism. We should have known all that would soon change.

Arriving at the shepherd's simple stone hut at La Vare, we ran into our old companion, Hugo, whom we hadn't seen for five days. After staying at the same Adelboden hotel, he'd wild-camped and then claimed to cover two stages in one. As usual, we were relieved to run into him and anxious to share our plans to continue to Pont de Nant that afternoon.

"Haven't you heard?" he asked. "This guardian told me it's burned down."

"Really? Maybe he just wants you to stay longer?"

"Well, funny you mention that. I always wanted to be a shepherd." He chuckled at his own joke. "I arrived here yesterday and may stay tomorrow. They feed me too well," he sighed, patting his belly.

If what he says is true and we continue, I thought, it's a five or six hour trek to the next refuge. It's just too far this late in the afternoon.

Then again, the hut did have a thriving side-business serving crêpes and drinks. Resigned to our fate, we relaxed with a large cup or *boule* of Brittany cider, and then watched other guests playing *boule* or *pétanque* on a special gravel pitch. It was an exercise in concentration. Two teams bowled silver balls as they attempted to get closest to a small colored one.

In the meantime, Hugo found an old multi-colored beach chair, stripped down to his skivvies, stretched out in the sun, and read a book—oblivious to the flock of curious, bleating sheep crowding around him.

"Bah, ram ewe. Bah, ram ewe."

Just once, out of curiosity, I had to ask a passing English couple if it was true about the refuge at Pont de Nant and they insisted they were just renovating the place. Who knew? But as a thick fog crept across La Vare, the issue became moot. We prepared ourselves for another night of sleeping on straw in the shepherd's stables. Fortunately this one was without the cows, constant clanging, or *o'dor cologne*.

Predictably, it soon started drizzling and thundering outside, but dinner more than made up for the weather. A Swiss couple and a quirky English family joined Cheryl, Hugo and me at candlelit tables inside the snug stone house. As soon as I'd noticed the English fellow that afternoon, I secretly called him "Duke" after a favorite comic character. His chunky frame was only partially disguised by an outrageous Hawaiian shirt that put the "moo" into muumuu.

His bald head, framed by aviator sunglasses, glistened in the sun. The only thing missing was his distinctive cigarette holder.

On the other hand, his wife dressed for dinner like she was going to some fancy soirée. Decked out in cashmere and pearls, she kicked mountain dining up several notches. And what a feast it was.

The shepherd and his girlfriend had grilled small steaks and tiny sweet potatoes fried in butter, which they heaped onto our plates. No sooner did we finish the first piece than they offered seconds, and then thirds. I now understood Hugo's reluctance to leave. As usual, we three hikers were happy to share stories about the Alps we'd grown to love. Maybe it was just the dim candlelight, but I imagined I could detect the far-off gaze of wanderlust in the others' eyes.

At one point the young Swiss woman from the city innocently asked, "How much do you carry in your packs on a trip like this?"

"Only seven or eight kilos," I stressed. "Even that's too much at times."

She shook her head in disbelief since she'd lugged several suitcases up there, and then asked, "But what do you wear on the trail?"

Without missing a beat, Hugo flew into an impromptu show-and-tell they'll never forget. He stood up at the dinner table and explained, "Well, I have this shirt." He unbuttoned his long-sleeved cotton top and took it off. "And I have this short-sleeved shirt." Taking it off, he threw it over his chair. "Then I have these long pants." He undid his belt, pulled down the zipper and suddenly dropped them to his knees.

Of course, Cheryl and I were used to Hugo's quirkiness, but the others looked on in a mixture of surprise and a little horror. Would he do the same with the tiny black shorts doubling as his underwear? I didn't wait to find out.

"I think they get the idea," I said with a laugh, hoping to end his striptease before he showed us the rest of his, er, gear.

"Well, she asked," he said, adding a nonplussed shrug.

At last, it was time for dessert and it was far better than the floorshow. Since it was another guest's birthday, we were served a four-layer cake topped with fresh berries. Then our host drew four bottles of schnapps from his cabinet and left them on our table, before wishing us all, "*Bonne nuit.*"

All night the rain beat a simple rhapsody against the tin roof of the stables. Yes, it was only a bed of straw, but all was right in the world.

At dawn, after our usual light breakfast, Cheryl and I set off down the mountain to Pont de Nant. Hugo remained behind, determined to stay, commune with the sheep, and sniff around the dinner table. And why not?

Once we confirmed the refuge at Pont de Nant was indeed toast, burned toast, we hiked through Nant Valley's beautiful Thomasia Alpine gardens with their 3000 plant species, then began a backbreaking ascent up Col des Perris Blancs at 2544 meters. What should have been a relaxing ramble, you might say a "time to smell the alpenroses," became another race against the storm clouds gathering once again.

This time we just made it to the summit as the fog rolled in, and then quickly slid down the other side to Cabane de la Tourche. As usual, there'd been no fountains to fill our water bottles all day during the excruciating climb—a cruel absurdity considering the endless rain we'd faced all summer.

The stone cabin balanced on the edge of the mountain was a minimal affair—but its door was open. A lady dressed in a flannel shirt and jeans sat outside reading on the deck. I assumed she was just another hiker.

While Cheryl hustled off to find a water tap, I asked, "Do they have food up here?"

The woman gave an ambiguous nod.

I poked my head inside. Funny, those places were usually cafés first and foremost, yet no one was there.

I went back out and asked, "You work here?"

She nodded.

"Have any food?" Bread and jam just didn't take us too far.

Her head bobbed again.

"Have a menu?" Her game of twenty questions was wearing me out.

She glanced up from her book and sighed, "I can fix an omelet."

"Okay, two please."

With that, she halfheartedly went into the cabin and then into a backroom, returning with a tray of eggs. Cheryl and I sat at a table outside on the deck and enjoyed a long drink from our liter water bottles. As we watched another endless dark swatch of clouds envelop the mountainside, we heard a "chic, chic, chic, chic, chic." Pause. "Chic, chic, chic, chic, chic" coming from inside.

"What's that?"

"Chic, chic, chic, chic, chic." Pause. "Chic, chic, chic, chic, chic."

"She's beating eggs for our omelets?" Cheryl guessed. We just had to watch. Besides, by now it started to sprinkle so we both ducked back inside.

"Chic, chic, chic, chic, chic." She beat eggs against her bowl with a metal spoon in a precise rhythm: five strokes and five strokes only. Meanwhile, we grew more ravenous. Finally, she poured them into a pan. They sizzled and popped. Blocked from our view, we could only imagine what wonderful ingredients she was tossing in.

"What do you think?" Cheryl asked. "Smoked ham? Mountain herbs? Maybe mushrooms? Of course, local cheese. Yum."

"These are going to be the world's best omelets," I promised.

We waited, pups salivating over leftovers. Then suddenly, the suspense ended. After a full fifteen minutes, she shuffled over to our table. And slid two plates in front of us. On each, a pathetic-looking scrambled egg looked back.

I swallowed a huge guffaw.

Cheryl looked forlorn, as if to say, "That's it?"

Just then, the musical "Chic, chic, chic, chic, chic." Pause. "Chic, chic, chic, chic, chic" began anew. This time, although we knew better than to hold out much hope, the woman surprised us and presented one large, flat omelet. There was nothing on it, nothing inside. But it was intact and we wolfed it down. It was fuel, if nothing else. It'd help us make it to the cabin at Col de Demècre— or so we hoped.

At that point, the Via Alpina follows an old mountain road totally exposed to the elements. No sooner did we step outside the hut than the rain began to beat our heads and shoulders. As the storm built in force, we followed the boulder-strewn road across the face of the mountain and managed to make it to Rionda before all hell broke loose. Spotting a one-story building, we found an open door and ducked inside.

It turned out to be an old WWII Swiss Army barracks. Troops had been stationed there just in case the Nazis changed their minds about Swiss neutrality, or made a run for their chocolate. It had that certain musty, time-forgotten smell like your grandfather's attic. But it also had a protective tin roof. From the old newspapers and bottles scattered around, we weren't the only ones over the past seventy years who'd sought shelter from the storm.

Since there was little else to do while we waited for the rain to pass, or talked ourselves into staying the night, I grabbed my flashlight and did some exploring. We were hunkered down in what used to be their sleeping quarters. Two dozen bunk bed frames lined the wall. On closer inspection, I found inscriptions the soldiers had scrawled into them or onto the doorjambs. "Jacques, Okt. '42." They were notes like bored soldiers anywhere might leave during a snowbound winter on a freezing summit—to pass the time or maybe just to prove they'd once existed. One even left his portrait, a silhouette sketch of a soldier's head.

For an hour or so while rain relentlessly pelted the roof, we seriously considered spending the night surrounded by all those echoes from the past. Sure, it was a "little boogedy," as Cheryl put it, but it was dry.

Fortunately, it never came to that. The rain eventually let up. We still had enough light to continue without accidentally tumbling off the side of the mountain. Besides, hunger's a great motivator. So, we set off once again in drizzle and fog hurrying toward Chalet Neuf. By that point, continuing all the way to Demècre was out of the question. We only hoped we could find the cabin before dark, and then again, we hoped it'd be open.

It was freezing. We were sopping wet and dispirited. I already wore my down jacket underneath my poncho, but it was soon soaked with sweat and little help. After trudging in rain most of the day, our boots were drenched. I've yet to find "waterproof" boots that actually keep the rain out, and I'd already taken them off once to wring out my socks.

Racing against the ever-fickle weather, it took forever to reach the forest below. And it was hours before we finally spotted the smoke filtering through the pines from Chalet Neuf's woodstove. Actually, "chalet" is a wild exaggeration. It was a cabin, nothing more, but welcome all the same.

Yves, a gregarious fellow with dark curly hair and a bushy moustache, greeted us at the door. At first, I didn't know whether he was the hut guardian or a fellow trekker who felt pity for us. It didn't matter. We were inside. Our needs were few. A big woodstove radiated heat. A kitchen promised food (without any "chic, chic, chic, chic, chic"), and beverages would do more than re-hydrate us. Yves led us to the bunkroom, gave us mattresses, and showed us where to hang our wet clothes.

"Want dinner?" he asked, and our hungry eyes shouted a reply.

Yves whipped up a huge pot of spaghetti Bolognese. While I had three plates before coming up for air, Cheryl looked just as contented and ready to roll over for a long summer's nap.

We weren't the only ones in the cabin that night. There were his two cute grandkids, plus three other hikers celebrating their friend's thirtieth birthday. They'd come prepared for some serious partying and had already cooked a coil of sausage outside on the grill. By 7:00 when my partner padded off to bed, unable to keep her eyes open any longer, the four Swiss fellows invited me to join them at their table.

Chris, lifetime best friend of the birthday boy, worked in Lugano, while their other friend organized safaris in Kenya. They joked that he was outside the cabin at daybreak every morning with binoculars, hoping to spot wild game. (Did marmots and Alpine salamanders count?) Even though relative locals, they wanted to hear about our long journey through their country.

At first, I was reluctant to go into much detail, but after a few glasses of red wine, I relaxed and laid out our map to show them the eight-country route we'd desperately tried to follow. Then eventually, they pulled out their cards and showed me how to play Jass, a kind-of Swiss bridge.

All in all, it was the perfect ending to a frigid, lung-numbing day. And one look at the birthday boy's glazed eyes told me he'd be glad thirtieth birthdays only happen once in your lifetime.

By dawn, it was mostly clear. Yves predicted good weather for the next few days. Although that was reassuring news, we found it difficult to leave the warmth of the cabin and to say *"Tschüs"* ("Bye") to the others. Those moments of fellowship sustained us. With cosmic synchronicity, they came at times when we were at our lowest. I'd seen it happen on other trips and was comforted to know we were still exactly where we should be, doing what we should be doing.

Fueled by that knowledge, and our carb fest the night before, our climb to Col de Demècre went smoother than imagined. In fact, we arrived just as the hoarfrost melted with the first rays of the sun. As we rounded the crest and spotted the refuge cradled in a bowl below, a man and his son bounded down from a nearby peak like steinboks. They met us at the hut with a hearty welcome and insistence that we come inside.

"Come, have a tea on the warden!" the fellow joked.

He was a volunteer up there, running the refuge with his family for two weeks. Their Alpine club had taken an old Swiss Army barracks, much like the one we'd seen the day before, and transformed it into a beautiful hut. While treating us to slices of chocolate cake his kids had baked on the woodstove, he proudly shared a photo album showing the cabin's renovation. What a challenge. I couldn't imagine the difficulty in getting all the supplies and workers up to 2361 meters for the task. We'd have loved to spend the night and at least help support all their hard work, but it was mid-morning and we knew we had a formidable descent of 2000 meters ahead.

My knees still ache at the memory.

After tea, we began a steep descent. We traversed more pastures than the average cow does in its lifetime. We crossed alpine meadows flooded with more flowers than several weddings and a funeral, as well as thick pine and deciduous forests offering a bounty of cherries, walnuts and chestnuts. Still, even at our breakneck pace, it took four hours to reach Vernayaz in the valley floor just north of Martigny.

Starting at the train station, knees still wobbly, we wandered through the tiny village for over an hour looking for a room. They were "out of season," I guess. Even most of the hotels were closed.

Finally, we dropped into a café and asked in French, "Does anyone rent rooms in town?"

An older couple sitting nearby looked up and said, "We'll help," in English. They led us to their Lexus and helped load our packs into their trunk where we spotted new hiking boots still in their original boxes.

Ah, fellow trekkers, that explains it.

At first, they drove us to a friend's who rents rooms, but they were booked. They called around town to hotels, including one at Pissevache Waterfalls, and then finally drove us back to the train station where we'd started. However, we didn't go to the hotel this time. He rang the buzzer at the house next door where a slim woman with short, smartly-styled hair greeted us. Sybil, a local schoolteacher, rents a spare room in her comfortable house. And yes, she had a vacancy.

Her place immediately felt like home to us. So much so, it didn't take long for us to decide to spend a day resting there, if she didn't mind. I could think of plenty of excuses. It'd been twelve days since our last break. Our 2000-meter descent had been exhausting. We needed to find better maps for France. I wanted to buy insoles and get a new pair of hiking socks to replace the ones that went walkabout in Gimmelwald. Plus, her shower had boiling water. Then again, we'd soon begin trekking west on a major dogleg around Mt. Blanc and could use all the extra energy we could muster.

After we were assured it would be no problem to stay the extra day, we had a bite to eat and then promptly slept for twelve full, glorious hours. What luxury!

The next morning, Sybil surprised us with a breakfast proving we'd made a wise choice. There was fresh-brewed espresso from the Porsche of coffee machines, warm buttery croissants, cheese, prosciutto sliced so thin it melted on your tongue, and a hazelnut chocolate spread.

Afterward she even gave us a ten-minute lift down the road into Martigny, set at a bend in the Rhône on the Dranse River. The one-time Roman market town is at the edge of Valais canton. Although it's famous for its variety of outdoor activities, finding the topo maps we desperately needed was out of the question.

"But *monsieur*, you are looking for French maps," the clerk reminded me. "This is Switzerland."

Oui, a baguette's throw away.

We did find insoles, however, and I splurged on the most high-tech hiking socks designed by modern man. They were labeled right and left for the totally obsessive and had the activity sewn into them—in case you forgot what you were doing. They promised all sorts of benefits, including added energy.

For the price, I expected a built-in masseuse named Wing-Li.

At daybreak, our hostess allowed us to print directions from the Internet for the next dozen French stages. They'd have to do until we found good maps again. Then, with an unexpected spring in our step, our journey began again—with a nosebleed ascent up an old mule track from Vernayaz to Salvan.

By the time we finally reached the picturesque village high above the valley, this old burro was bathed in sweat. The village celebrated Marconi's anniversary; his photo was plastered on every other wall.

"Now I can see why he invented the radio," Cheryl gasped.

Our route continued to wend up the mountain to Van d'en Bas where it led off through a serene valley scattered with holiday cabins. There the trail grew confusing where it merged with the Tour de Van. The mystery was solved only after we approached a few guys in colorful wetsuits who were canyoning, sliding like otters over rocky falls to the icy pool below.

"Yea, you're on the right route," they assured us. "Just go up there."

Up, always up.

We continued, reaching Lac de Salanfe at 1925 meters shortly after noon. It lay in the shadow of Dent du Midi with its symbolic seven alpine peaks. That reservoir holding 40 million cubic meters of water sparkled enticingly, but we stayed only long enough for a quick bite on its pebbled shore. We knew we still had to tackle a stiff climb to the Col (Pass) de Susanfe at 2494 meters and then a trek down to the cabin, which we stumbled into by late afternoon.

The stone hut was precariously balanced on a ledge beneath a melting glacier. Once inside, we bumped into the persnickety lady who ran the place and were greeted by the same first question out of every innkeeper's mouth.

"Do you have a reservation?"

"No. Why?"

"Never mind. Where are you going tomorrow night?"

"Tornay-Bostan, we hope."

"You have reservations?"

Now, I have to admit, that runs against our philosophy. You never knew what the weather or trail conditions will be like, who you might run into, or how far you'll hike on any given day—not to mention how well your body will survive the climb—or fall. This wasn't some road trip with rooms booked in advance by AAA. It was wild and spontaneous. It was the slow, soulful John Coltrane "jazz" of travel. It was improvisation, pure and simple. She wouldn't understand.

"No."

"I will call them for you. Later. It is much too busy now."

I looked around. It was empty. All the Brits trekking the Tour des Dents for a week were outside. Did she expect a sudden rush of phantom guests at 2500 meters?

Strangely, the whole operation was very proper. Not only were we assigned a bunk, but we were also given a small plastic grocery basket like you'd use to shop for milk and bread. That was to hold all our gear, including our packs. Fat chance. We were even assigned seats at a picnic table for dinner: fetid curry over uncooked rice.

No offense, but sleep is often impossible in huts filled by hikers who are fresh from the city, or who're on the mountain to party. I understand completely. Hey, they're the lucky ones who can sleep in late. You recognize them by their laughter like it's summer camp, while waving flashlight search beacons. That night, they just happened to be older Swiss misses.

"Are these our beds?" one asked, as if they'd never seen them before.

"Well, I think so," another replied. Then there was a long dialogue.

"You go first."

"*Non*, you."

"*Non, Cherie*, I insist."

More discussion. Eventually, all six lined up in single file, climbed up to the same bed, and then rolled across all the others, creaking all the way to the end, packed like Pringles chips. This took a painful fifteen minutes. Then they began to rummage through crackling plastic bags for, who knows, whatever.

A Pope is chosen with much less fuss.

We'd been through all that far too often to care much anymore. We'd just pull our sleeping bags up over our heads and think pleasant thoughts.

For once, at least, we didn't have THE SNORER in our room. There's inevitably one in every group. Now to be perfectly honest, most of us emit some combination of noises, burps, snorts, chortles, gasps, moans or farts at night. Sorry, I apologize in advance. But actually, I'm referring to those few who've elevated snoring to an Olympic-level art. It's more than sawing logs. It's taking a chainsaw to the Amazon. Sometimes they're even able to enlist the rest of us in the room in their snore-athon, like a Greek chorus.

If it's true, as someone once said, that snoring has evolved as a way for humans to keep the bears or wolves out of their cave, then perhaps these snorers are super-human, the finest of our species, the survivors.

Then again, maybe they just need to find a wife (or husband) with a sharp elbow.

France

Matterhorn
4478

Bourg-St-Pierre

Mont Blanc
4810

St. Leonard

Monte Rosa
4634

Corellaz

Valgrisenche

Ste-Foy-
Tarentaise

Tignes

Gran Paradiso
4061

Le Lac de Tignes

Dent Parrachée 3684

Termignon

Modane

Mt. Thabor

Granges de la Vallée Etroite

Névache

Barre des Écrins 4102

Le Monêtier-Les-Bains

Vallouise

Freissinières

Italy

Ceillac

Mont Dauphin

Maljasset

Larche

Bousieyas

St-Etienne-de-Tinée

Roya

Réf. de Longon

St-Martin-Vésubie

St-Sauveur-sur-Tinée

Belvédère

Col de Turini

Sospel

Monaco

Nice

Monte Carlo

Mediterranean Sea

11

THE ALPENHORN AT SUNSET

WE WERE UP AT DAWN WITH OUR STOMACHS CHURNING FROM the curry we'd eaten the night before. Relief wouldn't come for two more days. Since she'd been so busy in the kitchen, the guardian said she'd forgotten to call ahead for us, but promised to phone Tornay-Bostan hut after breakfast.

At the crack of dawn, we began pecking our way down the mountainside until the hut soon disappeared from sight. Before long, we reached a small reservoir and peered over it into a steep crevasse above Encel Pass. One false step and, oops, you'd find the fastest way to a valley floor is not always the best.

I was reminded of the joke about the fellow who jumped from the hundred-floor building. As he reached the thirtieth floor, he thought, "Well, so far, so good."

With any luck, we'd take the slow way down.

There were a few brave hikers climbing the other side of the peak at the early hour and we wished each other well in passing. Otherwise, we were alone with our thoughts, mostly of self-preservation. It was a precipitous path as we cautiously placed each measured step. We had to maneuver sideways, hanging onto fixed chains attached to the rock face, but hey, we were now seasoned alpinists. Besides, it wasn't even raining.

We slowly wound our way down into the valley and then began a slog again up the other side on the so-called Smuggler's Trail where, for a period of thirty years or so, folks bootlegged meat and salt to support their families during the wars. Afterward, the trail climbed past a small chapel built in memory of Austrian lumberjacks killed in a hurricane in the 1960s, then to Croix d'Incrène, and finally to Col de Coux at 1913 meters.

Once over that pass, we were abruptly in France, the seventh country on our odyssey. We felt a brief moment of accomplishment and sigh of relief since we spoke the language slightly better. We could handle a conversation with any four-year-old we met. Also, we were back in Euro-ville. Traveling was hopefully not as painful for those of us carrying dollars—whose value fell faster than the fellow who'd leapt from the building.

All afternoon we continued trekking in the impressive shadow of the snowcapped Dents Blanches in the Chablais Alps through several more climbs and descents, and then back up along shepherd and trader's paths to Col de la Golèse at 1670 meters. From there, it was only one more hour to the secluded Refuge Tornay-Bostan, a hut set amid the vast, traditional pastureland of the Samoëns.

It was the epitome of tranquility. The rugged mountain landscape was alive with bees and wildflowers of every hue. While steinboks and chamois still roamed the wild and craggy mountainsides, the refuge was modern, its sundeck welcoming. We even had a room to ourselves. There were just four other guests and we didn't have to fight over hot showers or a chance to wash our clothes and hang them on a line to dry. Better still, that evening a volunteer from the village cooked a fine traditional casserole of pasta, ham and cheese, cream of vegetable soup, and fresh yogurt with berries for dessert, all topped off with a French merlot. Life couldn't taste any sweeter.

By the way, the guardian at Cabin de Susanfe, creator of the killer curry, never did phone ahead to reserve a room. Did it make a difference? Nope. Maybe she understood jazz after all.

It was hot and clear again the next morning. At last, summer had arrived—in the middle of August. My re-vitalized partner and I caught a gravel road leading nearly from the hut's front door. It quickly descended 1000 meters or so through a rocky landscape, past more pastures and woodland, down into the village of Samoëns. These folks were hardly monkish, even though they owe their unusual name to the seven mountains given to them by the Abbey of Sixt friars.

The Haut-Giffre region was in the midst of a three-day fête. Streets bustled with vendors, rides, an accordion player and plenty of happy revelers from throughout the region. It was also a national holiday. So given our past sage advice to book in advance, we stopped into the visitor office to ask them to call ahead and save us beds in Salvagny. With the celebration, we thought their auberge, or inn, might already be filled to capacity. Since it was only a couple of hours away, I figured that was best in view of the crowds.

After pausing for an early lunch of quiche (yes, real hikers eat quiche and most anything else not moving), we followed glacial Giffre Stream and the GR5 out of town. We were already too familiar with the GR5. It's one of Europe's most popular long-distance paths. It's also our nemesis.

Several years earlier, Cheryl and I came halfway around the world with the dream of hiking the GR5 from St-Gingolph, Switzerland to the Med. It was mid-May and we were still under the delusion that normal people can hike the Alps in late spring. We'd leave a little early and miss the crowds. Well, we geared up, even had the foresight to bring heavier clothing just in case, and made it to the trailhead with no problem. However, as we now know, Alpine weather is more unpredictable than a Yugo.

We left St-Gingolph following those familiar red and white striped markings and made it all of about 15 kilometers (straight uphill, no less) before running into snow. This wasn't just a Jack Frost dusting of powder. It was a serious up-to-your-butt snowfall. It was piled so high that the meter-high trail posts were invisible. Still, not to give up too easily, Cheryl and I figured we'd hunker down for the night and look at it all more clearly in the early morning light. The hut we reached was closed, of course, but their woodshed was unlocked. So we ducked inside, rolled out our down sleeping bags on a bare wooden platform, and polished off a few slate-hard slabs of energy bars for dinner. We promised ourselves it'd all look better in the morning.

Well, it didn't. We poked our bleary heads out of the shed at first light. We were met by the eerie silence that comes with a fresh snowfall. No trail markers were visible. This was our first hint to make other plans. However, sometimes, just to give you an unmistakable sign, the Universe supplies a complimentary brick to the head. Ours was sighting an amazing steinbok standing statue-like on a rock outcropping, just throwing distance away. As we marveled at our luck in seeing this incredible creature in the wild, I noticed something odd. It stood on just three legs. One of its legs was broken, held off the ground. That was the ultimate warning sign.

Fine. We'd head south to catch the trail. Maybe there wouldn't be as much snow. Wrong. In Chamonix, naturally there's more snow. After all, it's a ski resort. Still, not wanting to give up, we caught a train to Nice on the coast figuring we could always trek the GR5 in the opposite direction. That didn't work either. Their alpine club told us we'd run into snow only two days outside of the Côte d'Azur.

So, at that particular point in time, hiking the GR5 wasn't in the cards. In search of warmer climes, we ended up going to the island of Ibiza off the coast of Spain where we knew there wouldn't be any snow and the only gear needed was a swimsuit. Then again, it did require a high tolerance for listening to the goofy, yet popular song *Macarena* playing non-stop—much to the delight of hairy Spaniards spilling out of Speedos.

No, this time the GR5 would be different.

On our ramble out of Samoëns, we passed rafters floating down the crystalline Giffre. Canyoners also suited up in neoprene wetsuits for a day of adventure. For us, it was just a relief to have sunny weather for a change. The trail was easy to find for the most part. There was plenty of signage, only none of it pointed to Salvagny. We finally ran into a young couple out for a day hike. They had a local trekking book, phoned their friend and confirmed, yes, we were headed in the right direction. As it turned out, we were only a kilometer from the tiny village tucked into Tines Gorge.

In a place that size, it's easy to find the only auberge in town. But any sense of victory in arriving early was short-lived. No one answered its door. We found the owner, a crotchety fella, in the backyard sipping cold drinks.

"No," he said, all too smugly. "You cannot check-in until five p.m."

What are we to do until then? Sit outside on the curb and work on our tans? We'd already been pretty badly sunburned the past two days.

So we set off, determined to find another place, and fortunately found a hotel just up the road. From the looks of their register, we got the last room, and settling in early gave us the chance to hike downhill into Sixt-fer-à-Cheval.

Admittedly, my French was far from perfect, but did its name have something to do with playing golf with a horse?

It's an area known for its *via ferrata*, or mountains with fixed ropes, ladders and bridges. They also had the only market or phone booth. We could pick up groceries and take care of business. It was a plan, or so we thought. Once we made it down there, we discovered the grocery didn't open for two hours and telephone booth didn't take coins, only phone cards. And the only place to buy one was, you guessed it, in the store that didn't open for two hours.

Shortly after sunrise, we left, hoping to beat the heat, knowing we'd be high and exposed with no idea where to find water all day. I especially worried about Hugo. We hadn't seen him since La Vare. Did he stay behind to become a shepherd after all? I was especially concerned since I knew he carried just a pint of water when he hiked, a plastic soda bottle tucked in his front shirt pocket. I'd teased him about it. How would he manage now that there were few watering holes or fountains on the French paths?

Just outside of Salvagny, we located the GR5 trailhead and reached a parking lot already filled with trekkers. It was Sunday and the end of a holiday, so we knew the pathway would be busy. We weren't used to seeing many people. Then again, we knew the kids returned to school in another week and we'd soon have the trails to ourselves.

Salvagny lay down-valley at 764 meters and we made steady if not swift progress to Lignon and its pastoral chalets at 1135. Since we'd been unable to find new maps back in Martigny, we were temporarily trekking without one at that point. Although we were deep in TERRA INCOGNITA, I wasn't worried. The trail was hard-to-miss with its red and white slashes and so many hikers had passed through. Its stones were polished till they positively shone from boot soles rubbing over them.

After passing the impressive Rouget Waterfalls, one of the largest in the French Alps, we finally emerged in a wide meadow ablaze with gentians, St. Bruno lilies, anemones and wild orchids at 1800 meters. From there, we trekked across a great bowl framed by sharp monoliths until we arrived, nearly out of water, at the Chalet d'Anterne. Sure, we could've overnighted there, but with the uncommonly good weather, we decided to push our luck and press on. After filling our water bottles, we continued to turquoise Anterne Lake to catch a quick lunch of leftovers from the night before.

Although Camembert may be a delicacy that grows better with age, that doesn't hold true for ripe cheese—in a backpack—on a hot summer's day.

Hoping to arrive at our refuge early, we set off on one last steep climb to the summit of Col d'Anterne at 2243 meters, which gave us an enticing sneak preview of the Mt. Blanc range. Then we bounded down the other side to the Refuge de Moëde-Anterne where we'd reserved beds.

It's a modern cabin built of wood and stone in the shadow of Mt. Blanc. It sleeps 130 (if you can still call it a cabin), and most of the hikers were outside soaking up sun and lager when we arrived. Given our last night cooped up in a bunkroom surrounded by plastic rustlers, we splurged on a private room for a few euros more. It was a small indulgence.

Dinner that evening made up for all the bad food along the way. We were introduced to corn polenta prepared in the local style, baked with mountain cheese and sausage. Light and fluffy, it was a taste of Alpine heaven.

Since they seated all the English-speaking guests together at one table, an Irish family joined us. They were an odd trio: a stern, somber fellow, his best friend, and his sister who was married to the friend. They'd just finished their first ten-hour day of hiking. One was near death; the other wished she were. Four seeping blisters put her in a prickly mood and she was full of complaints. Tiring of that, she eavesdropped on my conversation with a fellow from Montpelier. I didn't mind that so much, just her nagging interruptions to correct my less-than-perfect French, which he seemed to understand perfectly well.

Before heading to bed, as we indulged on fresh yogurt and pie, the refuge owner, a grand mountain woman, told us the colorful legend of Mt. Blanc.

"A local shepherd lived alone on the pastures of Mt. Jolly, just west of here. He loved the mountain so much that he decided to marry it. One day he went to a secret cave to visit an elf, Mt. Jolly's guardian. After pouring out his soul and revealing his love for the mountain, he asked for its "hand" in marriage."

That was disturbing even for elves, who've seen it all.

"He argued, 'It's impossible for a human to marry a mountain and against the laws of nature. Besides, Mt. Jolly has just separated from the Aiguilles du Midi.'"

There's nothing worse than a mountain on the rebound.

"Hearing this, the shepherd became despondent. He cried for weeks, and finally decided to leave Mt. Jolly forever. Disappearing down valley, he sobbed all summer. His flood of tears joined the rivers falling downstream. As time passed, his sorrow grew. By autumn, his rivers became torrents devastating the mountainsides. Three months later with the arrival of winter, he was still in tears. Only now they crystallized at his feet forming what became the Domes of Miage, as well as Bionnassay and Tre-la-tête Glaciers," she sighed with a sweep of her silver hair. "*Oui*, they say that behind every glacier is a sad tale, millions of frozen tears shed by shepherds over eternal love."

Sometime in the middle of the night, all hell broke loose. Relentless winds tried to blow us off the mountain. Thunder boomed like cannon fire. A bolt of lightning shook the large cabin to its foundation. The maelstrom hit once more. All that made us especially glad we were tucked inside for the night—and no, you couldn't blame it on jilted shepherds.

We were wide-awake by the time the first rays filtered through our bedroom window. Only one Irishman joined us at our breakfast table. I thought maybe he'd killed the woman to finally silence her. But no, his sister and friend had given up. He'd continue alone.

Cheryl and I were anxious to trek even closer to Mt. Blanc, so we wasted no time in setting off. Just outside in the cabin yard, we spotted a fellow who'd camped out the night before in his fragile tent. Honestly, I'd half-expected him to be swept away and on his way to Nice by then. We waved and flashed him a "thumbs-up" and he beamed at our encouragement.

On the trail, it doesn't take too much to make someone's day.

The Via Alpina headed straight down the mountain through soggy meadows. After crossing Diosaz Stream, swollen by the deluge, we began a steep climb toward Col de Brévent in the Aiguilles Rouges Nature Reserve. Just past the ruins of Arlevé Chalets, we had a rare treat and spotted two chamois as they nibbled sparse bits of green on the slope ahead. Just as shocked to see us, they disappeared in a flash, bounding to higher ground. Although we'd heard there's a wide range of wildlife in the region, they're masters at avoiding humans. Still, if you're lucky, you might see black grouse and royal eagles, steinboks, mountain hares, and of course those cute, pudgy marmots.

Then again, any creature would be dwarfed by those extraordinary surroundings. After cresting a rise to the Col de Brévent, all of a sudden, Mt. Blanc and its snowcapped court rose in a jaw-dropping panorama. The symmetrical crown of the Alps and the adjacent 4000+ meter mountains were radiant. Peaks encircled us as far as the eye could see. We fell silent. At that moment, we knew why the Via Alpina had taken its weird 10-day dogleg on its western loop. The vista surpassed anything we'd seen since leaving Trieste (and I could now understand the poor shepherd).

Although not nearly as high as Mt. Everest, its setting rivals the Himalayas. All that was missing were the classic strands of fluttering Tibetan prayer flags, although someone had done their best to create a facsimile with colored flags on sticks stuck atop a stone monument. To me, it was obvious why they place those pendants in such rarefied spots. It was sacred, a cathedral among the clouds.

At moments like that, words are redundant, meaningless. Cheryl and I hugged, and then took a few photos of us grinning ear-to-ear like fools.

A crowd already gathered on the pass. They'd arrived by cable car from Chamonix in the valley far below. As we approached, one English girl wearing a nose ring and Doc Martens stopped us to naïvely ask, "Is there a rubbish bin up here?"

Huh? It'd be one heckuva slope for the garbage truck to back up. I could just hear the "Beep, beep, beep, beep" echoing through the valley.

The tour group soon vanished. They had a schedule to keep. At last, we were alone in her magical sanctuary. As with many such places, experiencing the Alps means listening, remaining silent, watchful, patient, as you let nature unfold. And there couldn't have been a more ideal spot.

Eventually we began our heady descent along the Tour du Mont-Blanc trail leading to La Flégère at 1865-meters, a hut precariously hugging the mountain's edge overlooking Chamonix. It's a bird's nest setting, only flawed by the cable car terminus and constant parade of people coming and going off the mountainside. It was hot and we were famished, so we stopped for a snack under one of their café umbrellas.

Nursing our cold drinks, Cheryl and I chuckled to ourselves as we watched an Italian family sitting nearby. First, Grandpa went to the restaurant window and brought back beers. Meanwhile Momma, closely supervised by Grandma, made salami sandwiches from food she'd smuggled from home.

"No, you do it this way!" Grandma scolded. Or, "You know, Pietro likes more mayonnaise on his." She nagged, "No, you slice the meat like this..." And

poor Mama dutifully obeyed. It was hilarious to watch the group dynamics, but they were probably much the same in any culture.

Now I have to admit, by this time on our journey, we were tired of the stages ending at another resort, so we easily decided to trek on for a few more hours to reach a quiet village in the valley below. It'd put us closer to the next pass in the morning. Even still, it was strange when our trek downhill unexpectedly became bumper-to-bumper, an *autobahn* of the Alps.

We skirted past folks of all ages, sizes and physical abilities enjoying nature. I had to hand it to them. They were each doing it at their own pace, their own way, whether they were grandparents or five-year-olds. Some were outfitted like experienced trekkers, while others were dressed in red hotpants, deck shoes and gold jewelry, or carried designer handbags as if they were off to the mall. I was amazed by their diversity and the challenge a high-altitude trek must have been for them, especially when we reached a sheer cliff outfitted with more ladders and fixed ropes. I had to wonder how they'd made it up there in the first place. It was a nerve-shaking vertical drop and tricky even for us, as we maneuvered from ladder to ropes and back again on narrow ledges for a good forty minutes.

The tiny village of Montroc, just past Argentière, has several auberges and we stopped at the first one we found: The Windmill. The guardian was a gracious fellow who cooked a savory vegetarian dinner, a rarity on the trail of pork. Although our bunkroom was simple, it offered peace and quiet, an amenity far more appreciated than any pillow mint.

After a great night's sleep, we left for Le Tour, another ski resort with cable cars running to Chateau de Charamillon. From that station, a lift continues all the way to Col de Balme at 2204-meters. Although it was tempting to just hop a ride on those and forego the hours of sweat and strain, Cheryl and I actually relished our steep trek up the slope, as we passed cows grazing right on the runs.

Maybe we'd improved a little over the past few months. I enjoyed feeling the rush when your legs, lungs and heart all work in concert. Finally. There's a primal satisfaction, a sense of accomplishment, as well as a connectedness. To see we'd actually beat the estimated hiking time to the top, well, made it even more fulfilling.

Crossing the col, we were back into Switzerland, ready to begin our rapid descent to Trient. Border hopping is one of the more unusual aspects of the Via Alpina. The red route crosses between countries 44 times—sometimes several in a day. National borders are marked with little more than a plaque or surveyor's stone. Blink and you miss it. There's no customs post with suspicious guards, moneychangers, flapping flags, or souvenir stands selling chocolate and singing stuffed marmots. That's the modern European Union with its open borders, and I've got to say it certainly beats building more walls.

After all, mountains know no nationality. They're simply mountains; they salute no flag, march to no anthem, answer to no president or potentate. And they'll remain long after all of us and our so-called "countries" disappear.

Glaciers, on the other hand, are not so lucky. All day the legendary iceflows such as the Bossons, Argentière, Tour, and France's largest, the Mer de Glace at seven kilometers long and 200 meters thick, surrounded us. In earlier times, Mont Blanc Glacier stretched as far as Lyon. But today, climate and man have endangered them to the point of extinction.

Even as early as 1865, Trient Glacier was exploited as an ice factory. Workers slashed the frozen treasure from the flow and threw blocks into a channel flowing to a retention pond. Eventually a narrow-gauge railway was built to transport those giant ice cubes to Forclaz Pass where they trucked the harvest to Martigny and then on to Paris, Lyon and Marseille. Reportedly, around 20 to 30,000 kilos of ice blocks were removed each day for ten years. That's a lot of glasses of *pastis*. Today all that remains are expansive moraines where the mighty glacier once flowed.

Nowadays, global warming is the culprit. Scientists predict Alpine glaciers will nearly disappear by 2050, fifty years earlier than first thought. Reportedly, on average about three percent of Alpine glacial ice is lost each year, about one meter of ice thickness. So what? Well, glacier loss will not only devastate the ski industry and tourism, creating massive unemployment in many of the villages we passed, but it'll also dramatically limit the amount of water available for drinking, farming and irrigation. At the same time, warming increases mudslides and flooding. It has already happened in the Himalayas. This threatens the very survival of mountain villages, as well as those farther down valley. Also, it adds to the rise in sea level, which will devastate cities like New York, L.A., London, Sydney, and Mumbai. How long can you tread water?

Trient is one such town that survives by hosting hikers trekking the famous Mont Blanc circuit. It's in another picture-perfect setting and we enjoyed an incredible view of the sugar-frosted mountains from our dormitory or *dortoir* at the inn. After months, we finally phoned Nathalie at the Via Alpina network and, since she was nearby, she graciously agreed to join us for dinner.

We didn't know quite what to expect—or what she expected from us. She knew I was researching a book and, for better or worse, I'd tell the story of our Via Alpina experience. Was she looking for a glowing report? Constructive feedback? Or was she just hoping to actually meet someone hiking the path she helped manage from afar?

But there was a congenial connection from the start. Nathalie was young and enthusiastic with an easy smile. She was French, working from her English home for a group based in the Alps. She'd been with the organization several years and I was surprised to hear she'd actually hiked part of the trail. Much to our relief, she was personable and genuinely interested in our comments.

Okay, I admit we toned them down a little from what we occasionally wanted to scream on the trail. But to her credit, she listened patiently without becoming defensive.

Although we'd loved Slovenia's scenery, we'd already warned her via email about the danger of folks trekking its mountains in June, the problem in finding good maps, and its disappearing trails. We'd also alerted her to all the harsh weather we'd faced, forcing us to trek in Austria's valleys to escape rain, snow and lightning.

"If that's typical for the time of year," I said, "maybe you can suggest lower alternate paths for trekkers that parallel your own?"

"You're not the only ones," she confided. "As I emailed you earlier, others who started in Trieste this year had the same troubles with the weather. One fellow skipped ahead to Schwaz to get out of the snow and rain. And a woman switched to the yellow route in Italy hoping for better weather. Then again, I know you don't want to hear this, but another hiker who left in the opposite direction from Monaco told me they've had clear weather all summer. It's rained just two days."

Then she shared the most enlightening thing we'd heard yet about the trail. "You know, the Via Alpina is just a thread anyway," she said with a sympathetic smile.

A thread? Cheryl and I glanced at each other in disbelief.

"Yes, it was never designed to be a thru-route. We never thought many people would actually try to hike from Trieste to Monaco in one season. That's why people can choose from all these trails and create their own to discover the Alps in whatever time they have."

"So, it *is* like jazz? Constant improvisation?"

She smiled. We were right all along. Any regret we felt for deviating from the trail (even if it was to save our own skin) disappeared. Their concept matched our own. Still, you have to admit it's an unusual notion: a trail that's several paths, a trail without much signage at times, a cultural itinerary that skirts villages unless you choose to hike through them on your own alternate route. But that's okay. The goal's simply to "Discover the Alps." Nothing more.

It's Zen-like. "Be" the Alps.

[CUE GONG]

I guess we'd succeeded so far, after all.

It's amazing how we humans create routine of the most unusual activities in our lives. Just like normal people drive to work each morning or drop off the kids at school, we began each day following our own routine with a 1000-meter climb or descent, always headed for the next valley. It was our own odd wilderness reality.

After breakfast, we set off down the road and caught a trail steeply headed to Col de la Forclaz. Just when we thought we'd reached the summit, the trail veered east climbing through pastures to 2000 meters until we again descended into a valley just a few kilometers from Vernayaz—the same village we'd left five tough days earlier.

Champex sur Lac is a resort with one small market, one main street, and holiday rentals. From its emptiness, I had the feeling few locals live there. Its charming lake was typically Alpine: tranquil, turquoise and ringed by mountains cascading down to its shore. Ducks shared frigid water with sunburned visitors splashing and goofing around in paddleboats.

Cheryl and I took advantage of the pristine setting and chose an auberge right on its bank. After a fifteen-minute amble the length of town, we relaxed along the lake with a simple picnic dinner. Then as the evening unfolded, we talked about how we expected the Alps to change as we hiked south. We expected to climb smaller mountains, see different vegetation, smell new fragrances, and taste more French cooking. Likewise, as we continued toward the Med, we looked forward to meeting locals in something more traditionally Alpine than another vacation setting. It was our hope, anyway.

That evening at sunset, I sat alone on our room's balcony. Suddenly, someone across the lake in the murky shadows played a lone, soulful alpenhorn (one of those long wooden instruments best known to Americans by the famous cough-drop commercials). Although I couldn't see the musician, its deep tones echoed magically like a loon on a New England pond.

Here was traditional culture, enchanting, unearthly, and transcending time. Regrettably, many of the diners below in the outside café couldn't hear it amid the endless chatter and clanging of dishes. Sure, they came to see the legendary Alps, to relax over dinner, or maybe climb a mountain or two, and they undoubtedly went home with snowcapped images and memories of melted cheese *raclette* dancing in their heads.

But maybe, I thought, just maybe they missed its essence, its soul. They missed the alpenhorn at sunset.

12

SUMO COWS

AT DAYBREAK, WE LEFT TOWN SKIRTING THE LAKE, WITH THE sound of the mournful alpenhorn still echoing in my head. Cheryl and I hiked down toward the village of Orsières. It's set in beautiful Ferret Valley amid a fusion of cultures and traditions. We had a pleasant ramble through forest with little in the way of extreme climbs. Until just northwest of town, we came across a remarkable village that'll remain nameless in the hope that it stays pristine. It's traditional, featuring handcrafted timber houses and unblemished by tourism. Many townspeople still farm or have huge family gardens. The bus stop was once the village bakery and wooden paddles used to remove bread from its ovens now hang over its doorway.

It was also the first day we spotted the obvious signs of autumn, even though the calendar still insisted it was mid-August. Aspens already resembled cascades of butter patties lining our path. Our time was nearly up. No doubt, fall would be short with winter close behind. All too well, I knew we were racing time if we hoped to reach Monaco before the first snows covered the high Alps.

Based on the weather so far, it was anyone's guess how soon it would hit—or how hard.

Still, that particular afternoon was a reprieve. Sunlight dappled through the pine forest and we were alone in a primeval paradise. It was hot and sticky and we finally did what we'd promised ourselves we'd do for months. We stopped beside a clear mountain stream. Cheryl stripped off her clothes and plunged into a freezing pool with me close behind. It was glacial and bracing. The water was so cold it burned, but just for an instant before your extremities went numb. It was perfection.

The shrinkage would pass.

We were especially excited to arrive back in Bourg-St-Pierre, a hamlet at the base of Grand St. Bernard Pass leading over the mountains into Italy. The last time we'd been there was on a snowy spring day several years earlier while hiking a portion of the Via Francigena, a 9th century pilgrimage trail from Canterbury, England to Rome.

Back then, cold and hungry, we were welcomed into the church rectory by Pere Alphonse, a gregarious priest in his 80s. The fellow with a contagious smile wined and dined us, sharing several bottles from his own private cellar along with never-ending plates of spaghetti and genial conversation. Time and again, he encouraged us saying, "Eat! Eat! You're young!" Only once did we pause to come up for air when he unexpectedly excused himself to go say Mass. Happy to tag along, we joined him and ten ancient parishioners in the frigid stone church for what must be the shortest service on record. Then we continued joking and savoring toast after toast before retiring to one of his comfy, wood-paneled rooms for the night.

All that had changed over the past few years. We were sad to hear Pere Alphonse had recently suffered a heart attack and now lives in Martigny. There was no celebrating or catching up. There was no wine. There was no pasta.

There, in the tiny village where Napoleon and his 40,000 troops had once bivouacked, the sound of the church bell still rings at night. But its sweetest sound, the cherubic laughter of Pere Alphonse, is strangely absent and missed by all—especially us, two lonely pilgrims who'd once found solace from the freedom of the road.

To make up for lost time and calories, the next morning we splurged on a huge buffet at the Bivouac Napoleon: meat and cheese, four croissants, four or five coffees each, cereal, fruit, yogurt and whatever else wasn't nailed down. In fact, I was still eating as I walked out the door. After a near fast the day before, we weren't taking any chances. We had a huge climb ahead of us.

As we headed back through the village to begin our daily ascent, we thought one last time about Pere Alphonse and wished him good health in his new home. Though we'd missed a reunion, I knew he'd be with us in spirit.

Like our solemn mood, the weather also was overcast. For once, that brightened our day. A little cover would make our trek up the 2469-meter Grand St. Bernard Pass easier. Today, although its *autobahn* is a major transcountry thoroughfare, the same pass was used as far back as prehistoric times. During Celtic days, it was a dirt track. Then it was paved by the Romans to provide a major artery to the northern part of the empire. Julius Caesar tramped across with his Legionnaires in 58 B.C. Long after the Empire's fall, it continued to be one of the main arteries for crossing the formidable Alps.

Our trail was surprisingly well marked, following parallel to that road. Despite the fact the highway was chock-a-block with drivers headed to Italy, Switzerland or beyond, we were alone much of the morning on a southward trail hugging the mountainside. Just once, we ran into two other hikers coming from the opposite direction. With a formidable col to climb, there was little time to waste chatting, as it took us almost four hours to approach the summit.

Just before noon, nearly in sight of the crest, we stumbled upon a stone bivouac that was actually open. We'd passed several over the last few months, but they'd all been locked. I briefly poked my head inside the wall-tent sized hut to see a table, stove and wood supply—enough to sustain someone caught on that mountain in bad weather—and, man, they have their share. They had twenty meters of snow last winter in just one night. Fortunately, the same pass is also renowned for its St. Bernards. Those loveable, sad-eyed, slobbering dogs have been legendary for saving stranded travelers for 300 years or more.

The pass is even better known for its hospice. Back in 1050, Saint Bernard of Aosta founded a refuge that's become one of the most famous monasteries in the Alps, if not in all of Europe. Travelers, merchants and conquerors, including Henry IV, Frederick Barbarossa and Napoleon, have all welcomed its hospitality atop the foreboding col.

For once, just in case the weather or our condition turned for the worse, I'd made reservations up there from the roadhouse in Bourg-St-Pierre. Even though the weather was stable for the moment, upon reaching its peak, I grew more nervous about our impossibly long stage the following day.

We aren't in bad shape, it isn't raining or snowing, and who knows what tomorrow will bring? Why not continue?

Over lunch, when I casually mentioned the option of hiking on to St-Rhémy en Bosses, Cheryl and I had a heated argument, our first in a long time. I won't bore you with the details. Only in the end, she sullenly said, "Fine, you do what you want!"

I'd been married long enough to know what that meant.

"Okay, I'll go and check out the rooms here and find out what they charge. Based on that, we can decide whether to go or stay."

Jogging upstairs, I talked to the woman in charge of rentals and then returned to the café to break the bad news to my fuming partner.

We hiked on. Leaving the restaurant, we traced the lake, flew past the imposing pointing statue of St. Bernard, and then swiftly cut across switchbacks into the Italian valley on the other side. Just then, wouldn't you know, it began to storm. In frustration, we threw on our rain gear and slogged in silence.

"I told you so" rang repeatedly in my head. But guilt, another gift that keeps on giving, was short-lived. Skies cleared before we reached Ste-Rhémy less than two hours later. What's more, from the looks of the dry terrain, we'd stepped across a line into another climatic zone: wet on one side, dry on the other.

In spite of this, we'd trekked one mountain too far after all. There was no place to sleep. After searching for half an hour without any luck, someone finally suggested we continue to St. Leonard.

"And how far is that?" Cheryl asked.

"Just down the road. A few kilometers," they promised.

Now, that's not far away—if you're driving—or if you haven't already chased up and down a mountain or two already. In our case, it was another long hour. What choice did we have?

Exhausted, running on adrenaline fumes, we eventually straggled into St. Leonard to where we ultimately ducked into a bar. I found the owner, who knew a lady, who happened to rent a room in her house. We weren't a hard sell. It'd been one helluva day.

Even after unpacking, our rift remained. We ate in silence.

At daybreak, we rose in silence. We walked in silence, the way couples do when there's nothing left to be said. Then we stopped into a bar for a cup of coffee and croissant, meager calories to sustain us up the col we knew awaited again—no matter how much we wanted to wish it away.

Although it was easy to follow the marked path from St. Leonard, it disappeared once we reached the valley. Reluctantly we stopped at a farmhouse and asked a sleepy-eyed fellow for directions. He patiently explained in two languages that we were to cross two bridges and head up the mountain.

Easy, right? Wrong. Although we followed his advice precisely, there was no semblance of a trail. Nothing.

"Dammit, we're lost already" Cheryl cried, as though I'd misread my crystal ball.

"No, we're not. You're only lost when you don't know where you are. We know St. Leonard is up there, right, so *we're* not lost. The *trail* is lost."

My logic was lost on her.

Taking a chance, I forged uphill to what turned out to be a deserted stone house. There were a few other footprints and a vine-covered marker. After whistling for my partner who'd waited below to join me, I set off in what I figured must be the right direction until I eventually found a crumbling wall and the actual trail. It was easy, after all. If only we'd stayed another 100 meters on the dirt road, past *three* bridges, we'd have run into a sign pointing the way.

Once on the trail, it was a steep three-hour trek up to the col past a few dilapidated farmhouses and stables. We were greeted by a dozen black cows, their faces swarming with flies. Otherwise, in contrast to the popular Mt. Blanc route, we only met six other hikers all morning, all headed downslope. Fortunately, we found plenty of water, even if it was just snow runoff fed into the cattle troughs. It was enough to sustain us on yet another thousand-meter climb.

Col Citrin was stark. The path down the other side was poorly marked in contrast to the precise Swiss ones. We found trails marked 8A, 8B and 8C—all at the same time in different directions—while our topo map just indicated trail 8 or 118. As any experienced hiker knows, it can take a lot of creative problem solving or guesswork to get from here to there. But this one pushed it to the limit.

"So which are we supposed to follow?" I muttered to no one in particular.

We picked one and took our chances. As sharp as our ascent had been, the climb down was much worse. Trails were ragged traces of disappearing footprints across shifting sand and crumbled slate. It was like tracking a mirage.

Then wouldn't you know it, as we skidded our way down the meandering slope, Cheryl wrenched her knee again and started limping. We were mighty relieved to finally reach a dirt road that we knew led to Cérellaz. Even better was discovering the traditional country *trattoria* out in the middle of a farmer's field.

It was a humble, one-story stucco building with a tile roof. Much busier than I'd have thought, it was packed with families who'd driven up there on a hot summer's day. They enjoyed wine and food platters under bright parasols on the sunny terrace. For us, the cool, dark interior of the stone restaurant sounded much more appealing. Stepping inside, we were surrounded by tradition. Its thick white walls were decked out from top to bottom with a variety of wooden farm implements, shoe forms, and clogs made of wood. At that point, we'd have been delirious with just a cold drink and a snack; but after one look at the menu scrawled in Italian on a small blackboard, we splurged on the cheese platter.

While we cooled our heels, the wife of the owner/farmer presented us with a jar of honey and plate of rock-hard bread nuggets, a dentist's wet dream.

"Okay, so what do we do with this?"

Not wanting to appear ungrateful or look like the strangers we were, we figured we were meant to drizzle honey onto the gravel and crunch them like country granola. We did. It was awful.

So, you can imagine our relief when the lady returned, looked aghast at the odd sweet concoction we'd created, and then lectured us saying, "No, you eat the honey and bread with the old cheese—not mixed together."

(*Idiota!*)

All the same, she presented us with six enormous hunks of fontina cheese, about two-kilos of *formaggio* made right on their farm.

"The white cheese is fresh," the Italian patiently explained in English. "The yellow is one year old and the brown one is two."

Now to me, it looked like a science project left in the closet too long and tasted about the same way rust remover smells. Although the others were delicious, it was more food than we could possibly eat at one sitting and we saved the leftovers for later. They'd sustain us for at least two more meals.

Before long, we waddled back into the scorching sun and continued tracing the river directly down valley. All day we'd seen a major change in the surrounding terrain. The plants and trees were musky and aromatic, as in the Alpes-Maritimes. The ground was bone-dry. We'd tried to increase our water intake, but were equally parched. The searing weather, especially the wind, quickly dehydrated us, so we had to remember to be extra diligent in the days ahead.

I was shocked to see skin starting to hang from my calf muscles—not a good sign. But every now and then, we found unexpected relief. At one point, we came across a concrete sluice carrying fresh glacier water to the valley below. Cheryl and I stopped, pulled off our boots and socks, and plunged hot, tired feet into its icy goodness where we kept them until they were perfectly numb.

It was orgasmic!

From there, we made a swift descent to Cérellaz, a sleepy village of fifty-six inhabitants. There's no grocery. No B&B. No pension and one small hotel. Realizing it was useless to trek any farther in the heat, we checked into the Hotel des Alpes, run by a mother and her son. "Hiker-friendly," they went out of their way to drive us to the next village to a market where we bought bread and wine to eat with our cheese.

Still, after seeing how close it was, we had to wonder why the Via Alpina choose the smaller, less-equipped hamlet three kilometers away? Maybe the cows are to blame.

On the first Sunday in August, Cérellaz holds its oddly dramatic *Bataille des Reines* (Queen Cow Battle), a stirring sumo-like tussle between pregnant black Héren cows for the honor of becoming queen. True. We've seen photos. This is no small deal and it's a cultural novelty. Each year since the 1920s, the Haute-Savoie province, the Swiss canton of Valais, and Italy's Valle d'Aosta host cow queen fights that draw up to 50,000 spectators. They claim this breed naturally battles to determine herd dominance. Each fight lasts up to 40 minutes. Cows that back down are eliminated until one's left standing in the ring.

But don't bother to contact PETA; it's hardly a Death Match. With their horns blunted, the fights are more like a push-a-thon. At the end of the year, a grand finale is staged in Martigny where the six best from seven districts do battle in six weight categories. Afterward, the owner and his village receive kudos for winning. The "Queen of Queens" becomes leader of her herd, chooses the best pasture, receives a special royal bell, increases dramatically in value, and wins an all-expense paid trip to Cozumel.

Well, maybe all except the last part.

As usual, we were two weeks late.

We left the village at dawn's first light and headed down valley into Runaz where we stopped for the breakfast of hardened hikers: espresso and a cellophane-wrapped croissant. It's the French equivalent of our ever-popular golden, cream-filled snack cakes, also designed to survive any Alp-ocalypse. That was all they had in the tiny town at that hour.

After quizzing the eighty-year-old barmaid for directions, stomachs still growling, we set off on a steep climb once again. Sure, we could've saved hours by simply following the road another thirty minutes, but no, we strictly followed the Via Alpina the long way around to reach Reserve Naturale Lolair.

By then, the sun was high; no water was in sight. Trail markers vanished, and we were forced to stop at a house and ask for directions.

"I'm sorry," the young lady began, apologizing in broken German. "Hikers always get lost up here. Trail markings are no good. This is Italy," she added with a resigned shrug.

Following her directions, we inched constantly higher along a mountain dirt road to electrical towers; then hugged the mountainside through deserted villages, past stone houses and stables in ruins. In the energy-sapping heat, we kept our eyes peeled for water fountains. But there was no relief.

Eventually we reached Planaval where a huge banner proclaimed they were in the midst of a celebration. Although I could already taste their energizing white wine on my tongue, once again, we were a day late and a euro short. Fortunately, it just was a short trek to Valgrisenche, an ancient settlement that once bustled with copper mining.

Dragging into town, we settled into a dormitory in the old part of the village. Once an Italian Army barracks, it'd recently been transformed into a beautiful hostel. Pascal, the guardian, was lonely and especially sociable. After hearing we'd been trekking for more than eighty days, he gave us a room to ourselves. Then later, we learned a little more about the attractive border region.

Valle d'Aosta is a strategic gorge that's changed hands over the years. The valley originally belonged to the House of Savoy for 700 years until it was ceded to Italy in 1860. So interestingly, today, it's a melting pot. Many residents still consider themselves more French than Italian and speak a *patois* that's a combination of the two.

Likewise, Cheryl and I'd long-since made up. We still had too many mountains to climb. Besides, the secret to a long-lasting relationship depends on forgiveness—and a certain amount of selective memory loss. Given our difficulties during the past several days, we went all-out that night and treated ourselves to the refuge's feast of pasta, sausage and polenta, washed down with wine; then we moved the party back to our room.

The harsh early morning light arrived all too soon, and with it came a four-kilometer trek along Lake Beauregard to its 100 meter high dam doubling as a climbing wall. To build it, seven villages were evacuated in 1952 and submerged by water. Two reappeared when the water eventually receded. Today, five eerily remain underwater, an Atlantis of the Alps.

We made a long, relatively easy hike to connect with the spur heading west from the hamlet of Grand Alpe. Nepalese-looking, it's the rustic home of a few hardy herding families. Once there, we set off to climb another daunting 1000 meters over switchbacks to Col du Mont at 2637 meters. Travelers, traders and smugglers have long used the pass to move goods between Italy and the Haut-Tarentaise Valley in France. In 1799, it was also the site of a fierce battle between French and Austro-Hungarian troops. These days, once a year, villagers from both sides of the pass peacefully gather to celebrate the fraternity between Alpine people.

For us, the pass was eerily empty except for the burned remains of Seigne Barracks used by customs officials between the wars. At one point, we ran into a train of overburdened mules, guides and trekkers stumbling down. Otherwise, we were alone and made great time. We breezed over the summit back into France's Mercurel Valley and it was only 1:30 by the time we arrived at Refuge de l'Archeboc, a large timber and stone house sitting on a windswept ledge overlooking a sea of black shale. It was our stage stop.

As usual, we took off our boots at the door. Cheryl poked her head inside. Spotting a couple working in the kitchen, she innocently asked, "Do you have room for two hikers tonight?"

It was a simple question. We'd never had any difficulty finding a bed in a hut. From the looks of things, especially at that early hour, we were the only ones there. There were no telltale packs, poles, boots or bikes. Besides, we couldn't imagine it was busy. It was late August. The kids had returned to school.

So, we were a little surprised when the Frenchman indignantly shot back, "Do you have a reservation?"

We'd only reserved spaces a few times since starting in June. Anyway, this was a mountain hut, not a four-star resort.

"No," Cheryl replied, a little proudly. "We're hiking the Via Alpina."

Hearing that, he flew into a rage. "I am so tired of you Via Alpina people thinking you can arrive without a reservation! I hate you! I turned some of you away just yesterday."

Whoa. We were shocked. We'd never had that reaction before—quite the opposite. If anything, folks had always been supportive and interested in hearing more about our journey.

"But we don't have a mobile phone," I explained, entering the fray. I know that's unheard of these days in Europe. Then I added, "We've been hiking more than eighty days."

If nothing else, that never failed to cut us a little slack.

"Where did you stay last night?" he asked.

"Valgrisenche."

"Why didn't you ask them to phone?"

"To France from Italy? We didn't think they would. Would you?"

"You wait here," he snorted in perfect English. "*We* will have lunch. And then, *we* will decide if *you* can stay."

I wanted to laugh at his nonsense. Then again, Cheryl and I were annoyed by his attitude, especially to hikers seeking refuge in his "refuge." He'd obviously housed the group with the mules. They'd undoubtedly driven up there with their guides, but of course, they'd made reservations. His reaction seemed all the more bizarre since we'd been about the only ones staying at the refuge the night before. The lonely guardian actually seemed grateful to have our company.

The more we thought about his pomposity, the more it galled us.

Why stand around waiting for him to have lunch—only for him to say, "Go away, you stinking, filthy Via Alpinists!"

No, we wouldn't give him the satisfaction. Scouring our maps on the deck, I figured we could make it to Ste-Foy by sunset. Before leaving, we popped our heads inside just long enough to say, "Thanks for all your hospitality!" before setting off once again.

Not far down the mountain road, we bumped into a trekking French couple and asked if they knew where we could find fresh water. With the showdown at the hut, we'd missed filling our bottles. Well, without a moment's hesitation, they suggested we take one of theirs', as they didn't have far to hike. We politely thanked them and refused, but they insisted.

Spurred on by their generosity, it only took two hours to reach Ste-Foy-Tarentaise where we checked into their sole hotel. Heeding the rude bugger's advice, Cheryl made it a point to drop into their visitor office to reserve a room for the next night. Since the usual Via Alpina stop, Refuge le Monal, was already full, we decided to continue farther south.

At dusk, lost in thought, I stared outside our window toward the bell tower of the village church. As a golden yin-yang moon pierced the cobalt sky, I thought about those folks who'd shared their water. Sure, it was a simple act of kindness, but once again we'd been shown for every badass in the world there are many more good ones.

Just like that fellow's welcome, it stormed buckets all night. We woke to more ominous clouds.

"Look, since we're already in the valley," I suggested, "why make this any harder than it already is? Why climb another muddy mountain trail?"

Cheryl agreed. One glance at our map told us it'd save time and headaches to follow a more direct route down a small mountain road to Tignes Les Boisses. On paper, it looked good. What we didn't count on was the endless stream of traffic between Ste-Foy and the popular Val d'Isère.

I'd suffered through the dangerous exercise in road survival before. I'd even hiked across Serbia where you pass a memorial to fallen walkers or drivers every hour. But for my partner, it was a gut-wrenching experience—particularly once when a car flew over the centerline headed straight toward her. She flattened herself against the mountain wall as it swerved away at the very last second.

As they say, do NOT try this at home.

After too many tense hours, we connected to a side road leading down to the sleepy village of Les Brévières, a ski resort in its off-off season, before we continued uphill to another reservoir with an interesting past. In 1952, engineers created perfect little Lac du Chevril and its dam. Well, maybe not so ideal if you lived in the village drowned to create it. As you can imagine, the locals were not keen about the idea, even if their old baroque church was moved to the top of the hill in the new village.

It reminded me of a similar legend. A certain Savoie lake was well known for its cave fairies. They were always helping man, which was why they decided to build a bridge between Talloires and Duingt. It was a good plan—except for one small detail. The Lord of Duingt refused to move and then refused to pay them for their hard work. That didn't sit well with the industrious fairies who had the last laugh. Even today, some say, at dusk you hear church bells ringing from under the peaceful lake.

Moral of the story: Always pay your fairies fairly.

Tignes Les Boisses lay just above Les Brévières. It was equally shuttered. Even its youth hostel was closed. Knowing that bartenders can be a good local source for lodging and libation, we dropped into La Cordée where we met Mitch. Its gregarious owner was originally from Brittany. Over a beer, he told us how he'd arrived in the resort a few years earlier with "just 400 francs in my pocket" and rebuilt his life.

"This mountain is my family," he declared. "We take care of each other."

After hearing the story of our travels, he took care of us too, buying us drinks, and then directing us to his friends who ran the nearby cozy Chalet Hotel Les Melezes. Thanks to Mitch, our faith in real French hospitality was again gratefully restored.

That night, what began as a drizzle turned into yet another downpour. Thunder shook the hotel like a dog with a chew rag, but life looked far better in the morning. Autumn burst in full vibrant colors. Trees in those high elevations already donned Technicolor coats of gold, tangerine, and red, which made for a stunning hike along the lake and up to bustling Le Lac de Tignes.

It's part of L'Espace Killy, one of Europe's largest ski areas, combining Tignes and Val d'Isère. The popular resort set in the lap of snowcapped mountains offers every mountain activity imaginable, as well as a variety of restaurants, nightlife, and a very helpful visitor office.

The Brits running our hotel referred us to their friends who have an inn right on the lake, so it was an easy move for us. We relished relaxing for a few days, and it was a perfect spot to meet our friends, Ramon and Big Mac, his vibrant wife, who planned to drop by on their way home after touring Italy.

They're a dynamic couple. He's a modern Renaissance man: a writer, musician, composer and painter. She's Barcelona's freshest, funniest, up-and-coming rock diva. Running a little late, they pulled into town the following night and we looked forward to spending two days eating, partying, and just catching up.

Our first afternoon together, when we were on our way to the market, we just happened to run into Hugo. We hadn't seen the "seductive duck" for almost three weeks since our stay in the shepherd's hut. Scruffier than usual, he'd just taken a bath in Tignes Lake and was stretched out to dry in the grass.

"Hey, we thought we'd lost you," I said, walking over to introduce our friends. "Figured you decided to stay in La Vare and become a shepherd after all."

"Well, I considered it, but I finally finished my book. Nothing left to read up there," he said with a snort, "so I had to come down here to look for a Belgian newspaper. You haven't seen one, have you?"

It wasn't first on my to-do list.

"Where've you been staying?"

"I'm wild camping now almost every night. I got tired of the refuges. They just don't work for me anymore."

We'd talked about that earlier. But wild camping is often regulated on the Via Alpina, especially in national parks—not to mention the resorts. It's difficult to camp very "wild" in an upscale setting like that.

"What do you do for baths?" Cheryl asked.

"Streams or lakes," he said, pointing a bony finger to icy Tignes.

It was a strange choice, given the warmer options surrounding us. Then again, he was the same odd fellow who insisted that being swarmed by voracious flies reminded him of "being kissed all over by beautiful women."

He clearly didn't date enough.

"You camping here?" I asked.

"Well, I've been wondering. Where'd you think is a good spot?"

"Maybe you could try the other side of the lake above the golf course. It's close to the water, yet far enough away from people. You're not as likely to be arrested up there."

"Nah, too far from the water." He nodded toward a small log cabin not ten-meters away. "Actually, I was gonna camp right over there."

"There?" I couldn't believe it. "They run programs for the kids. I don't think they'd like you to sleep in their doorway."

He shrugged, saying, "Yea, that's real good."

On closer inspection, I could already see his pack, hiking stick and boots propped by their door.

Hugo, that friendly mutt-of-a-man, still loped to the beat of his own drum. We wished him luck, but hoped he'd exercise a little caution and not be run out of town—or worse. When we mentioned we were leaving in another day for Termignon, he was vague about his plans. But why? Looking gaunter than ever, we worried about his health. In his eyes, something had clearly changed during the last few weeks. Was it his energy? His willpower?

We wished each other well until we met again on the trail. Still, in my heart of hearts, I knew that day would never come.

That night, while sharing a bottle of Côtes de Rhône with Ramon and Big Mac on our balcony, we watched folks on the waterfront light candles inside colorful Chinese paper lanterns, which sent them levitating over that same lake. In the black of night, they appeared ethereal, a flickering globe mysteriously suspended in midair. Carefree, they rapidly soared, higher and higher, until the air grew thin, their flame blew out, and they plummeted to the inky lake far below.

13

A SECRET HANDSHAKE

HEARTFELT GOODBYES CONTINUED OVER BREAKFAST. RAMON and Big Mac would get in their merry Micra and bebop back to Barcelona, while we'd attempt to complete a double stage all the way to Termignon. Normally that'd be out of the question, but we were well rested and the stages (only) totaled nine hours in the best possible conditions.

We lost sight of our Catalon friends waving *Adéu* on the shoreline as we began our morning climb past the lift stations south of the lake, winding ever higher toward Glacier de la Grande-Motte and Col de la Leisse at 2729 meters. We'd heard our hotel manager went up there every morning with his buddies to snowboard the glacier. Supposedly, earlier that summer, someone had tumbled and was lost in one of the crevasses. There was talk of closing it to snowboarders, but they put the kibosh on that notion. Bad for business. So, for now, folks could still risk life and limb to slide that massive sheet of ice.

The trail was spectacular as we hiked like gnomes among frosted Goliaths. Our only company was the ever-present roly-poly marmots, barking their chew-toy squeal. Fatter than ever, they looked prepared for the long snows ahead. Winter was closer than we'd imagined.

Before long, we passed Refuge de la Leisse but didn't stop until we'd reached Refuge d'Entre Deux Eaux for a tureen of their pea soup. From there, it was a straight shot through the Parc Nationale de la Vanoise, so we pressed on. Crossing the Doron de Termignon River, we climbed steeply up the other side for another hour until we reached Refuge de Plan du Lac. A few folks were already out on its terrace soaking up the sunshine over a carafe of wine, but something told us they hadn't hiked there. Once again, we'd seen few people all day. You could drive there, or take a bus from the valley below.

Still, it didn't matter. We were happy to just read their interpretive signage and revel in the inspiring, wind-whipped vista of the Dômes de la Vanoise range, the wholly spectacular 3639-meter Dent Parrachée, and glaciers surrounding us to all sides.

For every "up" there's a "down" and ours was a knee crunching 800-meter descent along what was once a salt route between France and Italy. We skirted another cobalt blue lake, the third of the day, and then the ruins of stone houses and stables, past a waterfall, through forests, and finally down a river wash over huge polished stones on a path called "The Medicinal Trail" because of its trailside herbal remedies. Given its steep incline, you would've thought potions for blown knees would be a big seller, but no such luck, although we did spot a marmot cream claiming to work wonders.

It must take incredibly nimble fingers to milk one of those rascals.

After nine long hours, we reached Termignon. By the time we limped into town, our patience was frayed. The hostel and hotel were both closed, but miracle of miracles, the visitor office was open. Not only that, but they served samples of delicious local wine, cheese and sausage to passersby, right at their front door. Things were definitely looking up.

Elise, the cheery, dapple-cheeked girl who worked there, was also knowledgeable about the Via Alpina, a welcome change, and happy to find us a place to sleep at the campground. While Cheryl rushed off to buy groceries before the market closed, Elise demonstrated an interactive Via Alpina computer program allowing you to take a virtual tour of the route. With a joystick, you could zoom into any of the many national parks along the way.

"You mean we could've traveled like this and missed 40 days of rain?"

She suppressed a laugh and then repeated what the other hiker had told Nathalie. "We've hardly had any rain this season." Then she went on to explain how the route through there was once Napoleon's (as were most things in the region), but traders had also used it to market salt and their famous veined cheese, Termignon blue.

Speaking of which, I suddenly remembered Cheryl at the market. Thanking Elise, I jogged across the street to meet my partner, but was a minute late and more than a few euros short. She'd splurged 18 euros (25 dollars) on a rotisserie chicken. I was in shock.

"For one chicken?"

"I'm so tired of sausage and cheese. We've eaten little else for the past three months."

I was too, but we'd already spent far too much to sleep on straw or in huts, and to live on cold cuts and cheap wine. As she paid, I politely asked the clerk for a plastic bag to carry our treasure back to the campground.

"Free plastic bags are against French law," she smugly replied.

"How about golden chickens?

She grinned, as if to say, "Fool, you didn't have to buy it."

Cheryl tucked the warm fowl under her arm and we hiked to the nearby campground where we soon found ourselves seated around a dining table inside a warm trailer. True, it was a small extravagance. Then again, while licking the garlic from my fingers, I had to admit it was a damn fine golden bird, after all.

The icy blast of dawn was less welcome. Even though I wore my Polar Guard vest, we turned on the heater to thaw the small camper. Despite the calendar claiming it was still August, winter pounded on our door and crept through our windows.

My partner and I shivered into town to locate a place for an espresso and only found a bar open at that early hour. The lady who ran the place was in her late 70s, still svelte with an ebony-dyed pageboy haircut and red polished nails. Though I missed the era by a long shot, she appeared straight from the roaring twenties, transported to the high mountain town by a time machine.

The flapper was aloof when we entered, chatting to two local fellows nursing their hair-of-the-dog drinks. To her, we were just two more tourists. She'd seen her share. I drained my coffee in two sips and then studied the weathered photographs lining the walls.

Is she the little girl in the faded snapshot of the farmhouse and family? And what on earth brought her up here?

Eager to hit the trail, we stood to pay her and casually mentioned we'd nearly trekked the length of the Alps, all the way from Trieste. Well, that struck a nerve and her attitude and body language completely changed. The woman's eyes lit up with longing, as she asked all about our journey. We were suddenly all right. We shared her love. We weren't tourists, after all. We were alpinists.

We left Termignon via the newer part of the village, heading up its ski slope on the *Chemin du Petit Bonheur* (Path of Small Joy) between the timberline and lifts. This led us far above the villages below. As we trekked, we happened to pass an Irish wolfhound and I couldn't help but think of our buddy Hugo. We'd seen him briefly as we'd left the lake. He'd camped under the eaves of the kids' cabin after all, and complained his legs hurt.

That didn't surprise me. Long trails have a way of wearing you down in more ways than one. Figuring he had a mineral deficiency, I suggested chugging an energy drink for the electrolytes. Experience has taught me it's not enough to just drink water on long treks. Your body constantly loses minerals, which causes weakness and muscle soreness.

Now, with the cold snap and his weakened state, could he continue?

By mid-afternoon, the trail led us past the daunting Forts Marie-Christine, Charles Felix, and Marie-Therése, all built onto a rocky escarpment overlooking the valley. They were originally part of five fortifications called Forts Esseillon built from 1819-34. Back when the region was part of Sardinia, they defended the Piedmont against a possible French invasion. However, it was a short-lived buffer zone. The Franco-Sardinian alliance of 1857 soon made them obsolete.

From there, it was a short hop down valley to Modane. As it was Sunday, everything, including the market (and the chance to buy a golden goose) was closed. Luckily, we'd had the foresight to ask Elise to call ahead and reserve a place for us at the local campground. But as a friend of mine used to say, "Lucky? Unlucky? Who knows?"

We did have their so-called "chalet," a frigid hut, to ourselves, but since it was their last night open that season, the campground managers were less than cordial. Even their Cerberus kick-dog nearly loved us to death, snarling, baring its teeth, and promising to rip us to shreds every time we tiptoed past to the toilet.

The next morning, the campsite manager was packed and anxious to leave, refusing to sell us even a cup of instant coffee. To top it off, her husband gave us impossible directions to the trailhead, which we struggled to find. Sooner or later, we made our way steeply uphill, deep into ibex territory. We paused only long enough to visit a local pilgrimage spot, the Notre Dame du Charmaix, built in 1401. Dedicated to the Black Virgin, it hangs on the rocky face of a gorge.

Afterward, it wasn't far to Valfréjus, a deserted ski station, where we caffeine junkies were still unable to find a cup of java. Out of season, too, I guess.

Invariably, the trail continued winding uphill all morning through forests, then along unmarked trails toward the Col de la Vallée Etroite. At one point, we were surprised to find ourselves face-to-face with a bunker and turret, once part of France's useless WWII vintage Maginot Line. The huge string of concrete fortifications, machinegun nests, and artillery placements was constructed along France's border from Switzerland to Luxembourg. Named after French Minister of Defense André Maginot, it was reportedly built to buy time to either mobilize the French army—or to entice Germany to attack neutral Belgium instead (which must have certainly pleased the poor Belgians).

Nowadays, it's still somewhat intact, complete with retractable doors and deep trenches. With its well-disguised location, it's impossible to see from the top of the mountain pass. An enemy would run into heavy fire from either side, but that did little to stop the Nazis. As planned, they simply went around the line to invade Belgium—and then to occupy France itself—as unplanned.

During our steep climb to the col at 2456 meters, we only ran into four others all morning. An athletic, handsome German couple and two Frenchmen headed east to Mont Thabor refuge for lunch, while we doggedly continued sliding down the other side of the mountain. It was a far different backdrop from any we'd crossed so far. It reminded us of Utah's Bryce Canyon with its dry, jagged, unusually shaped monoliths. As is true of many of Europe's border regions, it's changed hands frequently throughout history. As you might guess, many folks speak Italian. As one wouldn't expect, we actually had the choice of staying in two different gîtes in Les Granges de la Vallée Etroite that evening.

Gîtes are the French equivalent of the pension, except most serve full dinners as well as breakfasts. They're very popular throughout the country. Given our stomach-led priorities, we settled on the Italian-run inn simply because it promised a larger dinner and half-liter of wine. While waiting for the feast, we beat a hasty retreat to the privacy of what we called their Gnome Room, a place under the eaves where we could never quite stand upright. But that made little difference. We spent most of our time horizontal, anyway.

You meet an international group of hikers and travelers at those refuges. We shared dinner with a soft-spoken Dutch couple. Willem and Bea, both tall and lean, came to hike the GR5 from Haarlem (Holland, not Manhattan). I could tell they weren't new at this game. Willem was as easy-going as he was strong, and Bea had an intense look punctuated by no-nonsense short brown bangs and stylishly retro horn-rimmed glasses. We also spotted those same fair-haired Germans, Berthold and Ingrid, that we'd run into earlier on our way to the col when we'd compared notes on one bit of unmarked trail. Surprisingly, there were many older Italian and French up there too on day hikes, plus six Englishmen who slept just down the hall. We overheard them going on for nearly an hour outside the showers as they teased each other like schoolboys about body odors and bowel movements.

All in all, it was a wonderful Italian evening, complete with aperitifs at a pre-dinner party followed by antipasto, polenta and sausage, and then dessert with espresso. It was oh-so-civilized and never more appreciated.

At daybreak, we set off on an easy climb past mountains named Gaspar, Balthasar and Melchior after the Three Wise Men, and then up to Col des Thures at 2194 meters. Its serene Chavillon Lake lay at the edge of a grassy, windswept plateau. The Dutch and Germans joined us briefly to yak about the latest in backpacks, maps and GPS gizmos (as gear geeks do everywhere), before we split in different directions. The Dutch couple, Willem and Bea, headed to Briançon, while the Germans continued to Névache like us.

The deafening silence at that altitude always surprises me, yet it's comforting in its own way. As you trek in solitude, your ears are serenaded by the most wonderful symphony. It starts with blood rhythmically coursing through your body, joined by exaggerated breaths, which keep the human machine humming. That's punctuated by irrepressible chirping barks from chubby marmots who inundate meadows with their condo burrows. Then there's the heady serenade of grasshoppers, more closely resembling the raucous rattling of snakes than any insect. But the most unusual sound and vision was one that Cheryl and I would mention to each other several days afterward.

As we trekked, a huge raven flew past in exaggerated cinematic slow motion. The sound of its swooshing wings long reverberated in our ears. To me, its odd appearance was almost symbolic, and I only wished I could read the hidden message in its wake.

After crossing the plateau past alpine chalets in the shadow of the 2545-meter Aiguille Rouge, we slid down into Thures Coomb beyond the gypsum quarries. All in all, it was an easy trek to sleepy Névache in the Clarée Valley and we arrived for lunch, a rare occurrence. Wasting no time, we checked in the Gîte Le Creux des Souches where we shared a comfortable dorm with Kevin, a lean Irish runner unbelievably in his 60s.

Of course, as usual, we shared hiking tales and techniques. Kevin was another bionic trekking machine, so our conversation naturally turned to Hugo. Actually, he'd seen our friend the day before. In fact, they'd sprinted together for a while, so we were reassured he was able to continue.

Naturally, the rest of the village was closed for a long lunch. I managed a quick tour of their humble church dating back to 1400, and then we tucked into the *gîte* garden for a little wine. In that heat, fortification was long overdue.

"A carafe of red," I asked our waitress.

"We don't serve wine without food."

"I don't understand," I said, with what must have been a stunned (or perhaps desperate) glare in my eyes. I mean, I knew what she was saying, but didn't understand. It couldn't be another silly French law like plastic bags. After all, wine's their national beverage. It's even served in plastic goblets at McDo, the name they use for those fast-food joints with the arches.

Sensing resistance was futile, she relented, whispering, "Fine. I'll just say you ordered crêpes."

Berthold and Ingrid arrived just in time to join the three of us for another delicious spread that night, and then we discussed our different, yet equally strenuous routes through the Alpes-Maritimes to the coast over the next two weeks. Not surprisingly, we each avoided mentioning our innermost fear of rising to the challenge. It was still a long trek to the Med.

Then again, I have to admit our morning ascents had become easier. At sunup, Cheryl and I left the others behind, tracing La Clarée River west only to climb sharply south on the GR57. It only took a few hours for us to crest stark Col de Buffère at 2427 meters where we enjoyed our first panoramic view of the Ecrins Mountains, as well as more gun emplacements and a bunker, which were another part of the Maginot Line. After that, all that remained was another quick march down a mountain dirt road and forest trail to Guisane Valley and then to Le Monêtier-Les-Bains, another spa/ski resort.

Its claim to fame began as far back as Roman times when it was known for its spa—in fact, its very name then meant "health" in Latin. For us, sorry to say, the village was mostly closed. But we easily found the *gîte* and patiently waited for Pierre, its guardian and chef, who arrived with five Belgian trekkers in tow.

Now frankly, France's gourmet *gîte* meals certainly gave us much more than a sausage and cheese sandwich (or golden chicken) to look forward to at the end of each backbreaking day. However, we found it difficult to sleep too soundly after feasting at 9 at night. Besides, they played havoc with our budget. As we knew all too well by then, the Via Alpina's a major investment for any thru-hiker who's on the trail for three to five months at a time. For most, it's no do-it-yourself Appalachian Trail of wild camping, chili and peanut butter sandwiches.

No, the Via Alpina's as much the Appalachian Trail as Wolfgang Puck is Rachael Ray. *Vive la différence.*

The next morning after breakfast, we popped into the kitchen to thank Pierre for his hospitality, the delicious dinner, and for even giving us a private room since they weren't busy. As we turned to go, he warmly shook our hands, and then said the oddest thing.

"You're nice people."

Huh? What'd he expect? Then I remembered he'd commented on our American passports when we checked in. Maybe he'd had a bad experience with a couple of our countrymen. It can happen; people are people.

Remembering the fellow back at Archeboc, we shrugged off his backhanded compliment, laughed, and replied, "Yea, you too."

Although we were eager to get an early start, we could tell two of the Belgians had painful blisters from their obvious limp. I hated to intrude, but blisters just happen to be my specialty. As the couple gingerly slid on their hiking boots on the front steps, I stopped to offer a little hiking secret.

"Try using Vaseline. It'll cut down the friction that comes from trekking so far each day."

The girl looked surprised, and then remembered, "Yea, my friend who's a marathon runner suggested the same thing," she said, forcing a brave smile. "I kidded him about it at the time."

"Nope, that's the best prevention. It's simple. Just rub a drop onto the bottom of your feet in the morning. It lasts all day. Haven't had a blister so far on this trip." And for me, that was unheard of.

"Isn't it messy?" she asked, screwing up her face.

"Well, it's tricky to get out of your socks and it smells a little." Cheryl could attest to that. "But it beats getting blisters. It's especially good to use in wet weather. Plus, you can find it just about everywhere. I even bought a rose-scented tube in Turkey."

With that, we wished them a good day's hike and sped off toward Vallouise, following a trail up the side of the Serre-Chevalier ski slopes. For once, we were energized after our dinner the night before and raced the thousand-meters to the summit in just two hours. We felt kinda proud. We weren't flip-flopping island slackers beat by feisty, yodeling Swiss nanas anymore. The Alps had finally whipped our sorry *okoles* (asses) into shape.

Although the mountaintop was deserted, the restaurant closed, and ski lifts empty, it was still a breathtaking tableau with Montagne des Agneaux glistening at 3664 meters. It was the perfect venue for taking a mini-Merz, before tracing the GR54 up to 2425-meter Col de Eychauda. It's a traditional passage between the Guisane and Vallouise valleys, overshadowed by the snowy summit of Cucumelle at 2698 meters and Rocher de l'Yvret at over 2800 meters.

When clouds predictably gathered over the mountains, we half-expected more rain, but our descent went smoothly along switchbacks and grassy, undulating slopes. We made it into Vallouise Valley without a problem. For once, on the descent, I didn't rely on my Nordic sticks for added support, even though Cheryl used hers and still faithfully wrapped her knee each morning, not wanting to risk another setback.

The valley's name originates from "Vallis Loysia" in honor of Louis XI. Back in the 15th century, King Louis tried to end persecution of the Protestants living there. Labeled heretics throughout France, many were arrested, forced to convert, deported, or sentenced to the gallows, and they were nearly wiped out by the 17th century.

These days, Vallouise is just another quiet village. It was easy to find the visitor office and our *gîte* whose owner upgraded us to a private room. After all the dorms, huts and listless nights on the journey, it was one small luxury we never took for granted. You never knew what waited at the end of the trail each day. If finding a place to stay is a nuisance, finding a nasty one is demoralizing. With that in mind, we broke our rules and had already made reservations for the next evening. We planned to trek a little farther than the stage-stop at Freissinières to stay at the presbytery in Pallon.

As Cheryl teased, "You know the secret handshake."

Now, even though our hostess gave us what we thought would be a far better map than our own, the next morning quickly turned into a nightmare. It began with a long, frustrating detour down an unmarked path on the mountainside. First, the trail markings disappeared deep in the forest, and then any telltale footprints as well, as we entered high brush. The only upside to the maddening diversion was spotting my first red fox.

Of course, it immediately caught my scent. Within seconds, all I could see was the white tip of her red tail as she bounded into the bushes.

It all fell to pieces from there. Soaked with sweat, I beat myself up for not following signs up the mountain to Puy-St-Vincent like Cheryl suggested. She was also testy by then since she lugged the leftovers from our dinner the night before. Until eventually, frustrated by the lost hour, lost energy, and our old friend Misdirection, I grabbed the food to lighten her load and stormed back down the mountain toward Vallouise.

I knew the GR50 and Via Alpina connected an hour away in Les Vigneaux, so I figured we'd follow the country road. It made sense. Unfortunately, I didn't know the trail headed west again from Les Vigneaux, back toward Puy-St-Vincent. (Apparently, like Rome, all roads lead there.)

So, after it was all said and done, we wasted two hours and a whole lot of anger over nothing. Then to top it off, it began to drizzle again, a near-freezing rain. Once again, we were forced into our ponchos just in time for one more tough climb up Col de la Pousterle.

We were a pair. In case you haven't noticed, my patience has its limits. I hiked a good half-kilometer ahead of my equally livid partner, all the better to fume alone. The length of the Via Alpina, foul weather, and grind after nearly 100 days had finally taken its mental toll. Every day seemed little more than anguish, as we sweated and strained up another mountain. Especially on wet, miserable days, we were left questioning why we continued.

We've already done more than most. Does stubborn tenacity keep us moving? Unwillingness to accept defeat? Or, just lack of common sense.

By the time we reached the pass, I shivered badly, trying to stay warm. So, when we spotted a refuge on just the other side of the summit, we made a beeline for its door. Opening it, we called inside and Jacques, a weathered alpinist with kind eyes, insisted we join him at his wooden table.

"Have anything warm to eat?" I asked, teeth chattering. "Soup?"

"This is my last day open for the season, but I'll see what I can find."

The hut guardian ducked into his kitchen and soon returned with two cups of hot water and packets of instant soup mix. While we savored its warmth, he enjoyed the companionship and seemed genuinely interested in hearing about our Via Alpina experiences. An Italian who'd also been trekking it stayed with him recently, so he knew about the trail.

Then, in French, Jacques shared his personal lament. As near I could translate, his refuge had been quiet that season. In fact, business had been slow the past few years.

"Not as many people are coming to the mountains," he explained. "Or if they do, they drive as close as they can, hike an hour or two, and then return home at night. That is their 'day in the country.' But most prefer to go to the beach anyway these days," he said, adding a half-hearted chuckle. "It's much easier than hiking."

"The call of the wild mai tai?"

He nodded. "They go to Greece or to the French coast."

It was sad. All summer long, we'd seen so few hikers on the Alpine trails, except for the Mont Blanc circuit. Then again, I'm sure many of those were on a day-hike and simply caught the chairlift up. Unfortunately, with the decline in business, how long would a place like his survive?

For us, our stop at Jacque's refuge came at just the right time. Warmed in body and spirit, we soon wished each other "*Bon journey*" and left, eager to descend the mountain and climb our second pass for the day, Col du Lauzes.

Now that the rain, personal gloom, and shivering had passed, I saw the bounty of Vallouise Valley and Pelvoux Massif with all new eyes. With its 900 plant species, rare yew trees, and Europe's largest blue thistle meadow, the news he shared seemed especially tragic. Many nature-lovers will never witness its grandeur for themselves. And it's hard to want to protect the Alpine environment when you've never experienced it.

Once down in Freissinières, we easily found the old mill visitor office, as well as Cherise, the lady we'd met the day before at the Vallouise tourist office. She'd promised to give us a lift to nearby Pallon Presbytery; true to her word, she closed up shop and dropped us right on their doorstep.

It was a large, rambling retreat surrounded by orchards in a sleepy hamlet. Georges, a can-do fellow who ran and renovated the place, met us at the heavy, weathered door. He showed us the kitchen where we could cook dinner, and then insisted we settle into a dorm room all to ourselves. Things were definitely looking up. After showering, I walked out on the balcony to ask him where the village restaurant was, since there's no market and Cherise had made reservations for us there.

Well, before long, we began talking about hiking and my recent trek on the Templar Trail. As I told him about the many folks who took us under their wings, Georges grew excited, until he finally insisted that Cheryl and I come up to his modest apartment to continue chatting. How could we say no?

Upstairs, his wife Mimi warmly hugged us and their young son Hervé, on their insistence, kissed us both twice on our cheeks, as is their custom. Then Georges opened a bottle of Sauvignon Blanc, sliced a sausage, and fetched saucers: one of black olive tapenade, one of capers and anchovies, and another of red peppers in olive oil, which he placed on the rustic tabletop. Meanwhile, Mimi sliced a crusty baguette and pulled up a chair.

The outpouring of instant warmth around their table made us feel like family. They quickly asked for all the details of our latest adventure, and then Georges emotionally told us about their recent relocation to those handsome mountains from Paris' Bastille *arrondissement.*

"I was riding the metro one day, looking around, asking myself, 'What am I doing here?' I do the same thing day after day, but 'What am I *doing* here?' Search as I might, I could find no good answer, so Mimi, Hervé and I left shortly afterward to start our new life here."

"Those small moments change our lives," I said, "maybe even the world a little bit."

"*Mais, oui.* So now we have come to this," he said, with a satisfied smile and a grand sweep of his arm to the beauty outside. "Our picture postcard!"

I knew exactly what he meant. We'd made a similar leap of faith. When it's all said and done, what do you have if you don't have your dreams? We also knew a little about his old neighborhood.

"I remember the first time we went to Paris, a beautiful city," I haltingly began. "We'd always heard about the Bastille and were anxious to visit it."

He nodded, patiently listening to my rudimentary French.

"Well, Cheryl and I rode the same metro as you to the Bastille stop and climbed the stairs to the street, expecting to be face-to-face with the old prison, so symbolic of the French Revolution. We figured it must have an interesting museum. The only problem was, we couldn't find it. We searched up one street and down another for an eternity, until I finally stopped someone on the sidewalk and asked, "Where's the Bastille?"

He started chuckling.

"Huh? Bastille?" they said, as if I was mad. "What Bastille?"

"It was only then I learned that it was stormed and torn apart by angry mobs during the revolution. I felt like such a fool."

We had a good laugh. Toasting each other and draining his first bottle of wine, our conversation turned philosophical when he asked to hear more about the Templar Trail to Jerusalem.

"The path we hiked was once taken by soldiers during the First Crusades," I began. "We wanted to reopen it now as an international path of peace for people of all nationalities, cultures and religions."

That struck a chord. Georges nodded and then rolled up his sleeve to show us a bold tattoo on his forearm: an international symbol of peace.

"*Exact*! I believe once we walk, eat, drink and share dreams (and blisters) with each other on the path, we realize how much we have in common—how much we're truly brothers. And as we both know, most people of the world truly want peace. If only their leaders will listen."

Georges beamed. Although my French is far from flawless, he said he understood perfectly well.

"*Inshallah*. If God wishes it," he sighed, placing his hand over his heart.

All too soon, we knew we had to leave, if only to make it to the restaurant before they closed. On parting, Georges' brown eyes welled up as he and Mimi embraced us as brothers in spirit, kissing us on both cheeks.

After it's all said and done, travel's a chance to touch lives and hearts. Perhaps that's the secret handshake, after all.

Leaving the family at 8:00, dinnertime in France, we wandered down the street in the dark and bitter cold to the village restaurant. It was pitch black inside. We rang the bell. Eventually a lady poked her head out of an upstairs window and said she'd expected us sooner. In spite of this, she shuffled downstairs, flicked on the lights, unbolted the door, led us inside, and then proceeded to fix the absolute finest ham and cheese baguette sandwiches known to mankind. All the while, she asked about the Via Alpina, showed Cheryl a local plant to relieve any future knee swelling, and even pulled out her own topo maps to tell us how to continue in the morning.

Once again, we'd seen how the Via Alpina's so much more than hiking mountains, although it has double its fair share. It's the people, sharing traditions and cultures, touching lives. Twice that same day, when our morale was at its lowest, we found extraordinary kindness. And if that wasn't already enough, we'd unexpectedly tasted a third.

It was another one of the Universe's metaphorical bricks to the head—just when we needed it most.

14

THE DREADED PATOUS!

EAVING PALLON IN THE MORNING MIST, WE SWIFTLY TREKKED A silent country road for three hours before spotting Mont-Dauphin Fort perched atop a distinctive butte far below. As we descended and grew nearer, the still mountain air was suddenly broken by the bizarre "cack, cack, cack" of automatic gunfire.

Cheryl and I glanced at each other, ready to duck for cover. From the bursts, it sure didn't sound like hunters, although we'd seen some earlier aiming at birds.

Where's it coming from? And why?

It was a mystery, until we rounded a bend in the village and were shocked to see a bearded fellow wearing an Afghan *pawkul* hat and traditional robe. He steadily walked toward a French armored troop carrier. A gunner on top aimed his mounted weapon directly at the stranger. Three others, a black, a white, and a woman soldier, stood staggered across the road, ready to fire.

Waving rifles, they screamed, "Stop! Stop! No farther," in English.

Still, seemingly oblivious to the danger, the fellow slowly crept forward, saying, "Come my friends. Come, have tea."

Tea was not on their minds.

It was all too surreal. It was as if we'd wandered onto some movie set. But this was no film. We were caught up in a national war game and he was acting the part of the potential suicide bomber. We'd read about an upcoming exercise at Ecrins Park several days earlier, but it was still weeks away. We figured this was part of the same program, as the French prepared to deploy more troops to Afghanistan.

Passing several more checkpoints into town, we nodded *"Bonjour"* and Cheryl even saluted as we skirted past, thankful we weren't pulled into their

melodrama. Still, I couldn't help but wonder how many of those young men and women would soon ship off—never to see those Alps, their homeland, again?

Our *gîte* was set in the walled city high atop a monumental fortress. Mont-Dauphin, an engineering wonder for its time, was designed by none other than the famed Marquis de Vauban. In 1692, under orders of King Louis XIV, it was built at the elbow of the Durance River to protect the Haut Dauphiné region from the Duke of Savoie who'd already sacked Guillestre, Embrun and Gap. However, before it could be completed, the region was traded to Savoie in exchange for Ubaye. So, the colossal fort never saw action then, or in any war since.

It was just noon when we arrived. The guardian was out to lunch, but she gave us a charming room after she returned. After a shower, we were anxious to explore the tiny village, home to a few hundred inhabitants. It's unique for its time, since it combined a military fort with all the necessities of civilian life.

In spite of that, these days its streets ring silent. The artisan shops were mostly closed, as were the arsenal, powder magazine, and most of the museums. What cost a fortune to build in its day was now an empty open-air museum.

At first light, we decided that creative improvisation, a little "jazz," was long overdue. We decided to trek directly to Ceillac in one day instead of two. To avoid the unnecessary ascent to the Refuge at Furfande, we'd head to Guillestre and then up the Gorges du Guil to Ceillac. On paper, (or on a 1:100,000 map), it looked possible, maybe even practical. After all, it was a Sunday morning, the weather was only cloudy, and traffic would be light. Or so we hoped.

In actuality, it meant making a four-hour constant climb up a perilous path of death. The road through the gorge is narrow, not much wider than two cars, very small cars, the kind you see clowns pour from at the circus. The stone walls built to prevent vehicles from tumbling a thousand meters into the abyss already missed telltale sections. Then, there were the drivers.

Instead of finding relaxed, easy-going, "Doh-Di-Doh," Sunday-in-the-country sorts, we squared off against A-type Andrettis of the Alps. They thought nothing of speeding 100 kilometers an hour around hairpin turns, only to barrel past slowpokes in blind spots on their way into unlit tunnels. One narrowly missed me by a hair's length, or so Cheryl screamed. And the tunnels? They were long, dimly lit, one-lane caves, unregulated by even a single traffic light to let through one side at a time, as we'd found in Austria.

I'm not exaggerating when I say we've never jogged faster through dripping, dark morasses in all our lives.

Several shaky hours later, years older, we arrived in the sleepy hamlet of Ceillac in one piece and checked into the *gîte dortoir* where we were the only trekkers. Looking for a less blood-curdling activity, we decided to explore the local culture. This took no time at all, since everything was predictably closed. We passed a few unique L-shaped houses with sundials, so we held out hope to see the sun again someday soon, but the village was deserted.

Nevertheless, we'd heard that area preserves its traditions in other ways. We'd read how the local *patois* was spoken instead of French until 1931, and the lady's traditional outfits with linen caps only recently went out of vogue. Even their time-honored dances, the *quadrille* and *piqua*, a type of polka, are resurrected for festivals. But no matter how hard we tried, we had no luck in finding its hand-made pasta, *manuis*, or famous blue cheese.

Too bad we missed them. As I said, French breakfasts are notoriously light, usually only bread, jam, butter, coffee (and maybe a pack of Gitanes, if you're French). Not exactly hearty alpinist fare. Fortunately, frigid weather does wonders for keeping your mind off hunger. By daybreak, the ground was dusted with frost. Winter would arrive before we knew it.

Fortunately, the Alps in that area offer plenty of pleasant diversions. That morning we climbed to two secluded alpine lakes. The first, Lac Miroir, is an aquamarine gem encircled by the jagged Font Sancte peaks, glaciers, and a scarf of green pine draping its shores. Having the picturesque spot all to ourselves, we took a mini-Merz and even took an extra five minutes to set up our tent to envision what it'd be like to camp there—steps from a CAMPING PROHIBITED sign.

From there, we made another steep climb to Lac Ste-Anne whose water is so clear it appears bottomless. The larger of the two lakes, it has its own stone chapel dedicated to St. Anne, guardian of sailors. Legend tells of two adventurous kids who set out on a raft until they became stranded in the middle of the lake. The scared out of their wits parents prayed to the saint until a breeze blew the raft to safety. Out of gratitude, they erected a chapel in her honor.

While we're on the subject though, St. Anne is also petitioned for rain in times of draught. Thanks to someone, she'd been working overtime for months.

From its shores, we climbed Col Girardin, our second col of the day, across loose shale on switchbacks up to its 2699-meter crest; and then dashed down the other side amid more condos than Daytona Beach—marmot condos, that is. Sometimes I felt like we'd become characters in our own private *Marmot Day* where each day kept repeating until we got things right. This time, we were able to get much closer to them than ever before, almost like they awaited treats. The frisky little fellas were especially chubby.

"Lookin' mighty tasty," a voice whispered inside my head. "After all, they eat them in Mongolia? Maybe roasted with a spicy barbeque sauce on a bed of fava beans? And a nice Chianti?"

Whoa! When Hannibal Lechter's cookbook comes to mind, you know you've been hungry far too long.

Fortunately for us, (and them), it wasn't far to Maljasset. The village has a 14th century chapel, but its gate was locked. Otherwise, there's a handful of crumbling stone houses built from local materials. Nothing more, except our refuge. Still, it put us into position to reach Larche the next day. As we unpacked and rolled out our sleeping bags in the hut's chilly, dank room, I was jazzed.

Tomorrow, we'll connect with the Via Alpina's blue route. We'll start our final press through the Alpes Maritime into Monaco. Sure, it might be freezing now, but the weather's bound to be warm and clear once we reach the sunny Riviera.

Now, let me be the first to point out the obvious. Nobody likes a whiner. Especially me. Nothing ruins a good trip faster than being around someone who gripes about everything. That said, even though I did my best to bite my lips and stifle complaining aloud even about the worst conditions on our journey, (some might say, saving it for this book), that evening an English couple joined us. And as you know, misery does enjoy company.

Reg and Jocelyn stayed at the same refuge. Although our room and bath had all the comfort of a 12th century monastery, we figured they'd make up for it at dinner, especially considering their chilling price. Well, supper began as a fiasco and swiftly went downhill from there. Everyone, wrapped in down jackets, sat huddled together at the bare wooden table. It was bone-chilling inside the stone hut, but they hadn't bothered to start a fire.

After a long string of small talk between us, the only guests, the "chef" eventually traipsed in and plopped a bowl of cold noodles on our table. It was followed by a plate with tiny hunks of mystery meat tied with string.

"What's this?" Jocelyn snapped.

"Looks like leftovers to me," Reg wagered.

Everyone agreed. Otherwise, how could it be overcooked and stone cold at the same time? Just as it registered that this was dinner, all there was to eat until supper tomorrow, the chef popped his head through the door and asked the compulsory, "Everything okay?"

"NO!" everyone cried.

"Huh-rumpf!" Reg added in a loud exclamation.

"Oh, that's so very British of you," Jocelyn chided.

Reg shrugged.

"Why? What is wrong?" Chef asked.

"Everything's as cold as a witch's tit in a brass brassiere," Reg said.

Unfazed, the fellow schlepped it all back into the kitchen. We listened closely. A metal door open and closed. A buzzer rang. Any bachelor or student knows that sound. Chef shuffled back with the food but it was little better than before. What could be so hard? After one more round, we finally gave up trying with him. It was DOA, beyond resuscitation.

Maljasset, whose name means "bad shelter" in *patois*, lived up to its name. After a hungry, teeth-chattering night, we left at daybreak. Although we nearly sprinted down a frozen country road toward the GR5 connection, it took more than an hour to reach the L'Ubaye River Bridge, and then a bit longer to the trailhead. Nothing was open in that village either, which meant we had to hike all day across two cols totaling 4700 meters on old bread, a solid honey cube, and weak coffee.

Oh, I nearly forgot. We did still have an emergency packet of dried salmon jerky that Cheryl's concerned mother bequeathed to us before we left. That was it, but what choice did we have? We couldn't count on finding village markets anymore. We'd just have to plan better in the future.

We set off, surviving on the beauty alone. At one point, I saw something scamper across the trail. It was about the size of a squirrel, but with a white face. I followed it to a rock where it slid into a crevice. Patiently I waited until it poked its head out. I snapped a photo. It ducked inside. It came back out. I shot again. It retreated. Curiosity called and he reappeared a third time. I fired one last shot. His body was dark, but his face was snowy white, cute and cartoonish with huge, wide eyes. It was a baby ermine!

But that was far from our only brush with Alpine nature. Just up the trail, we were engulfed by a flock of sheep who blended in with their rust-hued surroundings. Those three shaggy white dogs shepherded the herd en masse up the mountainside, but they were in no rush to move from one grassy patch to another. So we took our cue from them and moseyed too.

Late that afternoon, just shy of the col, we came across the ruins of old barracks tucked into a rocky pocket near the summit. From below, it'd been well disguised, sheltered on all sides. Actually, we didn't see it until we were upon it. Amid howling winds, we walked through a rusted, fallen gate and then around remaining walls, poking our heads inside the dining hall in search of forgotten relics (or meal rations). Even though the billet sat in the protective shadow of a battery designed by Vauban, the same fellow who'd built the fort at Mont-Dauphin, he knew nothing about modern air warfare. Both the Germans and Italians bombed it to smithereens during the war.

After summiting, Cheryl and I began our quick descent to Larche, a tiny village of less than two-dozen buildings. On our way, we came across four hikers lounging in the grass on the hillside. They watched as an eagle and two hawks effortlessly glided across the wide valley in search of prey. As we approached, we recognized one fellow who stood and waved. Berthold and Ingrid, the friendly Germans we'd left back in Névache, invited us to join them and then introduced us to a pair of strapping Kiwis: Simon and Phyll, his wife, both about our age with short-cropped hair. It sounded like we'd be traveling the same path over the next few days, so we looked forward to comparing notes later down at the hut.

Our *gîte* was easy to find, and after a shower, we moseyed over to the visitor center where their photo display told a shocking chapter in the history of the village. It hadn't always been so small. Back during the war, for reasons remaining a mystery to me, it was burned and then flattened by the Nazis. A tragic episode, it was yet another unforgettable and undeniable influence on Alpine life.

At first light, we awoke to summer frost on another bitter, cloudy day. The six of us, swaddled in down jackets, set a quick pace along a dirt road. It was hard to believe the Med was less than ten days off, but by then the warmth of the Riviera sounded especially appealing. Then again, we still had another dozen or so mountains left to climb, but who was counting?

Within two hours, we entered Mercantour National Park where the GR5 suddenly became wide enough for a car to pass. While the other couples took their time, Cheryl and I loped ahead toward a beautiful alpine lake where we stopped to enjoy lunch. Sitting at the water's edge, we could just barely discern a ragged path scarring the slag face of the opposite mountainside. There was no need to remind each other it was going to be one heckuva climb. Considering that, we decided to wait until the others arrived and had lunch before tackling it together.

Eventually we stood in unison, adjusted our packs, and took last swigs of water. Cheryl and I each popped a hard candy for energy. Then there was a long, pregnant pause while everyone waited for someone to forge ahead.

"Well, who's the penguin?" Phyll chirped with a mischievous grin. "Who's gonna be first to test the water for sharks?"

We sized up each other.

Finally I said, "Guess it's gonna be me."

We've seen worse, much worse, I thought. Cheryl and I've been climbing these for more than three months now. Besides, she's finally able to trek them without wrapping her knees. So, no worries mate.

We'd left our lumpy office-physiques far behind and were never in better physical shape. Actually, I had to laugh when I remembered our well-meaning, desperate efforts to get into condition the last three months before leaving Hawaii. Even the best trainer, an hour on a treadmill incline, and an hour with weights four times a week could never prepare you for eight hours of alpine mountain trekking each day. At best, it was a tone-up—or preview of the pain to come.

The slope was tricky with its narrow slag path constantly shifting beneath our feet, but there was no problem if you were careful. Of course, if you suffered from vertigo, you didn't want to look down. It was a long tumble to the lake. Nevertheless, after scrambling thirty minutes or so, Cheryl and I summited and then descended to a grassy meadow to await the others.

It wasn't very long before Berthold came scurrying down the path, screaming at the top of his lungs in mock alarm.

"Hurry! There's a sheep stampede coming!"

Stampede? Sheep? The pitter-patter of tiny hooves? Maybe something was lost in translation. I'd heard of buffalo stampedes, but sheep? And how'd he know? Did he put his ear to the ground like a scout in some John Wayne film?

Soon, a sea of sheep loomed on the horizon, but it was hardly a thousand pounds of stampeding revenge. It was more like a rising tide of flotsam and woolsam. Their guard dogs barked a warning and then we even met the white Grand Pyrenees when they came to sniff our packs for food.

"Ah, no ya don't!" Simon yelled, bopping one lightly on the nose as it attempted to snag a snack, as well as his glove.

Before long, that flock of a hundred sheep and goats engulfed us. We rode their crest out of the valley and up another col to more gun emplacements. As we descended, we were surprised to see the oddest climbing party approach. Two older couples were smartly decked out in expensive clothes and gold jewelry. They looked like they were off to a dinner party.

"They sure came dressed to impress," Cheryl said with a giggle, as they gingerly struggled past.

"Maybe their husbands promised them a night out. They just didn't mention it was out here."

Reaching the bottom of the second col, we arrived at deserted ruins called Camp de Fourches, which had once housed a mountain unit of 800 soldiers. Those famous Chasseurs Alpines were nicknamed "les Diables Bleus," or the Blue Devils. Their unique alpine training hoped to break the standoff of trench warfare in the French Alps. Unfortunately, the 1915 Vosges Campaign failed, even though they won commendation for their courage.

While the others caught their breath, Ingrid, Berthold and I wandered from building to building, trying to get a better picture of what life must have been like up there. We eventually found the rec hall and several revealing wall murals painted by bored, talented soldiers. One depicted a topless black dancer, maybe the celebrated Josephine Baker, emerging from a banana peel. It must have been drawn when she was all the rage of Paris nightlife. Another featured a chorus line of high-kicking dancers. I could just imagine the debonair Blue Devils, decked out in their distinctive indigo uniforms and capes, breaking hearts and conquering the City of Light.

Then again, another painting probably captured a more realistic portrait of the lonely life on that high outpost. A soldier stood up to his neck in a snow-drift. Only his helmeted head and rifle barrel protruded. Its sarcastic caption, "Perfect Powder," was every skier's dream.

Alpinists need to be especially careful what they wish for.

Our *gîte* waited at the base of that mountain. Bousieyas was little more than a name and all but deserted. There was no market, no other refuge, and the stone hut was bad news from the very start. Our dorm room was sub-zero. Its sheets looked like they were last changed when soldiers still camped up there. There was one shower for up to twenty, and a hole in the ground for a toilet. Though signs warned guests about the voracious flies, we were just as hungry.

"Ah, there's always dinner," we thought. After such a long, tiring day, we six, as well as the two Frenchmen staying there, were famished. No matter how bad the sleeping conditions, dinner had the power to make it right. Visions of *la belle cuisine* danced in our heads. So, with great anticipation, we sat at a long wooden table and waited. And waited.

What's it going to be? Polenta with gooey, melted cheese? Handmade sausages? Hearty alpine stew? Marmots in peanut sauce?

Our mouths watered in anticipation. Finally, the hut guardian, an urchin who'd been painting watercolors when we arrived, slid dinner in front of us.

What's this? Two plain omelets and a garbanzo bean casserole to split between eight hungry hikers? Why, it's hardly enough to feed two.

Before we could protest, she breezed out, barring the kitchen behind her.

Mutiny was in the air. Someone suggested raiding the soda and beer machine, but it was chained shut. Chained? Something told me this may have happened before.

Out of desperation, Cheryl offered to fix soup from a packet we'd squir-reled away for just such an emergency. In the process of looking for a pot, *voilà*, she found their entire cache of wine and beer. Being honest hikers, the thought of raiding their liquor cabinet would never cross our minds. Noooo! Then again, on that frigid, famished night, it was there for the taking—and we'd already been taken—so it presented a mighty big temptation.

But no, we suffered in silence.

Morning couldn't come too soon. Our *petit déjeuner* couldn't have been more so. Eight of us split a pot of coffee and bag of stale sliced baguette with a pat of butter. Nothing more. The guardian was nowhere to be found.

However, anger is another great motivator. We left the *gîte* at a break-neck speed through Mercantour National Park toward Tinée Valley. Mornings grew colder with each passing day and frost spurred us on. The trees and smaller plants already shed their leaves. Nature's confetti littered our trail. The six of us made a swift ascent of Col de la Colombière, a heady pass featured 19 times in the arduous Tour de France bicycle race, and then descended to St-Dalmas-le-Selvage.

In total contrast to Bousieyas, the village is charming with brightly painted building façades lining the plaza, and I was disappointed we hadn't pressed on and stayed there the night before. Whatever hour it was, we were just in time for lunch. Their *patisserie* was actually open and everyone enjoyed baguette sandwiches and beers in their deserted square, stuffing our faces as if we hadn't eaten in weeks. Their visitor office was surprisingly large, complete with life-sized exhibits of local fauna, including the reddish-brown wild sheep called mouflons, chamois (mountain antelopes), steinbok, wild black grouse and others.

Best of all, they offered to phone ahead to both Roya and the Refuge de Longon where we hoped to spend the next two nights. Yea, I know, we were breaking our rules, but we didn't want to repeat the catastrophe of Bousieyas.

Only one more col, a smaller one at only 1753 meters, separated us from St-Etiénne-de-Tinée. Clearing it, we skidded down the mountain to explore the quaint riverside village known for its medieval architecture. Walking down shaded streets ringing with children's laughter, we checked into a mom-and-pop hotel and then stocked up on provisions for the days ahead, vowing never to get caught flat-footed like that again. Still, even with as much as we ate each day, food was on top of everyone's mind, especially that night.

Dinner was a going away party. The other two couples would rest for a day before continuing to Nice. Phyll had taken a tumble while scrambling across scree earlier in the day, so they were anxious to take a break. As luck would have it, we also ran into Bea and Willem, the Dutch couple who'd been trekking the GR5. In that section, it corresponds with the Via Alpina again, so we decided to leave together in the morning.

Like wildebeest at the watering hole, there was safety in numbers.

It was a magical evening. The pasta was hot and plentiful. Wine flowed nonstop. As our cozy dining room overflowed, it was soon obvious we'd found the most popular nightspot in the tiny town. One unusual surprise came just as we finished dessert. An older distinguished gentleman, with neatly combed white hair and dressed in a starched shirt and tie, suddenly burst into song from his nearby table. Jean-Paul sang *a cappella* for an hour, crooning what could best be described as French torch songs, some bouncy but many full of longing. We were captivated. It was the first time in all our travels we'd heard such a thing.

At one point, Cheryl leaned over to whisper, "He's singing for his supper."

"Really? People still do that?"

Who knew? But if so, I'm sure Jean-Paul was well fed that night. And for musically inclined seniors, it sure beat working as a "greeter" at giant boxstore.

After Bea and Willem joined us in the morning, we left the village together along the river for another sharp climb up to Auron, the largest ski village in the southern Alps. By that time of year, the abundance of wildflowers, including edelweiss and génépi, were only memories. It looked and felt like snow would blanket the ground any day. Someone had warned us they'd had their first flurries last year on September 10th. It was past due.

As I viewed Auron's vacant streets of empty ski shops, boutiques and pricey resort restaurants, I was struck by one realization: For weeks, all of the villages we've passed have either been nearly deserted, or transformed into cookie-cutter ski resorts. How can there possibly be enough skiers to fill them all? Most dairy farmers and sheepherders have disappeared. They've either fled to the cities or now run ski lifts, tote espressos to tables, or hawk gewgaw to tourists. Even Auron, once famous for its wheat fields, now farms skiers. Is that the sad future of the Alps?

Threatening rain clouds approached once more and we picked up our pace, summiting the 2001-meter Col du Blainon in record time, before sprinting between sheep pastures, barns and chapels down to the hamlet of Roya, cradled in a valley of the same name. Bea and Willem arrived just behind us and we were grateful when the Québécois hut guardian opened the refuge doors ahead of schedule. Even though my body enjoyed their steamy shower, my mind couldn't help but wander.

With only a week remaining to the Med, I could already feel its soothing warmth, smell its lavender baking in the hills, and taste its tangy salt air.

About that point in time, our days had merged into one continual ascent-descent, which I made even in my sleep. Maybe that's the reason I felt especially lethargic the next morning. My body slammed into a wall. I was at the 99% point; so close, yet so very far. I lacked energy even though I'd certainly had plenty of calories the past two days. Despite the fact I'd lost ten kilos or so, I figured I had a mineral imbalance similar to Hugo's. Cheryl discovered one last packet of energy powder hidden in her pack and added it to our water. I hungrily gulped it down.

It was just our dumb luck to face three passes that day, as the trail joined the GR5 again, through Sallevieille Valley to pristine high-alpine meadows between 1800 and 2500 meters. Stopping after the first pass for a mini-Merz, we spotted a shepherd and his five dogs as they grew near.

At first, we were a little apprehensive. A Yukoner couple we'd met the night before had filled us with tales of vicious attacks by mountain guard dogs, *patous*, but those little guys hardly qualified as bloodthirsty Cujos. After swimming and slogging across a bog to reach us, two of the muddy pups headed straight for Cheryl's lap—to smother her with wet licks.

"So much for the ferocious *patous*!"

After they passed, we continued across the rolling barren landscape and climbed Crousette Pass at 2486 meters, and then Moulines at the entrance to Mercantour National Park. Clearing it, we could finally peer down at the bleak terrain below. That remarkably remote location had been chosen as the site to reintroduce the rare bearded vulture. And I could see why. A predator with a B-52 wingspan, it's known for its fondness for bones. It breaks them by dropping them from high altitudes.

An amazing skill, it has much in common with certain Slovenian mountains.

Just about then, we spotted huge thunderheads moving in from the west, so we picked up our pace and swiftly made it down to the river and then past the village, its Vignols Caves, and up the other side. As clouds closed in, we hustled to reach Longon Refuge before the storm hit with all its fury.

I've got to admit, I was surprised to find we'd added one more speed beside slow and slower to our hiking transmission. After three months, we now had semi-fast.

Not a moment too soon, we spotted a wisp of smoke rising from the alm and the former cowshed appeared as in a dream. We no sooner stepped across the hut's portal than the deluge began.

Inside, a bearded sinewy fellow and three children sat at a sturdy wooden table in front of a welcoming fire. The hut guardian was a shepherd and cheese maker, as I guessed by the large yellow wheel of goodness tempting me from his counter. Before we had the chance to sit down, he led us next door into one of three freezing rooms. They were two floors high connected by steep creaking stairs. Mattresses lined the floors. Wool blankets hung across the railings. It was clean, but any hope of a hot shower was chilled. They were solar heated. With that weather we were out of luck. After washing up as much as we dared, we ducked back into the main room to melt beside his fire. While it worked its wonders, the rains pounded harder than ever, occasionally punctuated by loud cracks of thunder.

We sat lost in a dreamy daze, and it was mid-afternoon before the front door creaked open again and in waddled the waterlogged Yukoners. Before long, Willem and Bea joined us. Finally, at nightfall, one last group of exhausted trekkers appeared. They'd left Roya that morning too, but by the time they reached the pass, it was snowing. In September!

After the others had changed into dry clothes, everyone gathered around the table to be entertained by the guardian's kids, ages 6, 4, and 19 months, who charmed guests, tended the fire, or slurped on fizzy green menthol drinks.

Meanwhile, wonderful aromas wafted from the kitchen, making us forget the rigors of the day. And what a feast it was. The guardian whipped up *socca*, a Niçoise specialty of garbanzo bean meal fried like a thin pancake in olive oil and served with a cold rosé wine. Next came a rare treat: wild nettle and potato soup, followed by a savory roast leg of lamb simmered with onions and tiny potatoes. To top it off, he proudly served three handmade fromages straight from his farm: a goat, an aged sheep, and a pungent cow cheese, followed by a tasty bowl of goat yogurt with berries for dessert.

The magical banquet held in a far-off alpine pasture was a culinary Brigadoon. As in the classic film, it'd vanish all too quickly in the morning mist; but we'd always remember that kind shepherd's delicious meal, his toasty fire, and especially his heartfelt hospitality served on an otherwise dreary night.

It cleared by morning and we set off to cover the short distance down valley to St-Sauveur-sur-Tinée. There was no pass to climb, a rarity, and we only had a 1000-meter or so descent. The other couples headed there too, but separately. For Willem and Bea, it was the end of their journey. They'd catch a bus to Nice, and then back to Holland. The Yukoners would continue on to Menton.

The trail down valley was steep at first, and then it undulated as we trekked through larch forests, perfumed meadows and past a deserted village of old stone houses. Tinée Valley bordered by Mont Gravières and Mont Autcellier spread before us.

There was a sensory explosion as we trekked across odd purple-hued slate and then through fragrant woods. Little can match the forest's aroma at that time of year, especially in the Alpes Maritime, an area abundant with herbs and flowers and brimming with tempting berries. In fact, we'd run into the Yukon couple the day before, as they gorged on wild blackberries. I sped past, but Cheryl paused just long enough to do what she thought was a good deed.

"Be sure to only eat the ones over your head," she cautioned.

"Why?"

"Foxes like berry bushes—and like to spray them with urine. Locals have already warned us twice. Fox urine carries a disease that harms your liver and kidneys."

The Yukoners glared at her, suspicious of her motives, but honestly, we weren't out to steal their fruit. If they chose to ignore us, well, we'd let natural selection take its course. Then again, if they couldn't swallow that news, we knew they certainly wouldn't believe us when we told them that wolves had also reappeared in the area.

Yea, we've got your wild *patous*!

After passing Roure, a village precariously balanced on the brink of a landslide, it was a short slide to our stage destination, St-Sauveur-sur-Tinée, set on a loop of the Tinée River. Although known for its fertile land and unique figs, the equivalent of French tumbleweeds rolled down the *rue*. As it was Sunday again, nearly everything was closed. After checking into the village's one-star hotel, we met Willem and Bea for one last drink before they caught their bus to the coast.

With any luck, and a strong tailwind, it'd only take us five days to trek what they traveled in two-hours.

We delayed leaving the next morning to wait for the visitor office to open. I was concerned. Although we were finally back on our topo maps, rain was forecast for the next few days. Why didn't it surprise me? It was anyone's guess if there was a place to stay at Col de Turini, the final pass we needed to cross before heading down into Monaco. Then again, if there was a refuge, would it still be open? Some were already shuttered for the season.

The only sure thing was the rain that'd relentlessly dogged us for more than three months since we'd started.

Just past the tourist office, the Via Alpina wound steeply uphill to connect with an old mountain road. We hugged a hillside covered with chestnut trees all the way to Rimplas where the trail promptly disappeared. The village of old stone houses with dark red slate roofs dates back 1000 years. But with the Ligurians long gone, it was a challenge to find anyone to ask for directions. However, we eventually caught scent of the path again and followed it snaking down one valley and up another mountain to St. Dalmas, a shire in the shadow of Cayre Gros peak. True to form, the farming town was closed for lunch, even its market, but luck was with us.

Outside the village, we spotted a lady amid boxes of produce in her garage. It was another one of those "Aha!" moments.

Famished, I asked, "Can we buy some fruit? Apples? Pears?"

Without a second thought, she reached into her crate and handed me four green pears.

"*Merci!*" I handed her a two-euro coin.

"No. It is free," she insisted with a beautiful smile.

"Really? You're very kind!"

As we walked off, I couldn't help but think, "You know, the road provides." Before long, we summited Col St. Martin, a ski slope where the trail markings again vanished. In frustration, we stopped into their visitor office and followed their directions down the ski run, past a lake, across a golf course, and through the forest, as if on a treasure hunt.

By then, I could sense the storm's approach deep in my bones and we picked up our already speedy pace. After the downpour and lightning the day before, we sure didn't want to get caught on the summit. While Cheryl did her best to keep up, we both nearly tumbled a couple of times, catching ourselves with our poles at the last second before landing spread-eagle in the mud.

It was tough enough for us. But as we neared the valley, we unexpectedly spotted a couple in their 70s far off the trail, climbing a steep river wash toward us.

Confused, they asked me in French, "How do we get to the resort lake?"

"It's quite a way. And this trail's very slippery."

"Oh, you speak English!" the well-coiffed lady sighed breathlessly.

"We like to think so."

Dabbing her forehead, she said, "We just walked up this riverbed from the village because the signs are marked 'Private Property.'"

"Don't worry. This is a GR trail and it's not private." Then I cut to the chase. "Look, there's a bad storm moving in. You both need to get back down to the village right away!"

"Oh, we're from Scotland," she said, giggling. "We're used to rain."

"Well, believe me. You shouldn't continue up to the lake in this weather. This trail's very steep and tricky. It'll take you hours. Plus, you don't want to get caught in lightning."

"Yes, perhaps it's best, Maggie," the gent coughed, clearly tuckered out.

"If it's anything like yesterday's storm," I warned, "you have about fifteen minutes until it really lets loose at 3:00. Try again tomorrow."

With that word of caution, Cheryl and I excused ourselves and nearly jogged down the trail. Even at that, we just made it to the first village houses before the skies lit up and the monsoon began—at exactly 3:03. Not a bad guess. Ducking under the eaves of a manor, we waited for the worst to pass before rushing the final kilometer into town.

Set amid chestnut and plane trees, St-Martin-Vésubie is a traditional fortified village of Baroque churches and stone houses framed by wooden balconies. It features a unique French *béal*, an open channel with water flowing down the middle of the street for local gardens. Our *gîte* just off the town square was packed with young trekkers and their guide. The air bristled with excitement like the night before Christmas in a family full of children. Eager anticipation glowed in their eyes. Many prepared for their first climb. They'd leave at 5:30 the next morning.

As we listened, their guide carefully gave them last-minute instructions: what to wear, what to pack.

"We may even get snow tomorrow!" he promised.

Snow? Cheryl and I shot each other one of those wide-eyed, "You've gotta be kiddin' me" looks. Did we just run out of time?

15

FLYING MONKEY SPIDERS

WE AWOKE TO MORE SHOWERS, BUT NO SNOW SO FAR, THANK God. Leaving St-Martin-Vésubie, the trail led through thick woodlands, as the sky grew dense with sinister clouds. We pressed on, trekkers on a mission to arrive in Belvédière before all hell broke loose. We only stopped for one quick mini-Merz deep in a primeval forest.

As we shared the last of our cheese, I casually flicked a spider off my arm. Ah, but this was no ordinary insect. No, this was a spider with wings and a Velcro body. It was difficult to remove. Its body stuck to mine. Then I found another, and then another on Cheryl's back. It wasn't enough to simply take them off. They stuck to your fingers. You had to pinch them in half to get rid of them! How'd they swarm us so quickly? And from where? Did they drop from the trees? Were they the flying monkeys of arachnids?

"Let's get out of here!" Cheryl screamed and we scattered, careening down the mountain, only to soon arrive in bustling downtown Belvédère, another ghost town. I'm sure it must live up to its name, "Beautiful View," on a clear day. I could just imagine the stunning vista across the Gordolasque and Vésubie Valleys. It just wasn't that particular day.

We walked down gloomy, narrow passageways past fountains and the 17th century church of St. Pierre and St. Paul, searching for someone, anyone. Finally, we ran into a woman sneaking a smoke in the rain outside the mayor's office. She just happened to work there. After one look at our sorry, soggy condition, she cut her break short to shepherd us inside, and then called around to find us a place to sleep.

There was a private *gîte* nearby, but off the trail, and we arrived just before the downpour hit in earnest. The dorm room was in the basement of their house, so it was chilly, even though the welcome was warm and we had it to ourselves.

No one else was so mad to hike in weather like that. We did have a chance to scramble outside through the deluge to the building next door for a slightly warmer shower.

While soaped up, I found another ten of those blood-sucking, flying monkey spiders on my body. Out of the corner of one eye, I even spotted one brazen enough to scamper across my cheek to escape the shower's flow. Afterward, back in our room, I stripped and asked Cheryl to check my body for any I may have missed—and she found several more—while hosting a few of her own.

The village market was closed for a week, so we made do with a trip to the baker to pick up the barest of supplies. By that time, I'd lost count of how many days we'd gone to bed hungry or slept on a floor mattress. I'm sure it's character building (and Cheryl could confirm I'd become a real character), but it always makes it difficult to perform at your best the next day.

Then again, to be fair, their *gîte* was better than many. It had a kitchen we could use and they were sympathetic to Via Alpina hikers. They'd met so few. That support counted for so much and was one of the few things that kept us motivated and moving when it would've been too easy to simply go back to the Südtirol to a soft down bed, a warm *schnitzel*, and a cold *hefeweizen*.

As usual, it poured all night. We knew our trail would be a slippery mire of mud. At daybreak, with the showers still raging outside, I stalled awhile to practice my French with the *gîte* manager. Actually, I hoped to glean any inside information what might help our trek for those last three days into Monaco. Yet, what wisdom the man offered, I didn't want to hear.

"In this weather," he warned, "I would not take the Via Alpina."

"Oh, we're used to hiking in this," I said, sounding a lot like the Scots couple. "In fact, if rainmaking were a career, we could make a fortune."

"You know," he claimed, "it has only rained four days all summer."

They were the same days since we'd arrived on "The Sunny Riviera."

"My friend, your trail is not well marked here. It is easy to get lost, especially in this. You should just hike the GR5. Many follow it. You will have a much better time. You will arrive in Menton and then catch a train to Monaco. Bam! In ten minutes, you are there."

It sounded very tempting. We'd searched for trails far too often on our journey. Showers only made it worse. Still, after trying so diligently to follow the Via Alpina for the past hundred-plus days, we needed to arrive in Monaco by foot, not train. That was no way to cross a finish line.

The rain didn't pass. If anything, it fell harder by the time Cheryl and I bundled up in our ponchos and trudged outside into the bitter weather and murky light. We followed the trail down slippery slopes from the village into dense woods. Dogs began snarling. They were big. And they were close. Though I couldn't spot them yet, they drew near as we struggled through high grass. Suddenly, the GR52A veered right to cross a small footbridge over the swollen river. We attempted to follow it, but after the first few steps, the bridge vanished—washed away. I was mighty glad we hadn't tried to complete that section in the dark. We'd have plunged into the drink, and I could think of far better if not faster ways to get down valley.

Dammit! This is nonsense! This is no day for dirt trails, especially when lightning can strike at any time. It's time for more improvisation.

In frustration, we backtracked to a mountain road we'd passed earlier and headed in the direction of the pass. We followed this dirt road around the mountain then up the other side to La Bollène-Vésubie, another hillside village. Rain hammered harder by then, so we quickly dismissed any thought of picking up the trail, reluctantly deciding to stick to the road.

Let me be clear. I normally loathe road hiking, but in that weather, we made an exception. Besides, there were few cars, maybe one every thirty minutes. Rational folks stayed inside huddled around a fire on days like that. Unless, of course, they're driving the Monte Carlo Rally.

Until recently, that same road up Turini was driven after sunset and called "Night of the Long Knives" due to the cars' beams slicing the darkness. Then again, maybe for hikers, it should be called the "Night of the Long Drop," as it was a long way to the valley floor—as well as a long way to the crest.

Yes, it was another 1000-meter climb or so over hairpin turns to reach Col de Turini, the former 17th century border between Savoie and France. That strategic summit symbolized the endless Franco-Italian wars.

For the two of us, it was a battle of a different sort. It was a death march up an endlessly winding road in the pouring rain. There was no place to stop, no reason to linger. There were no fountains, even though we quickly ran out of water. We could see little in that mess of mist: no scenic overlooks, incredible wildlife, or beautiful waterfalls. It was only one more mountain on a never-ending list; one more summit left to climb.

Only one more, I kept promising myself, and then it's mostly downhill to the Med. Must keep moving, must keep moving.

Cheryl lagged some hundred meters behind, as she dealt with her own private misery. Every twenty minutes or so I stopped to let her catch up. Together, we caught our breaths. Then all too soon, we'd start again, shuffling our frigid feet, sucking wind, and shifting our minds to sunnier days.

Our eventual arrival, hours later, at the 1607-meter pass was less than triumphant. There was no magnum of victory champagne waiting. Most of the businesses were closed between seasons, even the village gîte. There was no market. We were forced into the one hotel still open whose manager greeted us by saying, "Oh, you two. I passed you when I drove up the road an hour or so ago. I couldn't believe you were out walking in this. Glad to see you made it."

Thanks for the sentiments. That and two euros will buy an espresso.

We were drenched. What wasn't wet by rain was soaked with sweat from hours spent straining up the peak. Along the way, I'd stopped several times to pull off my boots and wring out socks, but it was useless. To top it off, there was no drying room in the hotel. There was no heat. It was out of season. Even though we stuffed newspapers into our boots and hung our clothes on hangers across both windows of our room, there was no chance they'd be dry by morning. Why'd it matter, anyway? More rain was forecast.

In spite of that, miracle of miracles, we awoke to a rare and wonderful occurrence. The skies were actually clear; it had warmed up and turned out to be the perfect day for trekking. Even so, considering the amount of rain those trails had suffered the past three days and the 26-kilometers we still needed to cover to reach Sospel, we opted to hike down the road over the other side of the mountain. Besides, it was closed to traffic for some reason and our boots and clothes were as wet as we'd feared.

This *is* supposed to be fun, right?

In the still tranquility of the morning air, we made good time. The incline on the far side of the mountain worked in our favor, as much as it had forced us to slog in snail-time just the day before. We descended the 1300 meters toward Sospel at six kilometers an hour, a Grand Prix-like clip for us, all without breaking a sweat. In no time at all, we arrived in Moulinet and combed its abandoned streets in search of a café—or at least someone to ask.

Eventually, I spotted a white-haired woman as she poked her head out of a shuttered second-storey window.

"*Bonjour, madame!*"

"*Bonjour, monsieur, madame.*"

"Is there a café here?"

"*Non.*"

"A market to buy bread?"

"*Non,* it is Thursday. There is no bread."

No bread? We'd forgotten how many French shops are notoriously closed on Thursday. Why? Imagine, a French village without baguettes? It's like an American town without a burger joint. *Quelle horreur!*

So I changed tack. "Anywhere to buy food?"

"*Non,*" she said, and then rambled on, until a man inside interrupted.

"Oh, that's right," she suddenly remembered. "Go to the main square. There is a hotel and bar. They may have something for you."

Thanking her, we were off in a flash and found an inn where life hadn't changed since the 1920s. Faded photos and posters lined its walls. Weathered wooden chairs circled a few glass-topped, rusted iron tables with cigarette burned Pernod ashtrays. An equally wizened woman shuffled back and forth behind the counter. We were her only customers.

"Have any food?" I asked, offering the sincerest of smiles. "Sandwiches?"

"*Non* bread. It's Thursday!"

Oh, that again. "You have a restaurant, but no food?"

She shook her head.

"No chips?" Cheryl chimed in. "Cookies?"

"*Non.*" She thought for an instant and then remembered she did have something in the kitchen, and shuffled off.

Cheryl and I looked at each other. What could it be?

The woman soon returned, waving an old fruitcake.

"Want this?"

"*Oui!*" We snapped it up. Then spotting one of those timeless metal peanut dispensers at the end of the counter, I asked, "Does that still work?"

She nodded, adding, "It only takes these."

With a gnarled hand, she placed a couple of old ten-franc pieces (pre-euro) on the bar. Like I said, not much had changed in decades. Not the money, the peanuts, or maybe even the fruitcake. Thank goodness for their indestructibility.

Our visit also answered one of the great mysteries of life. All those unwelcome holiday fruitcakes keep getting passed around until they end up in some small French village at a bistro on a Thursday. Come to think of it, maybe Moulinet is the fruitcake "happy hunting ground."

Fortified, we continued our trek down the closed road. Serpentine, it snaked another hour or so. Its peaceful stillness was shattered only by the odd occasional grinding and gnashing, like a giant's trip to the dentist. Eventually even that mystery was solved when we spotted three landslides, tons of slag, blocking the road. Crews chiseled, ground and set explosives atop the adjacent mountain to loosen any other boulders before cleaning up the three mini-mountains that'd cascaded below. They'd worked on it for over a year, effectively cutting off villages up the mountainside.

Well, after snowfields, icefields, deluges, mountains of mud, sheep patties, washed-out bridges, flying monkey spiders, crying marmots, and all the rain we'd endured, we weren't about to let a few landslides stop us. I grabbed my Nordic poles, Cheryl snatched a nearby tree limb, and we began to climb the heaps of loose, shifting rocks. They were only ten meters high, but any false move could send you tumbling into the ravine. Still, there was no time to worry about that. We needed to get past it all before the workers spotted us and forced us to climb down into the gorge to trek along the river anyway.

Scrambling the first two impasses went fine, but when I was just halfway across the last one, before I knew it, my feet slid out from under me. Only my poles still connected me to the mound.

Then, we heard screaming from atop the mountain. We were spotted!

Oh, it's probably just the foreman yelling at his men to stop drilling and blasting while we pass. Anyway, what can he do? Climb all the way down the mountain to physically pull us off? Fat chance.

In the meantime, I managed to stand back up, crawl the final two feet, and slide down the other side. Cheryl, having seen my stumble, took it slower, leaned on her stick, and made it across without any problem.

After all that, anything's simple and we raced the final few kilometers into Sospel and back onto the Via Alpina red route for the final stages into Monte Carlo.

Sospel is Mediterranean in design. The epitome of "charming," it's a 5th century medieval village lined with brightly painted buildings of rust, tangerine and ochre. Some Gothic homes feature *trompe-l'œil* paintings around their windows or doors, creating three-dimensional illusions, while banana trees and palms frame others. It's in a picturesque setting along the Bévéra River crossed by Pont Vieux Bridge, which once collected caravan tolls. It has long hosted travelers. As early as the 1300s, the town flourished under the protection of the Counts of Savoy. Then in the 16th century, it grew in prosperity as a stage stop on the royal route from Nice to Turin. In 1860, residents finally voted to become united with France.

Upon reaching the visitor office, another helpful woman made reservations for us at a nearby auberge and then called ahead to Nice to reserve a room. The Sospel room was 50 euros (nearly 70 dollars), and a little dear for a room with no breakfast, since we were paying the same in Nice. However, she was quick to remind us we were now on the Côte d'Azur and that was "the price of paradise."

I couldn't help smiling. They use the same tired line in Hawaii. Still, with luck, we hoped to reach Monaco the following afternoon.

Our modest room in the old building was quiet and overlooked the river. We were finally able to dry our clothes, especially our waterlogged boots, visit a market, and we looked forward to a good night's sleep. The only snafu came when I went to pay for our room. Knowing they'd be closed at dawn when we left, I always made it a point to pay the night before. It wasn't as if we were going to make long distance calls, raid the mini-bar, or order from room service—not even if we tried—especially not in that modest place.

When I went downstairs to settle-up, the manager asked me the strangest question in French. "Do you want this separate, or all together?"

What an odd question for a couple.

"Together is fine."

He wrote out a receipt for 100 euros and handed it to me.

"A hundred? The visitor office said it's fifty." They were long since closed.

Quickly losing his patience, he sighed, and then pointed to a sign behind the restaurant counter. It read, "Double—50 euros."

"Exactly. So, what's the problem?"

Growing more agitated, he led me out into the street and sternly pointed to another sign posted on the building itself.

"See," he began, slowly and loudly, lecturing me as if we were standing on an airport runway. "It says, '36 euros single, 14 euros supplement p/p.'"

"Yes," I agreed, raising my voice to match. "And 36 euros...plus 14 euros... equals 50 euros for two. Right?"

I'd only been in the mountains, not over the hill.

"Ah-ha, right!" he triumphantly shouted, with a "See-there" nod to his wife who watched the drama unfold from the hotel doorway. He'd reached the fool.

"Well, there are just two of us."

He paused. "Two?"

"Two."

"But you are in room eight."

"No, room three."

His partner shot him an icy glare that wives reserve for special occasions, as if to say, "You're the dumbass."

"Yea, we all look the same."

The fellow sheepishly apologized, led me back inside, and then gave us a carafe of red wine to make up for the ordeal. It was very decent of him.

Back in our room, as I came in, Cheryl leaned up on one elbow and sleepily asked, "What was all that noise outside? Did you hear it?"

"You might say that."

"Was that you?"

"Yes. We had a misunderstanding, but everything's okay now."

"Good. And you brought back some wine. How nice."

It was. But honestly, for me, the taste of success was even more delicious. I'd won my first argument in French. Life's made of those small moments, victories along the way. Savor them. I sure did.

16

Just the Tick-Talkin'

WE ROSE WITH THE MORNING HAZE. OLD MEN WITH BROOMS made from bushes swept the street outside our hotel door in the peach-hued morning glow. Our hearts raced, anxious to reach Monaco by day's end. Fueled by adrenaline, we sped off over the surrounding hills and were barely out of town when it began to drizzle. Again. I had to laugh. It was a fitting conclusion to a journey that'd been plagued by bad weather for months. To top it off, the trails played their disappearing act one last time, just like when we'd first started back in Muggia.

We *were* living *Marmot Day*, after all. Muggia Marcus poked his head out of his burrow, saw rain, and ducked back inside, meaning six more weeks of terrible weather.

It turned out the GR52 wasn't nearly as hiker-friendly as the GR5. Though I'd already kicked myself several times for not following that trail into Menton as the fellow advised back in Belvédère, we still wanted, especially on that last day, to stick to the Via Alpina. And now we were back on the last stages of the red route to Monaco.

Leaving Sospel on our way to the first of several passes, we ran into some kids on their way to school. It was comical. They darted back and forth, desperately trying to catch a lean black dog they called Bud. We figured the shepherd-sized mutt must be the so-called "village dog," since he didn't answer to any of the boys. Strong-willed, he loved to run and you could see the obvious thrill in his clever brown eyes. For some unknown reason, the big fella latched onto us. We couldn't shake him no matter how hard we tried to send him back to the kids.

That dog had a mind of his own. He answered to no man. Bud trotted a hundred meters ahead of us on the trail, and then sprinted back with an expression

like, "What's taking you two so long?" Every now and then, catching a scent or a birdsong, he'd gallop off to check it out, but always returned before we'd gone too far ahead.

The pure joy reflected in his eyes reminded me why I take to the trail. It's the fresh air, the heart pounding, air-gasping pace; it's the lure of something new around each bend and the freedom to explore. It's the sweat and strain to accomplish something measurable each day. It's the memorable views from a mountaintop. It's reducing life to its primal essentials and finding satisfaction in the smallest things: a hot shower, a warm meal, a soft pillow, or word of encouragement. It's the new people you meet every day and experiences shared. It's the personal peace you find when you reconnect with nature and the Universe. Could life get any better?

I've always thought Henry David Thoreau described it best, when he said:

> "I went to the woods because I wished to live deliberately, to front only the essential facts of life, and see if I could not learn what it had to teach, and not, when I came to die, discover that I had not lived."

Bud was the perfect guide on that particularly wet, slippery, unmarked path. He could leap a three-foot slope without missing a beat. Solid and muscular, he was a perfectly honed hiking machine, in better condition than we were after all those months. I was envious of his prowess, humbled by his raw athleticism. Why, if he'd been with us the past fourteen weeks, who knew how soon we'd have finished? But it's the journey, right?

We set a record time over St-Jean Pass, only to dip back into another valley to begin our climb again up to Baisse du Pape. By then, it began raining harder, and with it our nerves grew frayed. Would the nasty weather prevent us, even with Bud, from completing the two final stages today? We knew it was an eight-hour trek—if we could find the trails.

Still, Bud was patient, waiting for us as we pulled on rain gear one last time. As always, we were on a path, but uncertain we were on the right path until we met a fellow out gathering berries with a large wicker basket.

"Yes," he assured us with a friendly grin. "Peille is just two or three kilometers." Pointing upward, he added, "Just climb the mountain."

Another mountain.

And so it was. We reached the quaint hanging village of Peille by midmorning—and promptly lost the trail. Absolutely no marks led from there to Peillon, at least any we could find after nearly an hour of fruitless searching.

Wandering rain-slicked streets, the three of us wound our way through the sleepy village until we finally arrived at the mayor's office.

"Wait, stay here," I told Bud in both French and English, knowing he'd go ballistic if hitched to a railing. Then Cheryl and I quickly ducked inside where we tried to explain our dilemma to a group of curious staff and bystanders.

"Where are the markings to Peillon?"

The workers shrugged in unison. Even though they had an official Via Alpina map spread across their office wall, they knew little about the trail.

"If this is the Via Alpina and we're so close to Monaco, why no signs?"

The manager apologized, but she was quick to caution, "The markings get even worse from here. All I know is you must go down in the valley and back up over another mountain. But with this weather and the trails..." She slowly shook her head. "I think you two should take the road from here."

Her office companions quickly nodded in agreement.

"How far is it?"

"Twenty-four kilometers."

If true, that could take us another five or six hours or so in this mess.

Downcast and discouraged by the conditions so close to the finish line, we thanked the ladies and then slogged back out into the hammering rain—only to discover that Bud the Wander Dog had moved on. He was more impatient than we were, I guess, and not used to being slowed down. We missed him already, but imagined he'd return to Sospel in time for dinner, or at least find a new home with an active couple in Peille. Then again, I half-expected to find ol' Bud waiting for us just down the road, wagging his tail. Or to see him dashing toward us with that eager gleam in his eyes, as if to say, "What took you guys so long?"

However we crested one hill and then the next, and yet another, and one more, but never saw his toothy grin again.

More disheartened than ever, Cheryl and I struck out along the lightly traveled road. The rain pelted heavier on our backs. Our boots were drenched. Each labored footstep was like fording a deep river. The kilometers slowly ticked past on posts lining the road toward the hillside village of La Turbie, where we knew it was, in fact, all downhill from there. We hoped that seeing the Med, our first sighting since Muggia in June, would give us a final dose of endorphins to help us complete our long journey.

Will it come soon enough? As thunder cracked around us, I couldn't help but remind myself: The lightning bolt you see never kills you. Pure physics, right? But you know, after some 40-days of rain, somehow, it just didn't matter any more.

It was another long hour or more before we finally caught sight of the sea on the horizon. All it took was a sliver of blue for my partner and I to cry out in unison, "Ah! Yes!" as we collapsed into each other's arms.

[MUSIC SWELLS] Well, only in our minds.

Those last few kilometers to Monte Carlo, that chic village by the sea, flew by. We soon entered La Turbie, a cliffside town boasting the remains of a monument dating back to the 7th century B.C. Its Trophy of Augustus once featured a statue of the Emperor perched on a limestone cylinder surrounded by columns, symbolizing the Roman defeat of the Gauls and forty-five alpine peoples. Back then, the Empire constructed a highway running all the way to the Rhône River and west through the Pyrenees. Ironically, only four of their victory columns remain, while parts of their road network still exist today.

Likewise, our Via Alpina markings also resurfaced. We followed an old cobbled path down the steep hillside through ancient fruit orchards and olive groves, past stucco villas with red-tiled roofs and swimming pools, using the sea as our compass. Monaco was such a bizarre finish line for our journey after months of so many cabins, floor mattresses and cow patties. It was the other extreme: a vest pocket of world-class hotels, swank shops, casinos, and even a palace with a real prince and princesses. It's been home to the Grimaldi Family for nearly 700 years, since François Grimaldi seized the fortress by disguising himself as a Franciscan monk.

As is typical for these treks, arriving in Monte Carlo on September 18, 2009 was a bit anti-climactic. No 21-gun salute welcomed us, only in our own minds.

Then again, as Cheryl pointed out, "Come to think of it, there *was* a particularly loud clap of thunder when we first entered the Principality."

You know, that was somehow more fitting. After all, it was the Alps.

We completed our 1800-kilometer or so, eight-country, 110-day, rain-plagued Trans-Alpine odyssey at Monaco's Palace Square, trying to appear respectable beneath a nearly-hidden plaque commemorating the conclusion of the Via Alpina. At first, we couldn't find the final marking. (At least, we're consistent.) We had to ask the Palace guards to point us in the right direction. Upon hearing about our journey, they insisted on having someone take their photo with us. Afterward, while trying to connect with the Via Alpina's Monaco bureau, we dropped into the mayor's office.

Now, this was not your run-of-the-mill town hall. This was Monaco. As you might guess, its entrance looks more like the foyer to a grand ballroom. On that particular afternoon, some VIPs were celebrating their wedding. Ladies were dressed in their finest jewels and gowns, and gents posed like mannequins in sleek tuxes. Meanwhile, in traipsed two wet, slightly disheveled Via Alpinists looking like, well, looking like they'd just spent nearly four weary months trekking and climbing across the Alps. Try as they might to quickly scoot us out of there, the mayor's office was unable to find the Via Alpina coordinator, but they did offer to stamp our passports.

Why? We knew we'd arrived.

I've got to admit, I'll always cherish the memory of our grandiose exit. The wedding party had circled the bottom of the stairs waiting for the happy couple. Pink rose petals lay scattered across the fairytale tableau. Paparazzi stood with their cameras poised at the ready.

And who should appear? Tah-dah! Two Via Alpinists with ponchos flying.

We strolled down the red carpet as photographers snapped our picture. Some folks clapped at the absurdity; others simply looked aghast. Personally, I grinned and just barely resisted giving all a regal wave. If they only knew what we'd been through, I like to think they'd smile too. In any event, our photo was bound to liven up someone's otherwise staid wedding album, or society page.

From Monaco, it's a short train ride to Nice, a place we once called home after a harrowing trek across Tibet. It seemed appropriate to return. She was more beautiful than ever, transformed by renovations and a public outcry over her famous dog droppings. We wasted no time in checking into a hotel in the heart of the city. The matronly, bleached blonde at the front desk couldn't be bothered. She had a manicure to finish. To her, we were just two more weary travelers, two more names on a register.

It didn't matter. We were content. We'd discovered the Alps, one-step-at-a-time. It's a land of much more than mountains, cheese and gnomes. It's a revival of the senses. It's the crisp freshness of the air, the scent of pine, the riotous splash of wildflowers, and the taste of sweet milk straight from the cow. It's history ever-changing, culture ever-evolving. It's the chance to free yourself and seize the most from life, day after challenging day. It's the humbling realization that we can never tame nature—only cooperate and hope to mutually survive. It's more than bagging peaks; it's the folks and experiences along the way. It's a land of legends, towering giants, well-hidden gnomes, and an independent frame of mind. It's the ultimate in tranquility. It's the closest you can come to touching the stars.

Go. See it now. Preserve it. Live it.

By the way, for those who keep score of such things, as close as I can figure, even with our valley detours, we climbed a vertical total of 104,661 meters (343,376 feet) and descended a total of 106,860 meters (350,591 feet) across the Alps. If Mt. Everest is 8,848 meters (29,028 feet high), we summited the equivalent of almost twelve Mt. Everests from sea level.

No wonder I'm so tired.

As I write this in Brixen, snowcapped peaks outside our window remain an inspiration and constant reminder of the magic and freedom of high, pure places. A bit of the gnome still resides in us. And the peace we discovered remains until the time when we return. Yes, as they say here, "*Alles Gute!*"

Well, almost. The tick infestation remained in my blood and took another round of antibiotics after my return to the Südtirol. So, who knows? Don't blame me. Maybe all of this, well, maybe it's just the tick talkin' one last time.

Note: Since our journey, the Via Alpina network, regional and national Alpine clubs, and Via Alpinists themselves have all made great strides to provide better information, markings, maps and resources for those planning future treks. This information is constantly changing. For the latest, visit their website: www.via-alpina.org.

CONVERSIONS

Meters to Feet

100 meters	328 feet
300 meters	984 feet
500 meters	1640 feet
1000 meters	3281 feet
2000 meters	6562 feet
2500 meters	8202 feet
3000 meters	9843 feet
3500 meters	11483 feet
4000 meters	13123 feet

Kilometers to Miles

1 kilometer	.62 miles
5 kilometers	3.11 miles
10 kilometers	6.21 miles
20 kilometers	12.43 miles
30 kilometers	18.64 miles

Kilos to Pounds

1 kilo	2.2 pounds
5 kilos	11 pounds
7 kilos	15.43 pounds
10 kilos	22.2 pounds

Centigrade to Fahrenheit

0° C	32° F
5° C	41° F
10° C	50° F
15° C	59° F
20° C	68° F
25° C	77° F
30° C	86° F

At the time of this journey
one euro = $1.40 -1.43 USD

GEAR

GoLite Pinnacle backpack
GoLite down sleeping bag
Gossamer Gear Squall Classic tent
LEKI Super Makalu Air Thermo
Nordic sticks
packing cube with:
2 GoLite wicking t-shirts
2 pr. GoLite air-eator socks
GoLite Reed waterproof pants
rain poncho
convertible pants
nylon shorts
2 pr. hiking socks
cotton kerchief
synthetic towel
cotton hat
gaiters
down jacket
MagLite (small)
plastic foldable cup
10 yds. nylon cord
compass
GPS backtracker
toilet paper
Zip-Fizz energy powder
waterproof matches
Olympus U700 digital camera
Montrail Continental Divide shoes
(so-called) waterproof hiking boots
altimeter watch
Swiss Army knife
journal & pen
30 topographic maps (split)
water bottle
nylon pouch with passport
debit card
med kit with:

antibiotic cream	athletic bandage
small mirror	petroleum jelly
aspirin	naproxin
muscle cream	deodorant
earplugs	analgesic cream
athletic tape	small sewing kit
shaving cream & razor	soap
nail clippers	sunscreen
toothbrush	blister wraps

approx. pack weight
15 pounds total (7 kilos)

SPECIAL THANKS

For their moral and logistical support:

Siegi Gostner
Peter Merz
Dr. Luis Durnwalder, President, Bolzano-Alto Adige Province
Nathalie Morelle, Association Grande Traversée des Alpes
Senator Robert Gstalder
Piero Palocci
Dr. Franz Wenter
Paul and Arlene Buklarewicz
C.B. Gilberti
Karl and Sonja Hofer
The People of Brixen
Teri Kahan

For gear, maps and fitness support:

Andy Burgess & Tiffanie Beal, GoLite, www.golite.com
Grant Sible, Gossamer Gear, www.gossamergear.com
Russell Guy, Omni Resources, www.Omnimap.com
Jan Sears, Izaak and staff at Upcountry Fitness Maui,
www.upcountryfitness.com

For local history and legend contributions:

Osterreichischer Alpenverein (OeAV, Austrian Alpine Club)
Grande Traversée des Alpes (GTA), France
Deutscher Alpenverein e. V. (DAV, German Alpine Club)
Amt für Wald, Natur und Landschaft (AWNL,
Office of Forest, Nature and Landscape), Liechtenstein
Regione Piemonte (Piedmont Region), Italy
Schweizer Wanderwege (Swiss Hiking Federation)
Hiking & Biking Slovenia /Pohodnistvo in kolesarjenje giz
Club Alpin Monégasque (CAM, Monegasque Alpine Club), Monaco

And to the countless others who added to the Via Alpina website

About the Author

BRANDON WILSON is an author and photographer, explorer and adventure travel writer. His other books in this series include: *Along the Templar Trail*, a Lowell Thomas Gold Award-winner for Best Travel Book, *Yak Butter Blues*, an IPPY Award-winner, and *Dead Men Don't Leave Tips: Adventures X Africa*. His story about a year spent living in the Arctic, "Life When Hell Freezes Over," appeared in *They Lived to Tell the Tale: True Stories of Adventure from the Legendary Explorers Club*.

His photos have won awards from National Geographic Traveler and Islands magazines; his pictorial essay was featured in *Naive and Abroad: Spain: Limping 600 Miles Through History* by Marcus Wilder.

A voracious explorer of nearly one hundred countries, over decades he has trekked many long-distance trails, including: the Camino de Santiago across Spain, the Via de la Plata, and St. Olav's Way across Norway. In 1992, Brandon and his wife Cheryl were the first Western couple to complete the 1100- kilometer trail from Lhasa, Tibet to Kathmandu, and he was the first American to traverse the 1850-kilometer Via Francigena from England to Rome. In 2006, he and his French friend re-blazed the 4500-kilometer Templar Trail from France to Jerusalem to establish it as a path of peace.

Wilson is a member of the prestigious Explorers Club and a graduate of the University of North Carolina at Chapel Hill.

Other Books in the Travel Series by Brandon Wilson:

Along the Templar Trail

Walking in the nearly forgotten footsteps of the legendary first Knights Templar, an American and a 68-year old Frenchman embark on a mission all their own. Traveling simply and trusting in the kindness of strangers, they set off to carry a message of peace along a route historically used for war. Their incredible journey leads them thousands of miles across eleven countries and two continents toward Jerusalem.

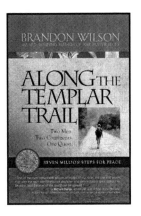

After the outbreak of war, everything becomes uncertain—except for their steadfast and perhaps life-threatening resolve. This inspiring tale is a powerful testimony to the courage of the human spirit.

Lowell Thomas Gold Award winner for "Best Travel Book" (SATWF); Also named a *ForeWord Reviews* Book of the Year finalist

"A fascinating testimony of faith and gumption that inspired two men to take seven million steps for peace. A must read..." ~ Arun Gandhi, M.K. Gandhi Institute for Nonviolence, University of Rochester, NY

"More than the mere adventure of two brave men, it is a grand and noble quest for peace, as well as a spiritual voyage that will leave readers emotionally and intellectually replenished... His writing combines a marvelous sense of Zen with good humor, and his personal style makes you feel as if you were there taking part in it all." ~ Mayra Calvani, *Midwest Book Review*

"Brandon Wilson is strictly fast-forward in his exhilarating *Along The Templar Trail*... Wilson's remarkably attractive account will galvanize couch potatoes..." ~ *ForeWord Reviews*

"A vivid and eye-opening blend of history, adventure, religion, mysticism and modern conflict... Simply one of the most remarkable adventure stories of our time..." ~ Richard Bangs, adventurer, author/host of the PBS TV series *Richard Bangs' Adventures With Purpose*

YAK BUTTER BLUES

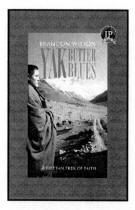

What does it take to survive? Yak Butter Blues exposes the raw challenge of traveling deliberately, one-step-at-a-time on an incredible 1100-kilometer (680-mile) trek across the unforgiving Tibetan plains. Join a daring and somewhat crazed man and woman with Sadhu, their horse, as they set off to attempt to become the first Western couple to trek this ancient Himalayan trail across the earth's most remote corner.

Their true story tells a riveting tale of human endurance. It also provides a candid first-hand look at the lives of the Tibetan families who secreted them into their homes—and at a culture teetering on the edge of extinction. Nothing could prepare the couple for what would become the ultimate test of their resolve, faith… and very survival.

An Independent Publisher IPPY Award winner

"Recommended for adventure travel and Tibetan culture collections."
~ *Library Journal*

"A moving and emotional testimony, and a travelogue that is the next most vivid experience to hiking upon the trail oneself." ~ *Midwest Book Review*

"A high-altitude tale of synchronicity, divine providence, begging monks, trigger-happy Chinese soldiers and dehydration." ~ *Pittsburgh Post-Gazette*

"I came under the spell of Brandon Wilson's lively and vivid prose. He is a fine writer—perceptive, funny, a great way with words—making the book a whooping good read." ~ Royal Robbins, renowned mountain climber/kayaker

"Told with humour and insight, this vivid narrative allows you to vicariously experience life at true Tibetan pace, one step at a time: so close, you can smell the yak butter." ~ Michael Buckley, author of *TIBET: the Bradt Travel Guide*

"A soaring travel diary. It places the reader in the thick of the action every bit as well as Marco Polo transported Italians to China and, as it seems to me, better than Lowell Thomas led readers in the dust of Lawrence of Arabia."
~ Joseph W. Bean, *Maui Weekly*

DEAD MEN DON'T LEAVE TIPS: ADVENTURES X AFRICA

What does it take to follow your dream? Quite a bit, if it means crossing Africa. That's what a couple discovers when they leave on a seven-month, 16,000-km. overland journey from London to Cape Town, South Africa. Against their better judgment, they join a do-it-yourself safari with a bizarre band of companions. After their dream quickly turns into a nightmare, they set off across the continent alone—and that makes all the difference.

Wilson, in a style one reviewer described as "a hybrid of Paul Theroux and Tom Robbins," takes you onto the crazed roads of Africa and into the hearts and lives of its people.

Meet mountain gorillas face-to-face. Melt down during a Saharan breakdown. Hunt dik-dik with Pygmies. Climb Africa's highest mountain. Hop the "gun-run" through a civil war. Rush down thundering Zambezi rapids and dive into South Africa's cauldron of turmoil.

Join us for a raw look at the real Africa—one far removed from the usual postcard perfection.

"Journeys of body and soul in every sense of the word… Interlaced with this honesty and detail are Wilson's beautiful prose, obvious passion for adventure and a deep inquisitiveness about other cultures, making this book a pleasure to read. Highly recommended."   ~ Mayra Calvani, *Midwest Book Review*

"Honest, gritty and insightful. Best of all, it makes the world's most exciting continent read just like that."   ~ John Heminway, author of *No Man's Land: A Personal Journey into Africa*

"A masterful crossroads of characters, exotic places, history and human drama in a rig that never stalls."   ~ Richard Bangs, author of *Mystery of the Nile*

"A monument to those who would take on the challenges of land travel across one of the most dangerous, unhealthy continents in the world."
~ *Heartland Reviews*

"His exciting writing style keeps you on the edge of your seat… The best travel writing I've ever read and his adventurous spirit is inspiring."
~ *The Rebecca Review, Amazon Top Ten Reviewer*

CPSIA information can be obtained at www.ICGtesting.com
Printed in the USA
BVOW08s1927091213

338615BV00002B/378/P

9 780977 053629